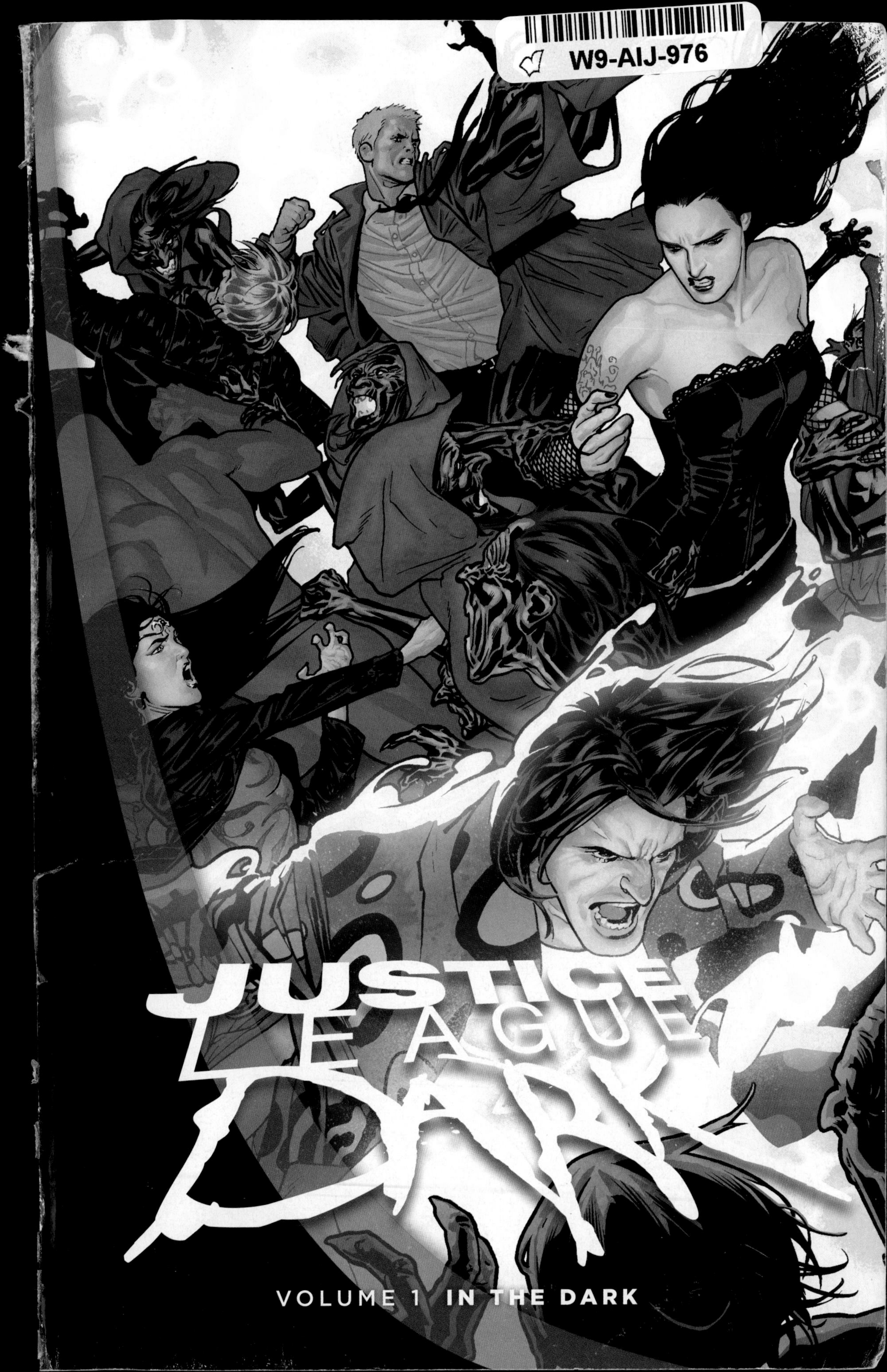
JUSTICE
LEAGUE
DARK
VOLUME 1 IN THE DARK

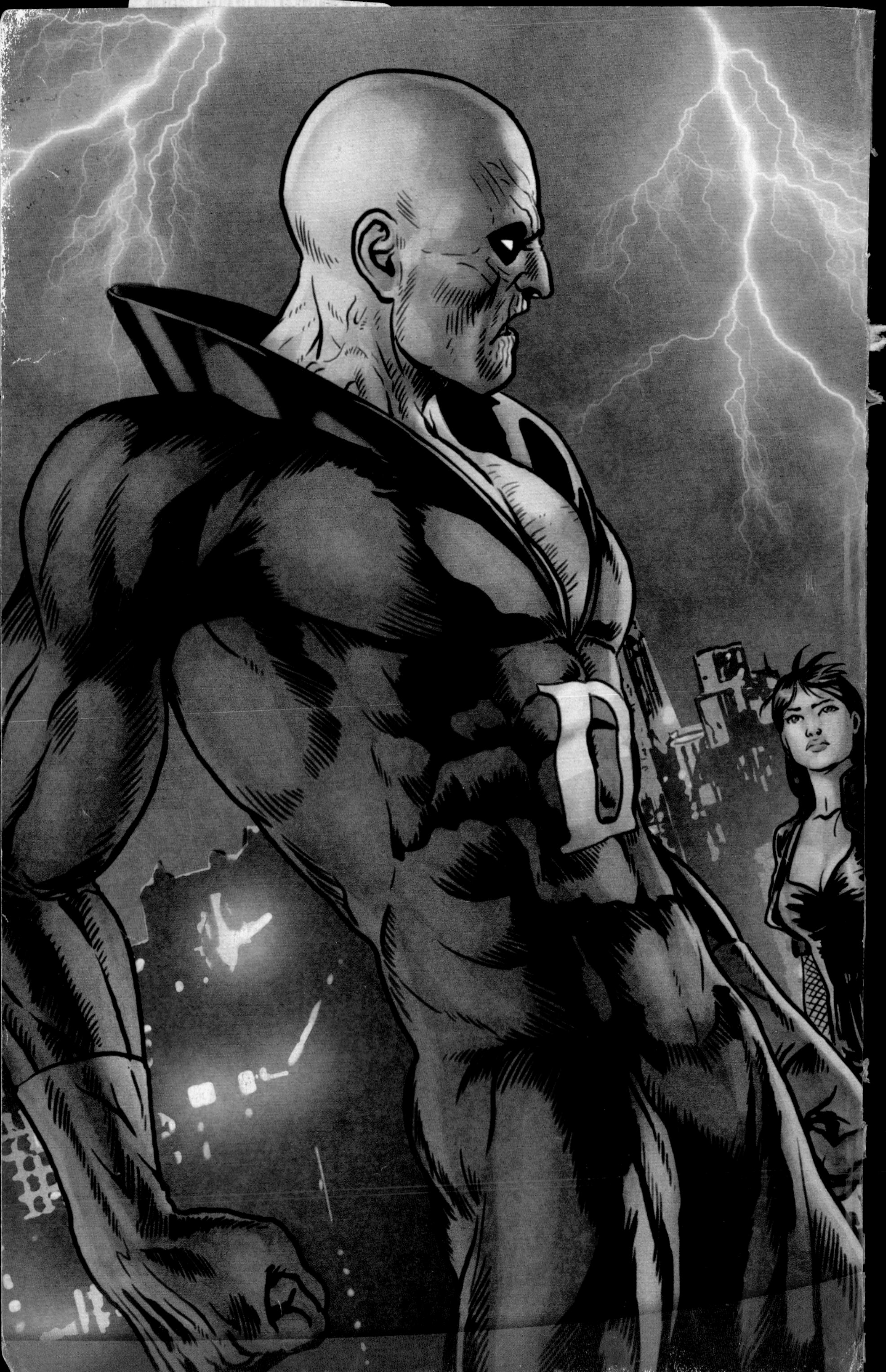

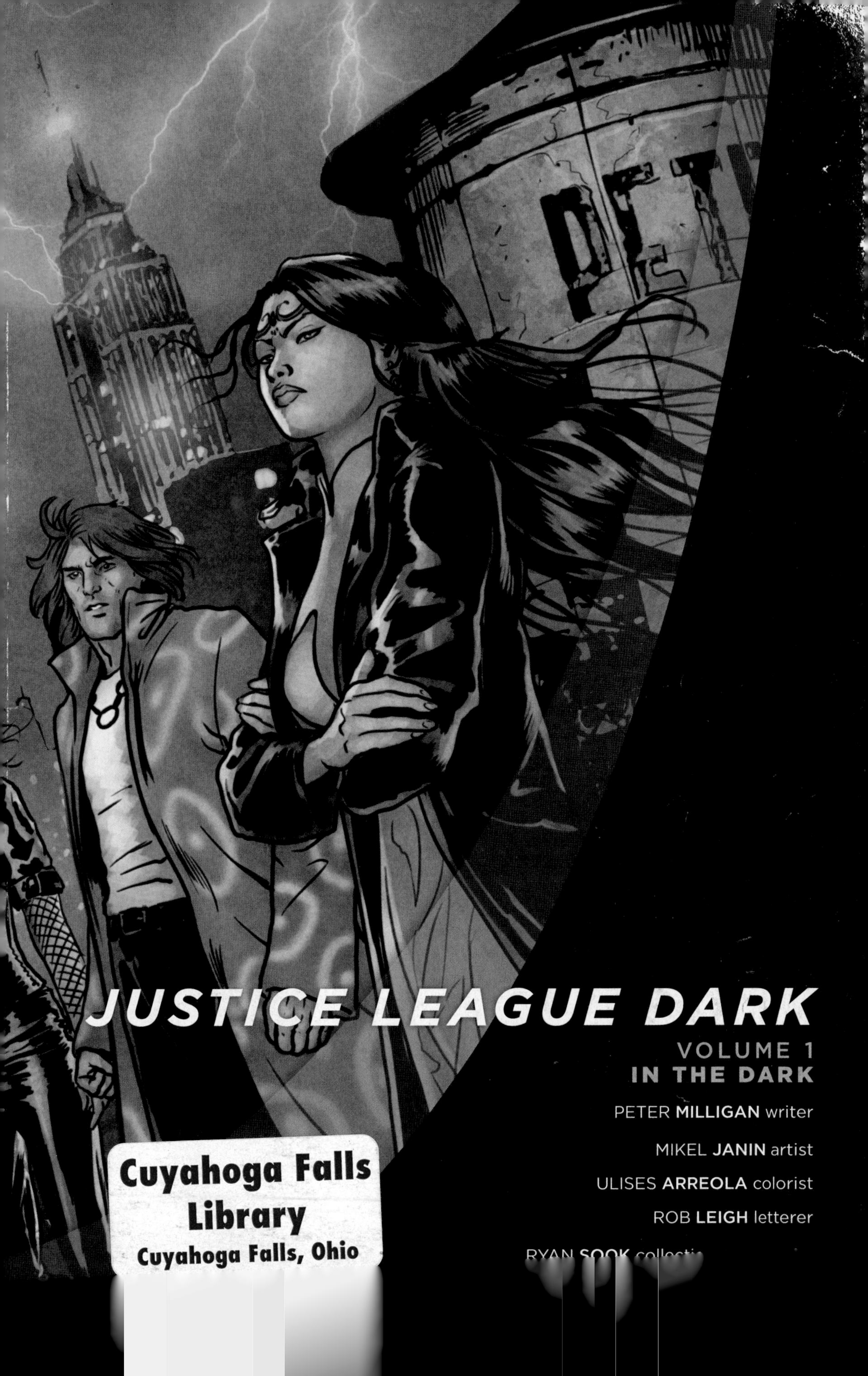

JUSTICE LEAGUE DARK

VOLUME 1
IN THE DARK

PETER **MILLIGAN** writer

MIKEL **JANIN** artist

ULISES **ARREOLA** colorist

ROB **LEIGH** letterer

RYAN **SOOK** collecti

REX OGLE MATT IDELSON EDDIE BERGANZA Editors – Original Series CHRIS CONROY Associate Editor – Original Series
PETER HAMBOUSSI Editor ROBBIN BROSTERMAN Design Director – Books ROBBIE BIEDERMAN Publication Design

BOB HARRAS VP – Editor-in-Chief

DIANE NELSON President DAN DIDIO and JIM LEE Co-Publishers GEOFF JOHNS Chief Creative Officer
JOHN ROOD Executive VP – Sales, Marketing and Business Development AMY GENKINS Senior VP – Business and Legal Affairs
NAIRI GARDINER Senior VP – Finance JEFF BOISON VP – Publishing Operations
MARK CHIARELLO VP – Art Direction and Design JOHN CUNNINGHAM VP – Marketing
TERRI CUNNINGHAM VP – Talent Relations and Services ALISON GILL Senior VP – Manufacturing and Operations
HANK KANALZ Senior VP – Digital JAY KOGAN VP – Business and Legal Affairs, Publishing
JACK MAHAN VP – Business Affairs, Talent NICK NAPOLITANO VP – Manufacturing Administration
SUE POHJA VP – Book Sales COURTNEY SIMMONS Senior VP – Publicity BOB WAYNE Senior VP – Sales

JUSTICE LEAGUE DARK VOLUME 1: IN THE DARK

DC Comics, 1700 Broadway, New York, NY 10019
A Warner Bros. Entertainment Company.
Printed by RR Donnelley, Salem, VA, USA. 9/7/12. First Printing.

ISBN: 978-1-4012-3704-2

Library of Congress Cataloging-in-Publication Data

Milligan, Peter.
Justice League dark. Volume 1, In the dark / Peter Milligan, Mikel Janin.
p. cm.
"Originally published in single magazine form in Justice League Dark 1-6."
ISBN 978-1-4012-3704-2
1. Graphic novels. I. Janin, Mikel. II. Title. III. Title: In the dark.
PN6728.J87M55 2012
741.5'973—dc23
2012022428

SUSTAINABLE FORESTRY INITIATIVE
Certified Chain of Custody
At Least 25% Certified Forest Content
www.sfiprogram.org
SFI-01042
APPLIES TO TEXT STOCK ONLY

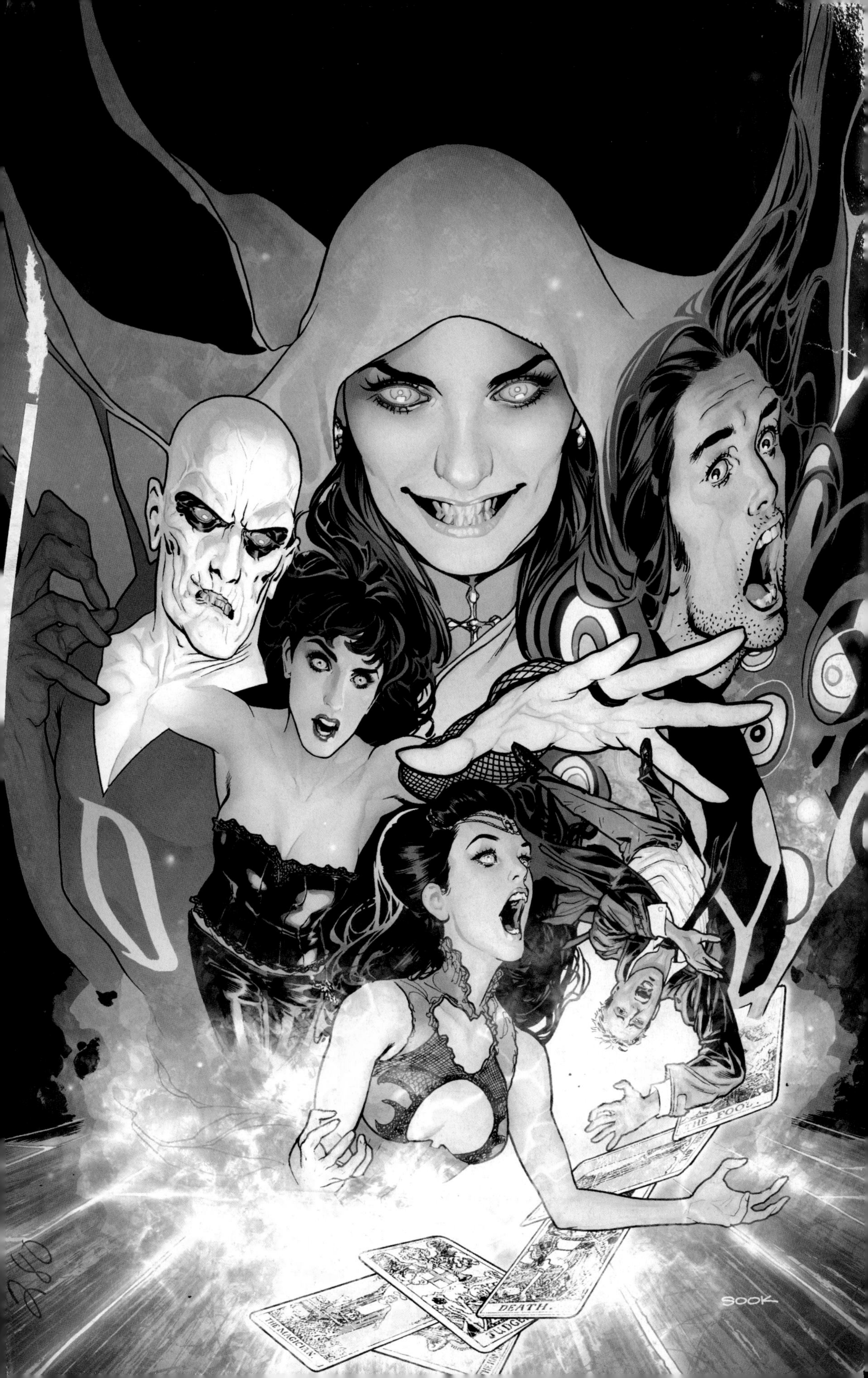
THE FOOL.
DEATH.
SOOK

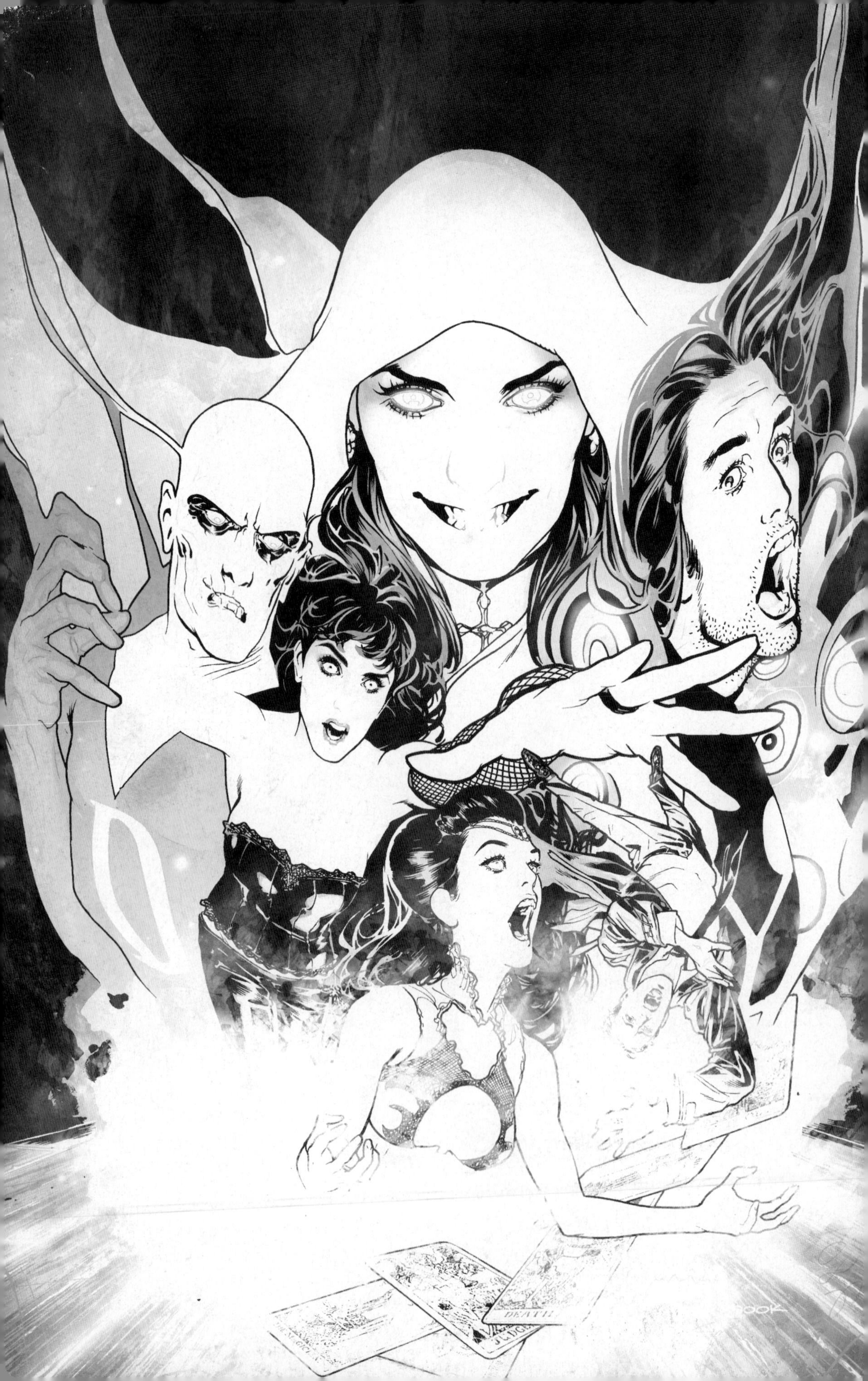
DEATH

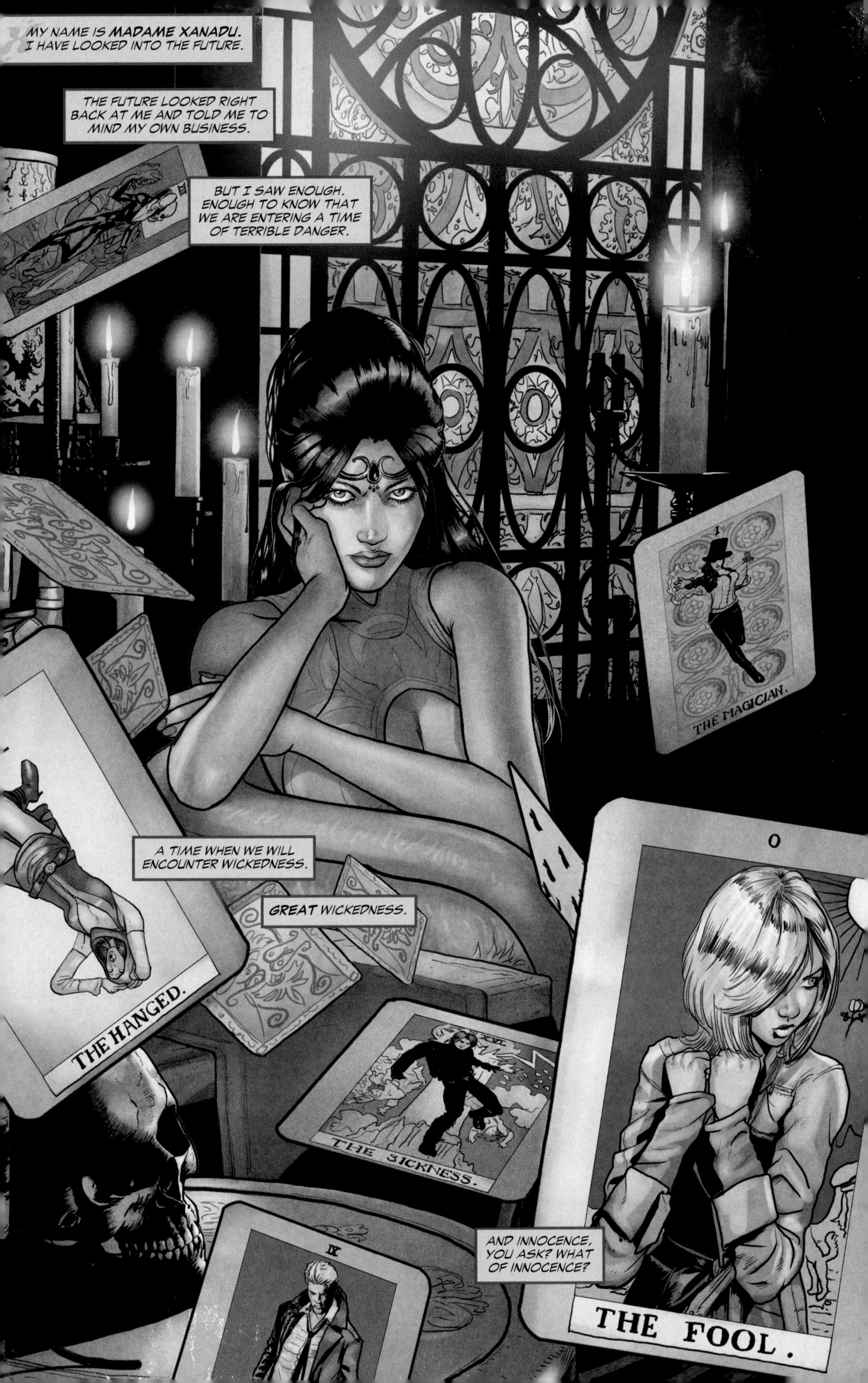
MY NAME IS MADAME XANADU. I HAVE LOOKED INTO THE FUTURE.
THE FUTURE LOOKED RIGHT BACK AT ME AND TOLD ME TO MIND MY OWN BUSINESS.
BUT I SAW ENOUGH. ENOUGH TO KNOW THAT WE ARE ENTERING A TIME OF TERRIBLE DANGER.
THE MAGICIAN.
A TIME WHEN WE WILL ENCOUNTER WICKEDNESS.
GREAT WICKEDNESS.
THE HANGED.
THE SICKNESS.
AND INNOCENCE, YOU ASK? WHAT OF INNOCENCE?
THE FOOL.

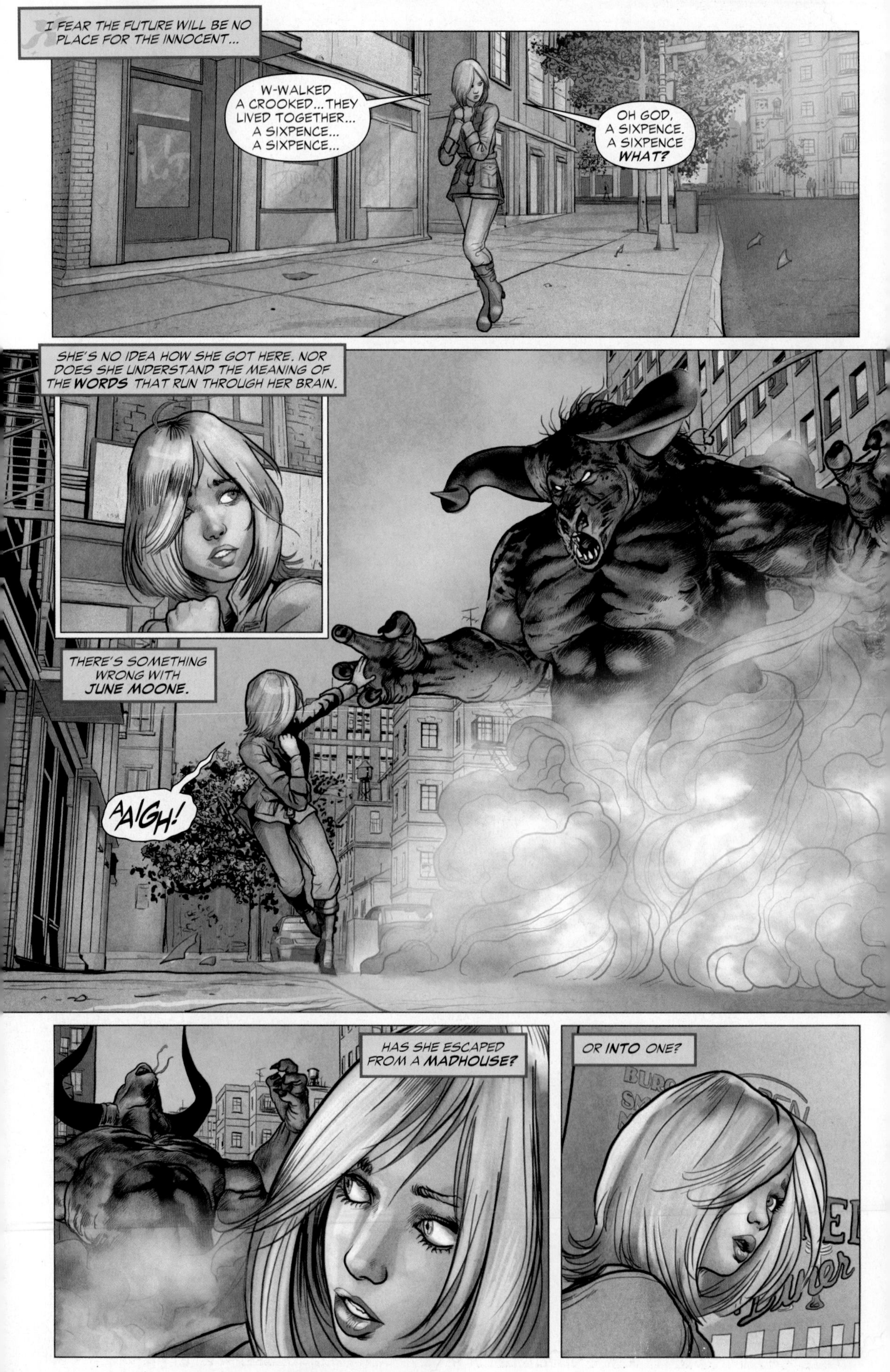
I FEAR THE FUTURE WILL BE NO PLACE FOR THE INNOCENT...
W-WALKED A CROOKED... THEY LIVED TOGETHER... A SIXPENCE... A SIXPENCE...
OH GOD, A SIXPENCE. A SIXPENCE WHAT?
SHE'S NO IDEA HOW SHE GOT HERE. NOR DOES SHE UNDERSTAND THE MEANING OF THE WORDS THAT RUN THROUGH HER BRAIN.
THERE'S SOMETHING WRONG WITH JUNE MOONE.
AAIGH!
HAS SHE ESCAPED FROM A MADHOUSE?
OR INTO ONE?

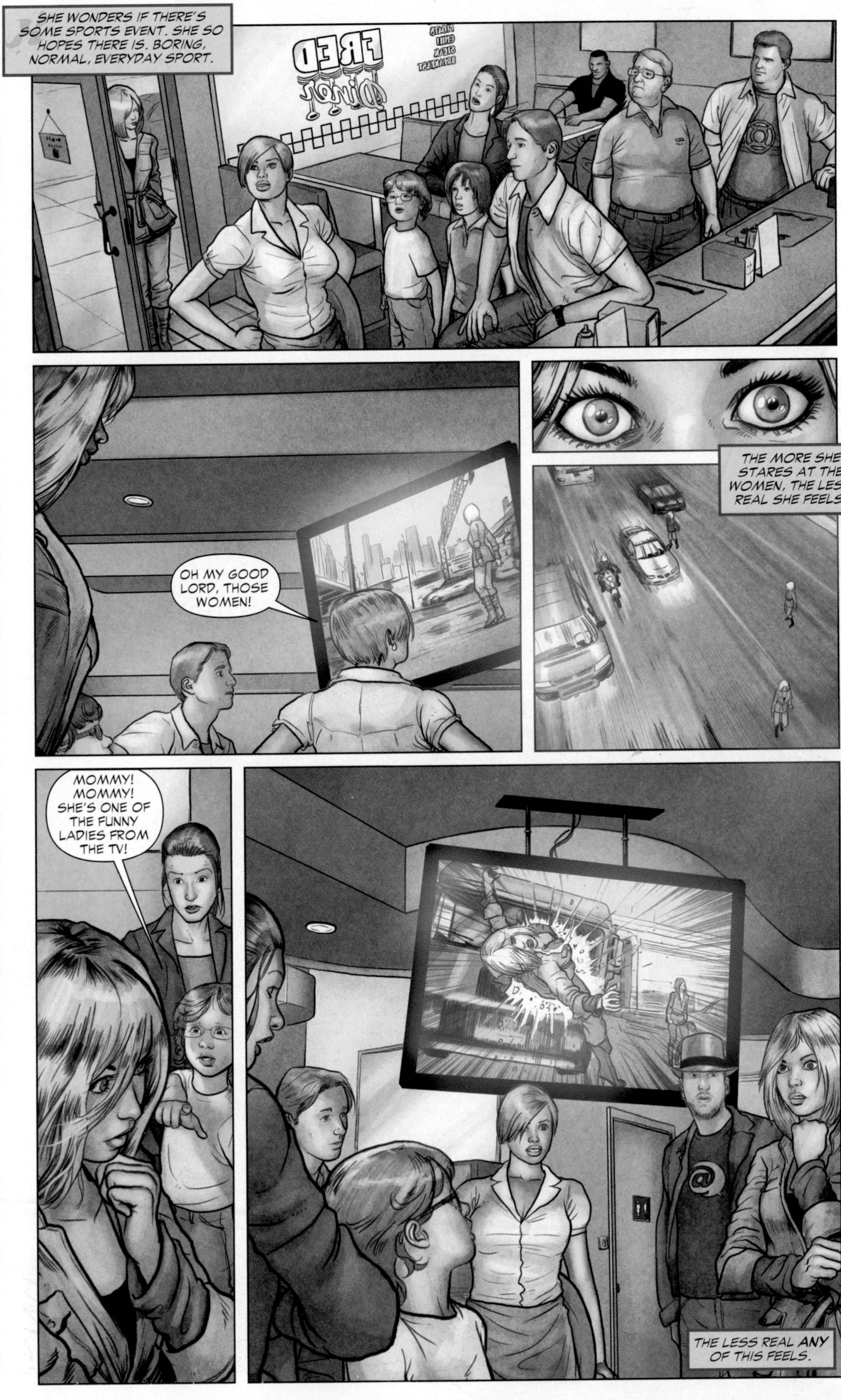
SHE WONDERS IF THERE'S SOME SPORTS EVENT. SHE SO HOPES THERE IS. BORING, NORMAL, EVERYDAY SPORT.
FRED Diner
OH MY GOOD LORD, THOSE WOMEN!
THE MORE SHE STARES AT THE WOMEN, THE LESS REAL SHE FEELS.
MOMMY! MOMMY! SHE'S ONE OF THE FUNNY LADIES FROM THE TV!
THE LESS REAL ANY OF THIS FEELS.

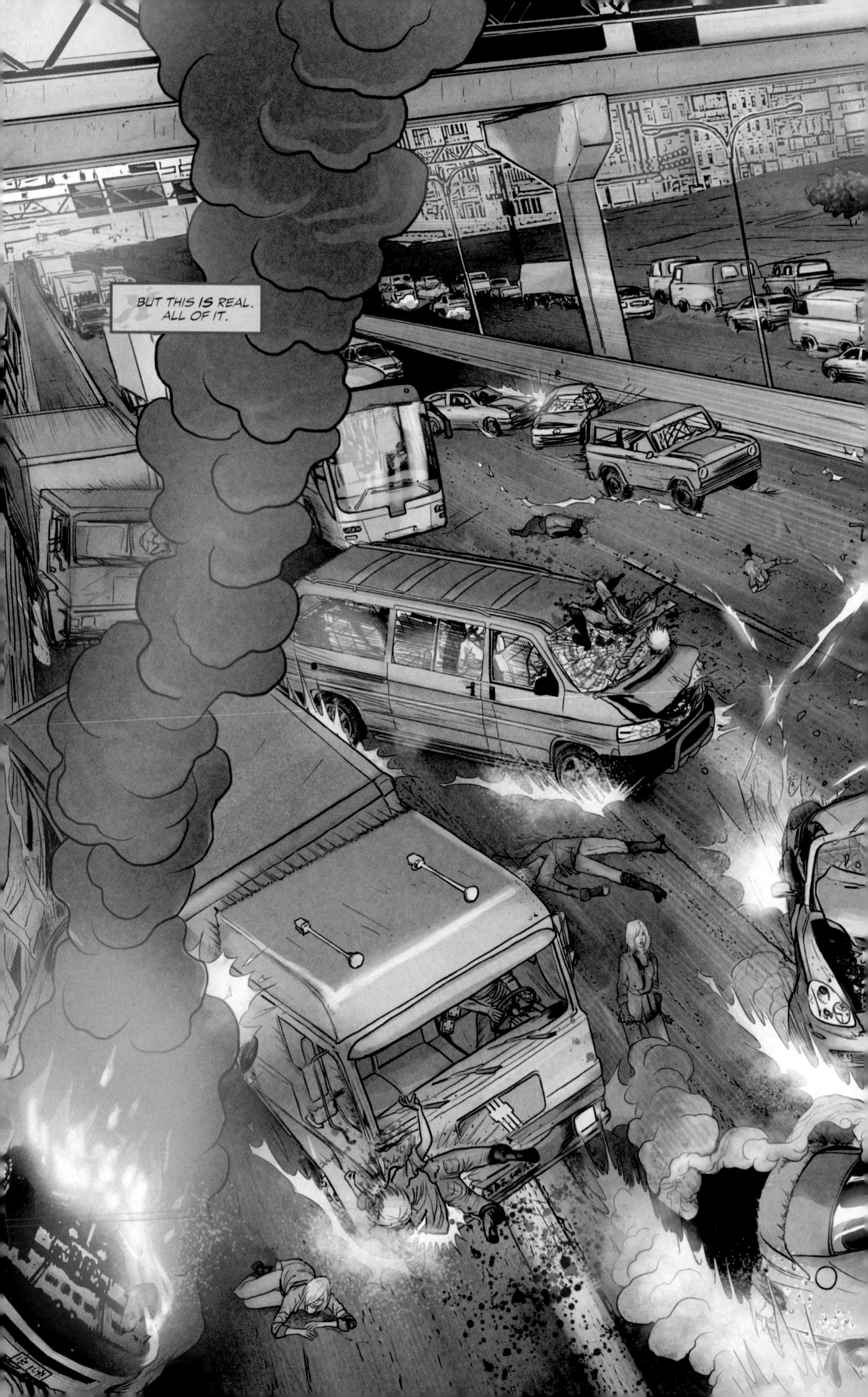
BUT THIS IS REAL. ALL OF IT.

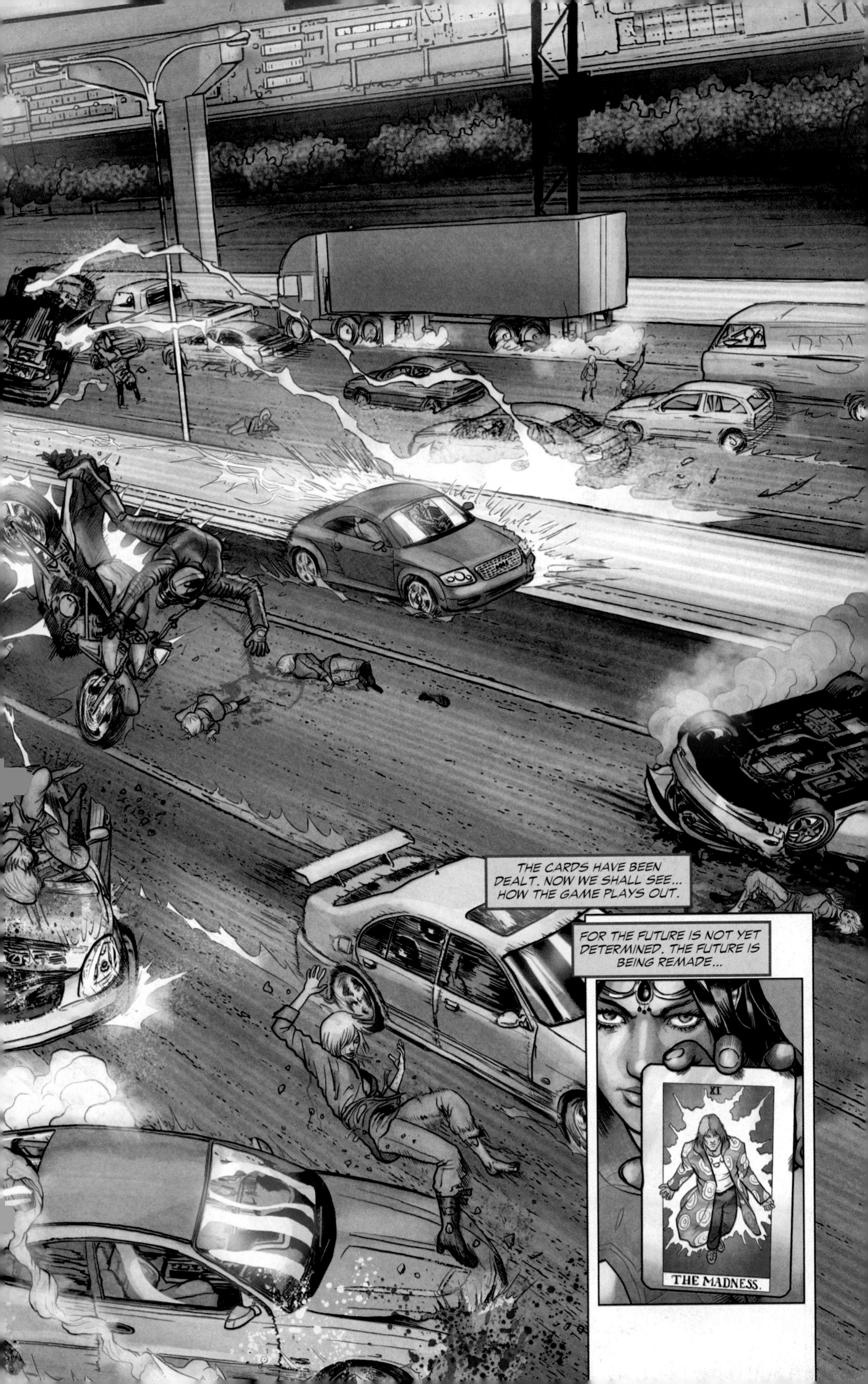
THE CARDS HAVE BEEN DEALT. NOW WE SHALL SEE... HOW THE GAME PLAYS OUT.
FOR THE FUTURE IS NOT YET DETERMINED. THE FUTURE IS BEING REMADE...
XI
THE MADNESS.

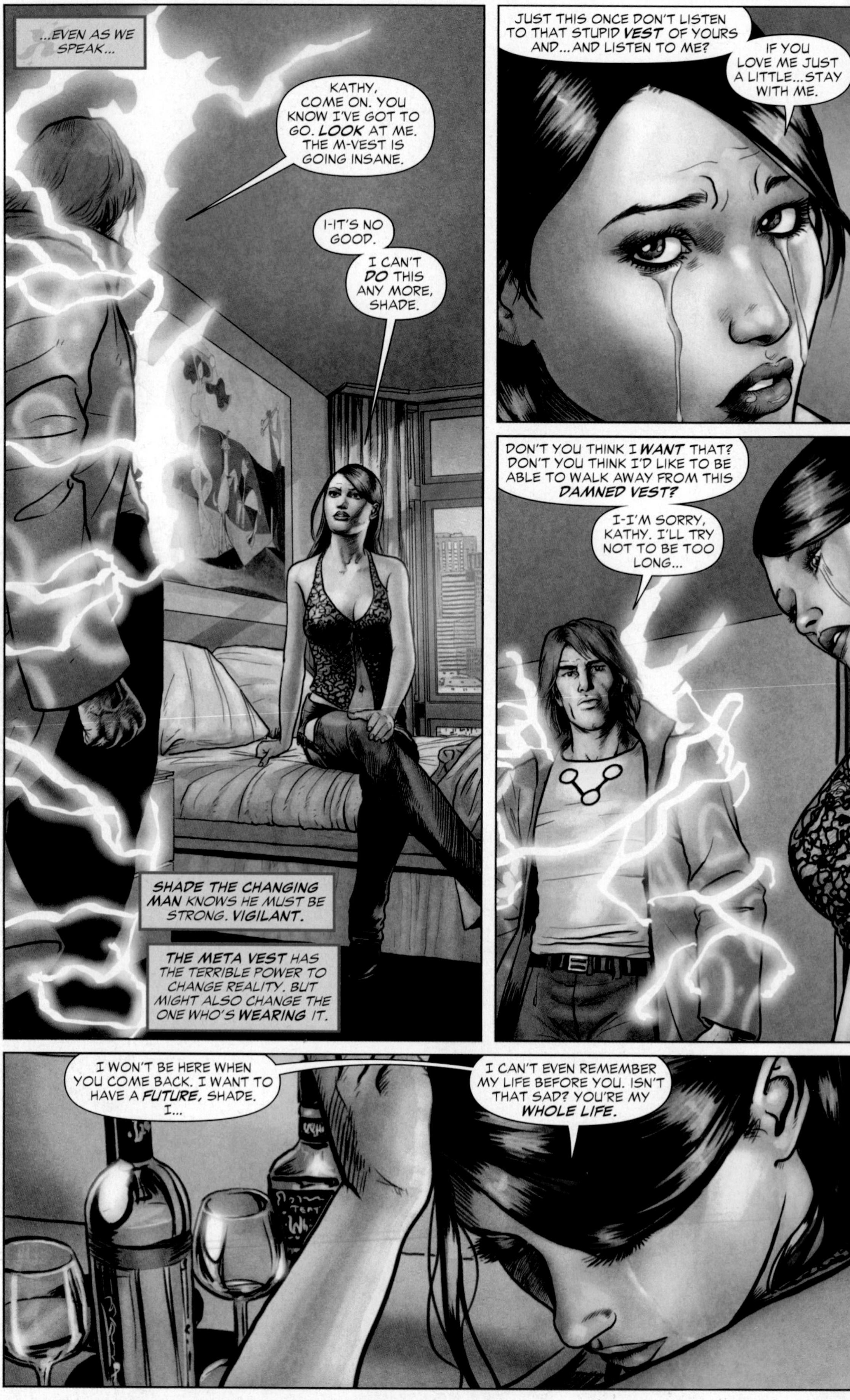
...EVEN AS WE SPEAK...
KATHY, COME ON. YOU KNOW I'VE GOT TO GO. LOOK AT ME. THE M-VEST IS GOING INSANE.
I-IT'S NO GOOD.
I CAN'T DO THIS ANY MORE, SHADE.
SHADE THE CHANGING MAN KNOWS HE MUST BE STRONG. VIGILANT.
THE META VEST HAS THE TERRIBLE POWER TO CHANGE REALITY. BUT MIGHT ALSO CHANGE THE ONE WHO'S WEARING IT.
JUST THIS ONCE DON'T LISTEN TO THAT STUPID VEST OF YOURS AND...AND LISTEN TO ME?
IF YOU LOVE ME JUST A LITTLE...STAY WITH ME.
DON'T YOU THINK I WANT THAT? DON'T YOU THINK I'D LIKE TO BE ABLE TO WALK AWAY FROM THIS DAMNED VEST?
I-I'M SORRY, KATHY. I'LL TRY NOT TO BE TOO LONG...
I WON'T BE HERE WHEN YOU COME BACK. I WANT TO HAVE A FUTURE, SHADE. I...
I CAN'T EVEN REMEMBER MY LIFE BEFORE YOU. ISN'T THAT SAD? YOU'RE MY WHOLE LIFE.

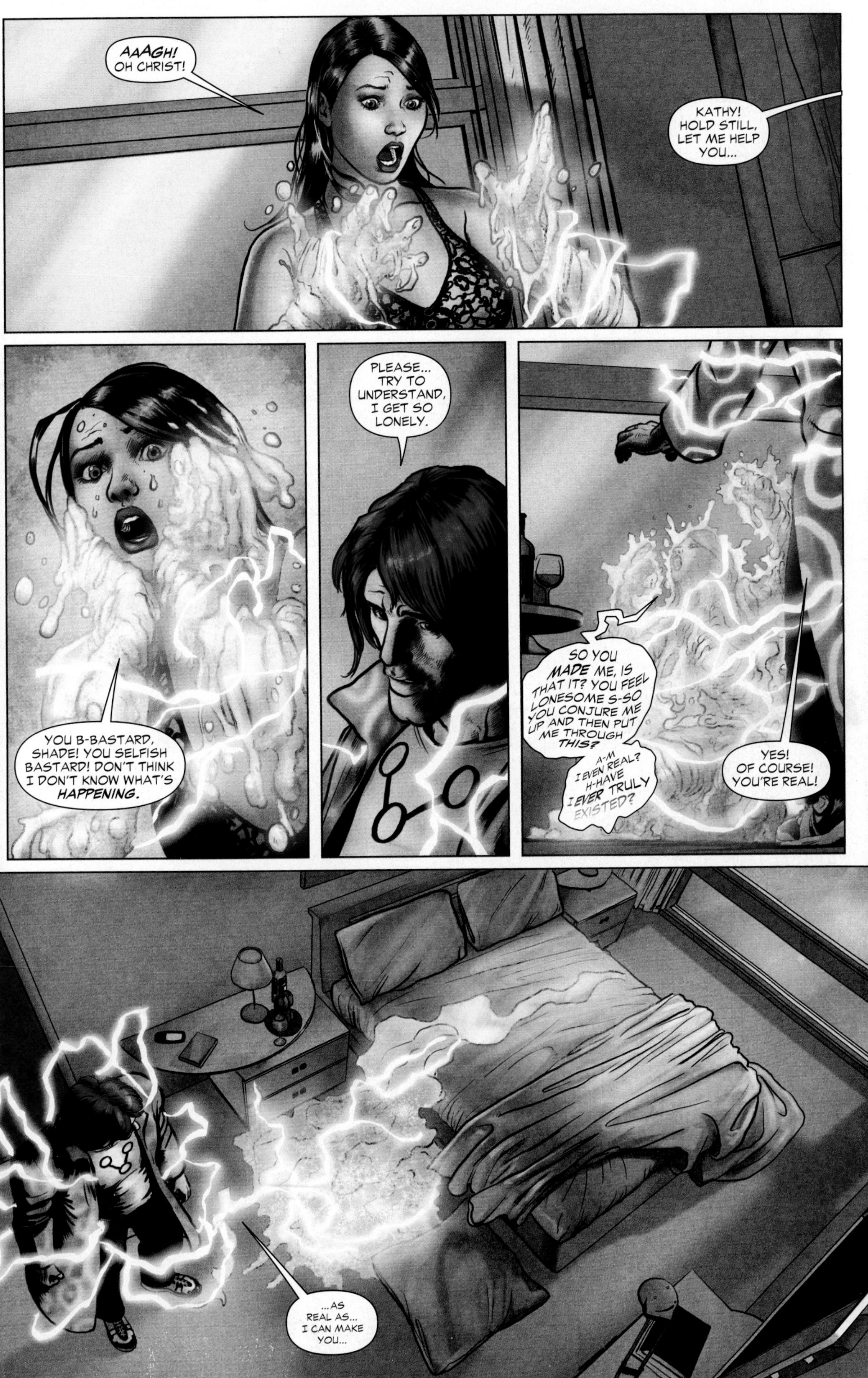
AAAGH! OH CHRIST!
KATHY! HOLD STILL, LET ME HELP YOU...
YOU B-BASTARD, SHADE! YOU SELFISH BASTARD! DON'T THINK I DON'T KNOW WHAT'S HAPPENING.
PLEASE... TRY TO UNDERSTAND, I GET SO LONELY.
SO YOU MADE ME, IS THAT IT? YOU FEEL LONESOME S-SO YOU CONJURE ME UP AND THEN PUT ME THROUGH THIS?
A-M I EVEN REAL? H-HAVE I EVER TRULY EXISTED?
YES! OF COURSE! YOU'RE REAL!
...AS REAL AS... I CAN MAKE YOU...

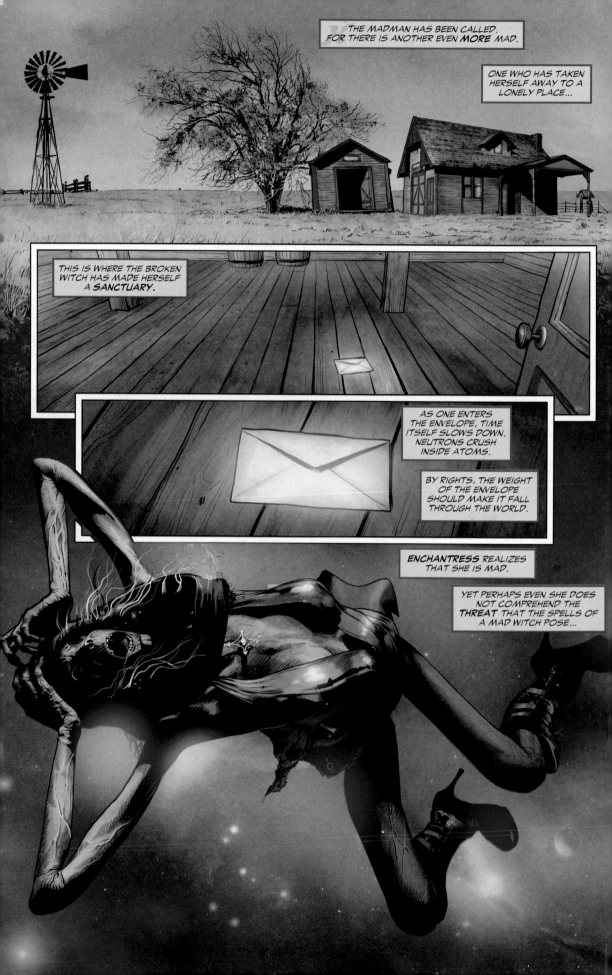

THE MADMAN HAS BEEN CALLED.
FOR THERE IS ANOTHER EVEN **MORE** MAD.

ONE WHO HAS TAKEN
HERSELF AWAY TO A
LONELY PLACE...

THIS IS WHERE THE BROKEN
WITCH HAS MADE HERSELF
A **SANCTUARY**.

AS ONE ENTERS
THE ENVELOPE, TIME
ITSELF SLOWS DOWN.
NEUTRONS CRUSH
INSIDE ATOMS.

BY RIGHTS, THE WEIGHT
OF THE ENVELOPE
SHOULD MAKE IT FALL
THROUGH THE WORLD.

ENCHANTRESS REALIZES
THAT SHE IS MAD.

YET PERHAPS EVEN SHE DOES
NOT COMPREHEND THE
THREAT THAT THE SPELLS OF
A MAD WITCH POSE...

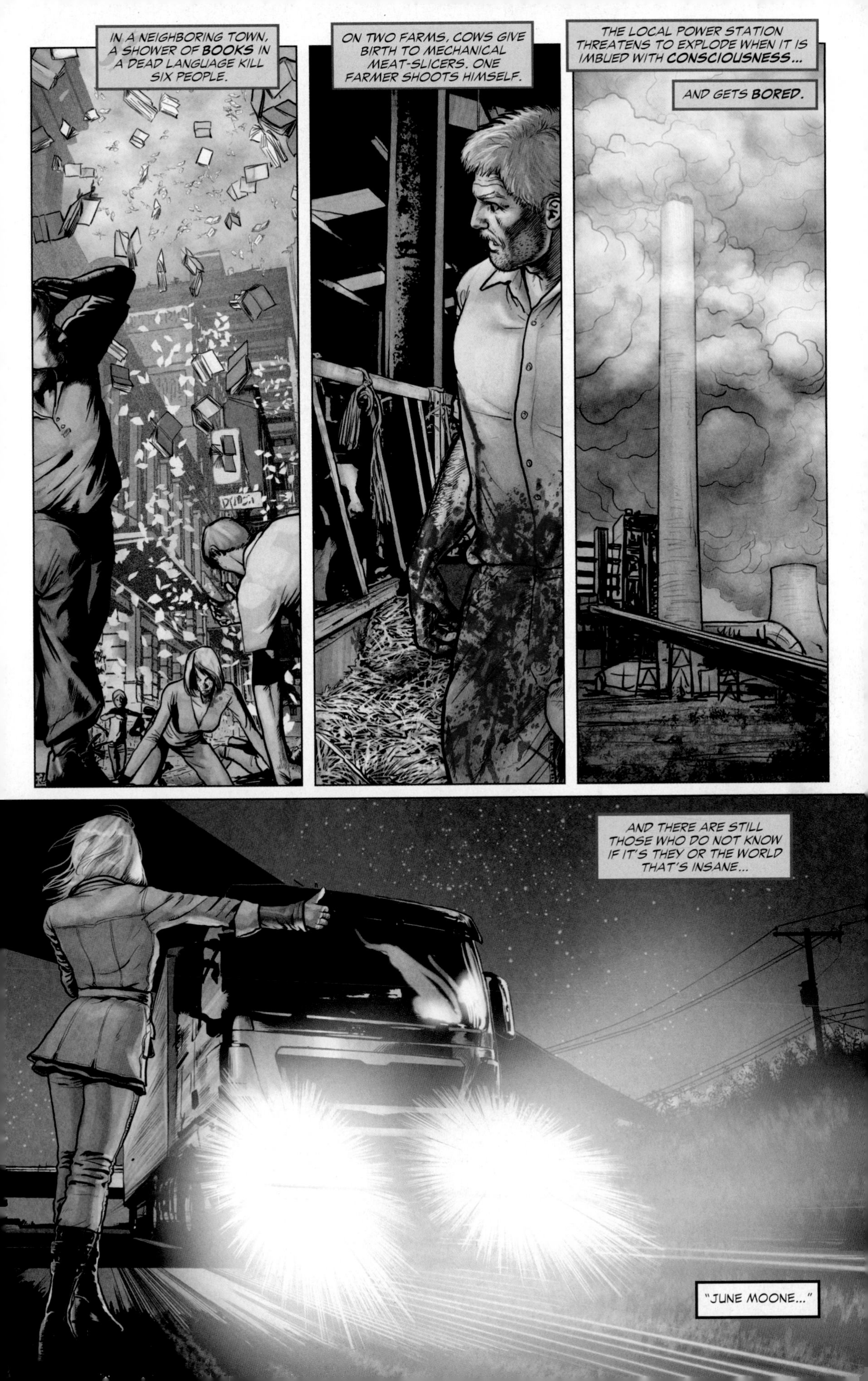
IN A NEIGHBORING TOWN, A SHOWER OF BOOKS IN A DEAD LANGUAGE KILL SIX PEOPLE.
ON TWO FARMS, COWS GIVE BIRTH TO MECHANICAL MEAT-SLICERS. ONE FARMER SHOOTS HIMSELF.
THE LOCAL POWER STATION THREATENS TO EXPLODE WHEN IT IS IMBUED WITH CONSCIOUSNESS...
AND GETS BORED.
AND THERE ARE STILL THOSE WHO DO NOT KNOW IF IT'S THEY OR THE WORLD THAT'S INSANE...
"JUNE MOONE..."

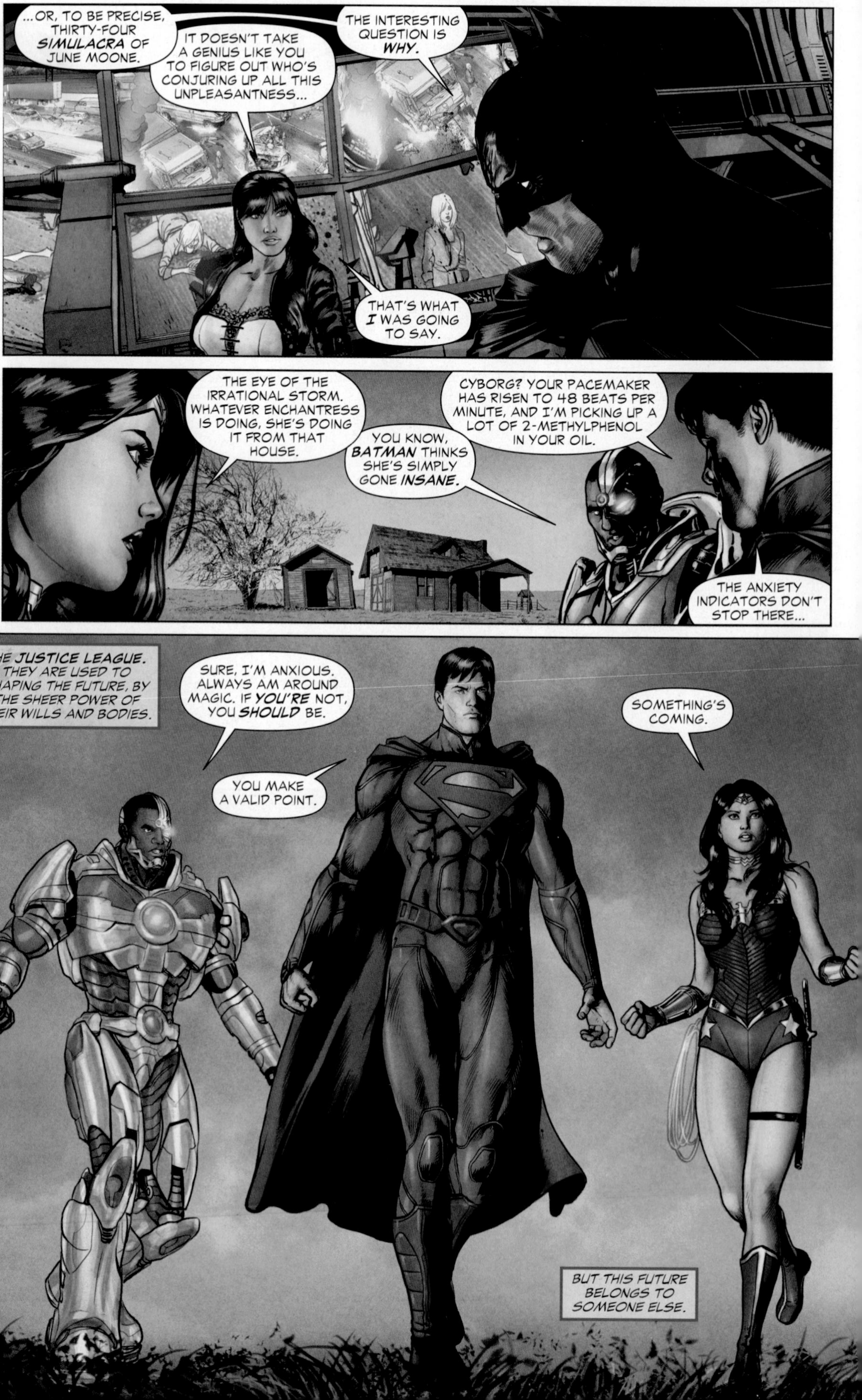
...OR, TO BE PRECISE, THIRTY-FOUR SIMULACRA OF JUNE MOONE.
IT DOESN'T TAKE A GENIUS LIKE YOU TO FIGURE OUT WHO'S CONJURING UP ALL THIS UNPLEASANTNESS...
THE INTERESTING QUESTION IS WHY.
THAT'S WHAT I WAS GOING TO SAY.
THE EYE OF THE IRRATIONAL STORM. WHATEVER ENCHANTRESS IS DOING, SHE'S DOING IT FROM THAT HOUSE.
YOU KNOW, BATMAN THINKS SHE'S SIMPLY GONE INSANE.
CYBORG? YOUR PACEMAKER HAS RISEN TO 48 BEATS PER MINUTE, AND I'M PICKING UP A LOT OF 2-METHYLPHENOL IN YOUR OIL.
THE ANXIETY INDICATORS DON'T STOP THERE...
THE JUSTICE LEAGUE. THEY ARE USED TO SHAPING THE FUTURE, BY THE SHEER POWER OF THEIR WILLS AND BODIES.
SURE, I'M ANXIOUS. ALWAYS AM AROUND MAGIC. IF YOU'RE NOT, YOU SHOULD BE.
YOU MAKE A VALID POINT.
SOMETHING'S COMING.
BUT THIS FUTURE BELONGS TO SOMEONE ELSE.

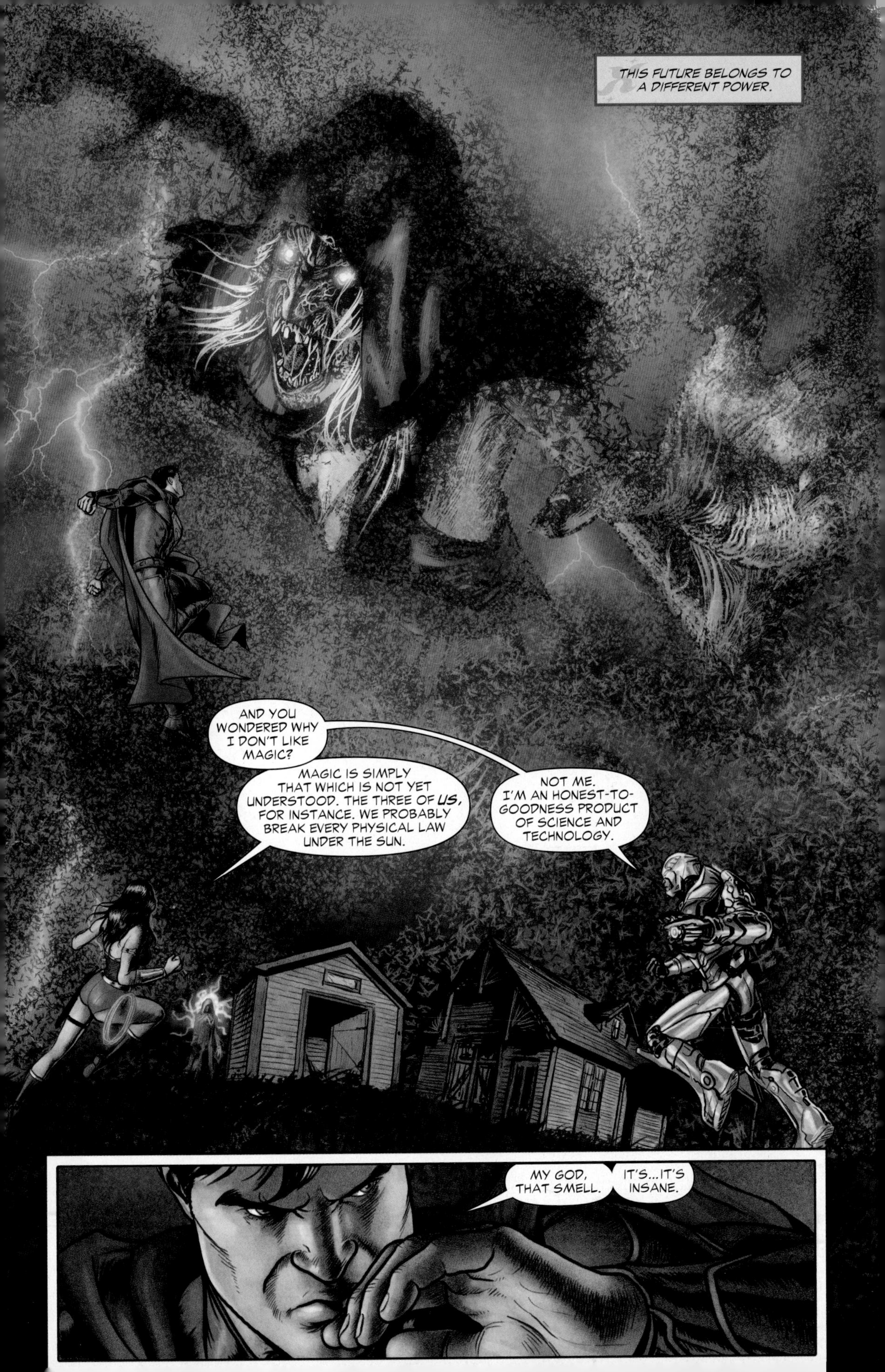
THIS FUTURE BELONGS TO A DIFFERENT POWER.
AND YOU WONDERED WHY I DON'T LIKE MAGIC?
MAGIC IS SIMPLY THAT WHICH IS NOT YET UNDERSTOOD. THE THREE OF *US*, FOR INSTANCE. WE PROBABLY BREAK EVERY PHYSICAL LAW UNDER THE SUN.
NOT ME. I'M AN HONEST-TO-GOODNESS PRODUCT OF SCIENCE AND TECHNOLOGY.
MY GOD, THAT SMELL.
IT'S...IT'S INSANE.

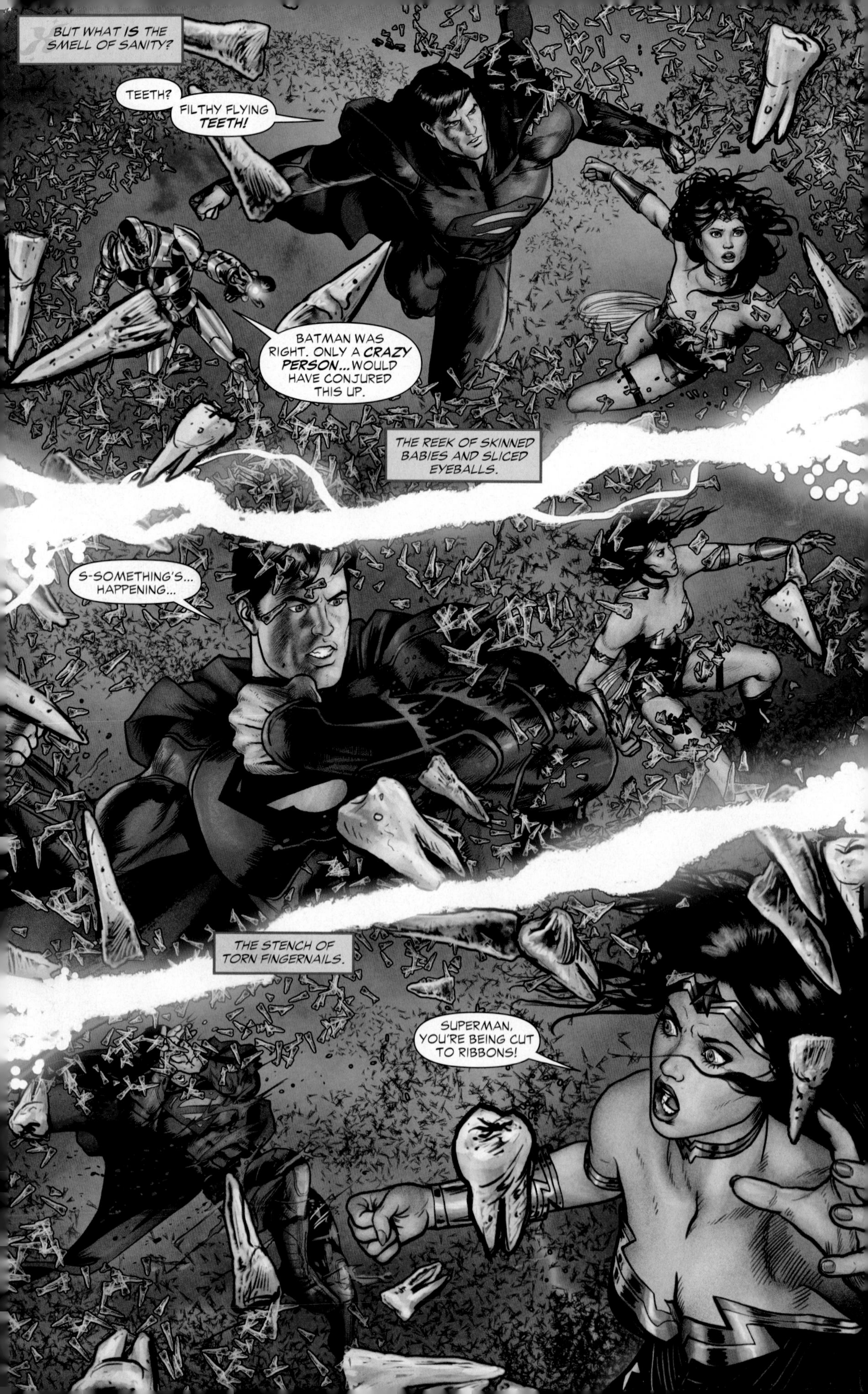
BUT WHAT IS THE SMELL OF SANITY?
TEETH?
FILTHY FLYING TEETH!
BATMAN WAS RIGHT. ONLY A CRAZY PERSON... WOULD HAVE CONJURED THIS UP.
THE REEK OF SKINNED BABIES AND SLICED EYEBALLS.
S-SOMETHING'S... HAPPENING...
THE STENCH OF TORN FINGERNAILS.
SUPERMAN, YOU'RE BEING CUT TO RIBBONS!

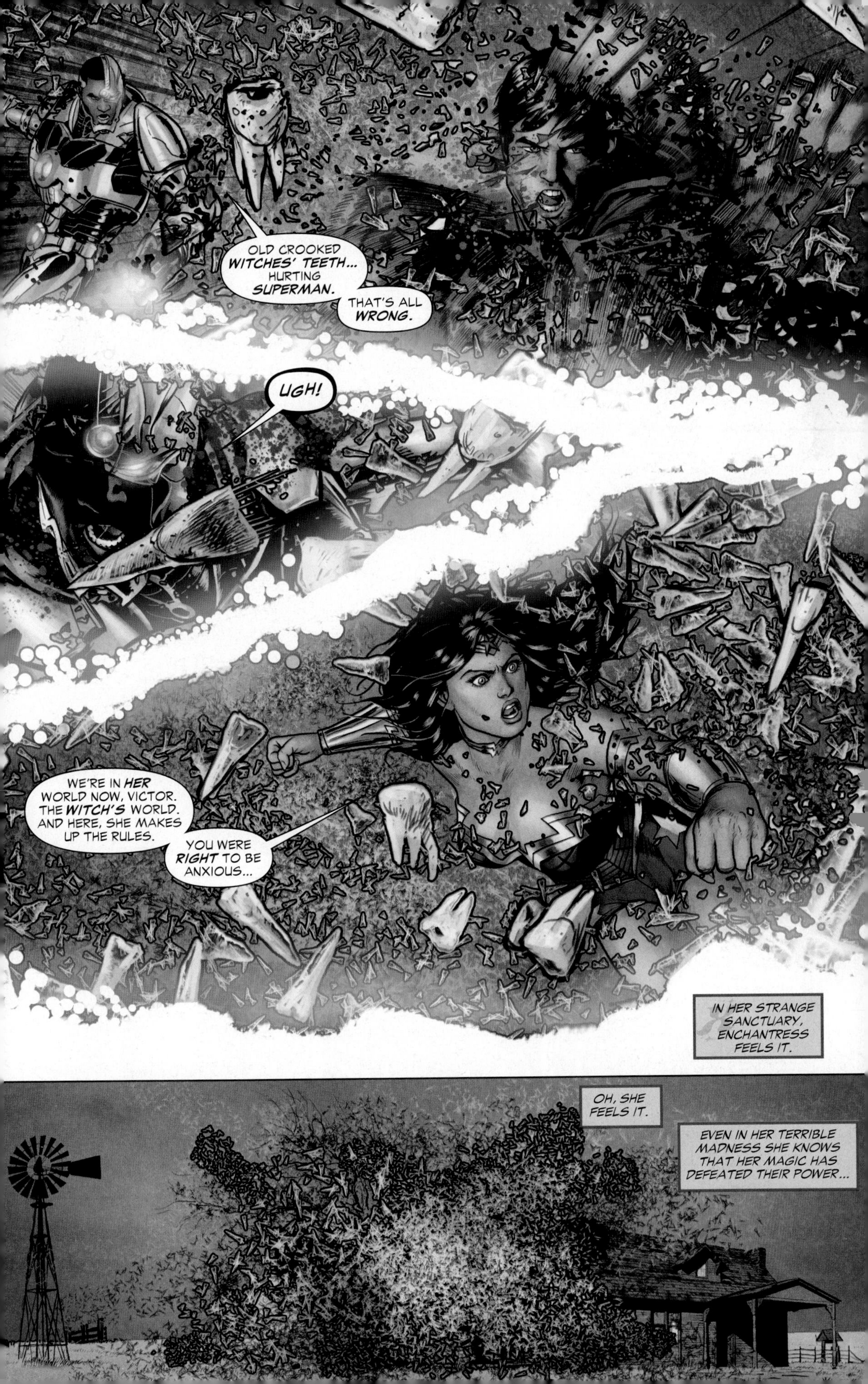
OLD CROOKED WITCHES' TEETH... HURTING SUPERMAN.
THAT'S ALL WRONG.
UGH!
WE'RE IN HER WORLD NOW, VICTOR. THE WITCH'S WORLD. AND HERE, SHE MAKES UP THE RULES.
YOU WERE RIGHT TO BE ANXIOUS...
IN HER STRANGE SANCTUARY, ENCHANTRESS FEELS IT.
OH, SHE FEELS IT.
EVEN IN HER TERRIBLE MADNESS SHE KNOWS THAT HER MAGIC HAS DEFEATED THEIR POWER...

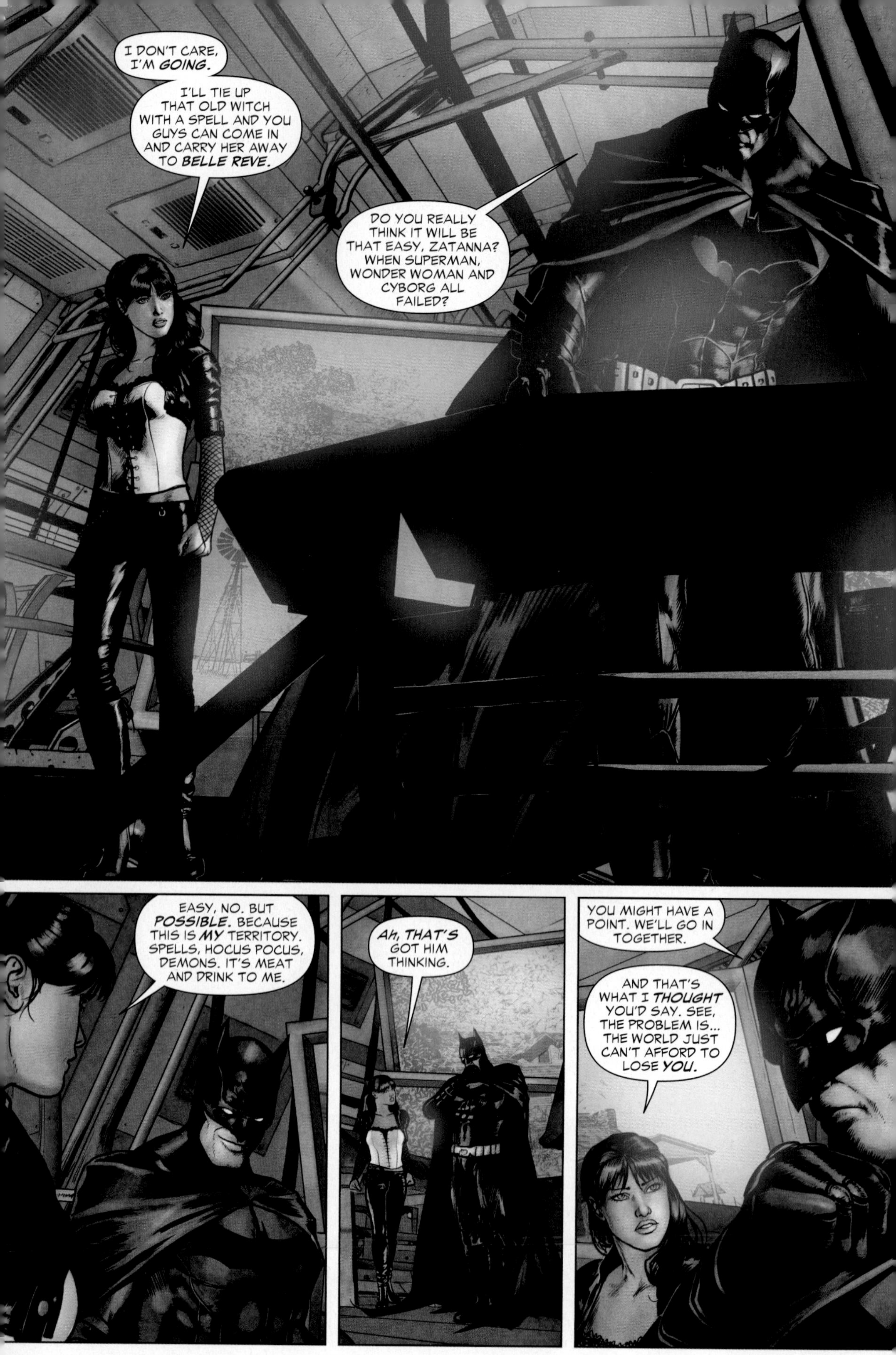
I DON'T CARE, I'M *GOING.*
I'LL TIE UP THAT OLD WITCH WITH A SPELL AND YOU GUYS CAN COME IN AND CARRY HER AWAY TO *BELLE REVE.*
DO YOU REALLY THINK IT WILL BE THAT EASY, ZATANNA? WHEN SUPERMAN, WONDER WOMAN AND CYBORG ALL FAILED?
EASY, NO. BUT *POSSIBLE.* BECAUSE THIS IS *MY* TERRITORY. SPELLS, HOCUS POCUS, DEMONS. IT'S MEAT AND DRINK TO ME.
Ah, THAT'S GOT HIM THINKING.
YOU MIGHT HAVE A POINT. WE'LL GO IN TOGETHER.
AND THAT'S WHAT I *THOUGHT* YOU'D SAY. SEE, THE PROBLEM IS... THE WORLD JUST CAN'T AFFORD TO LOSE *YOU.*

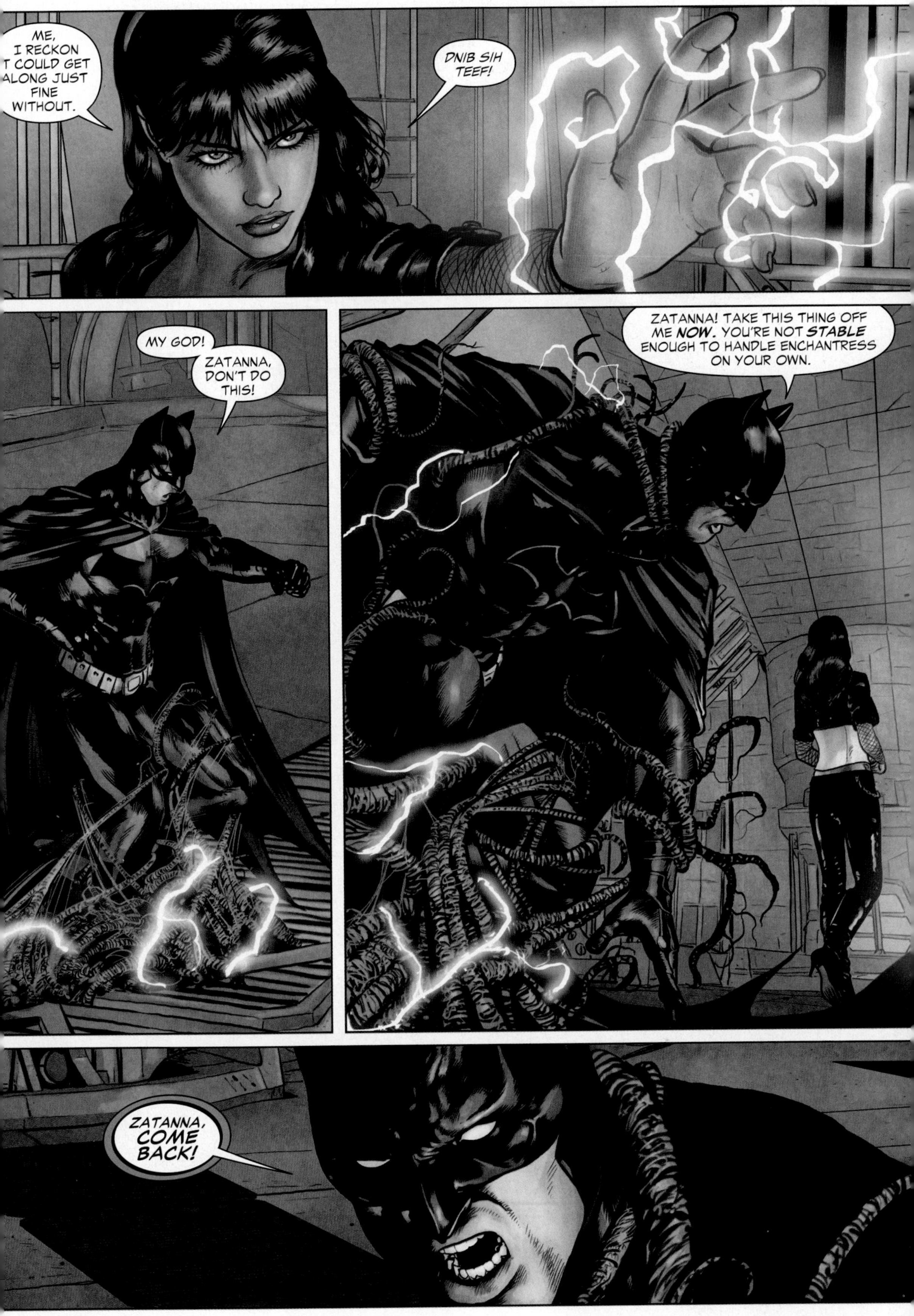
ME, I RECKON I COULD GET ALONG JUST FINE WITHOUT.
DNIB SIH TEEF!
MY GOD!
ZATANNA, DON'T DO THIS!
ZATANNA! TAKE THIS THING OFF ME NOW. YOU'RE NOT STABLE ENOUGH TO HANDLE ENCHANTRESS ON YOUR OWN.
ZATANNA, COME BACK!

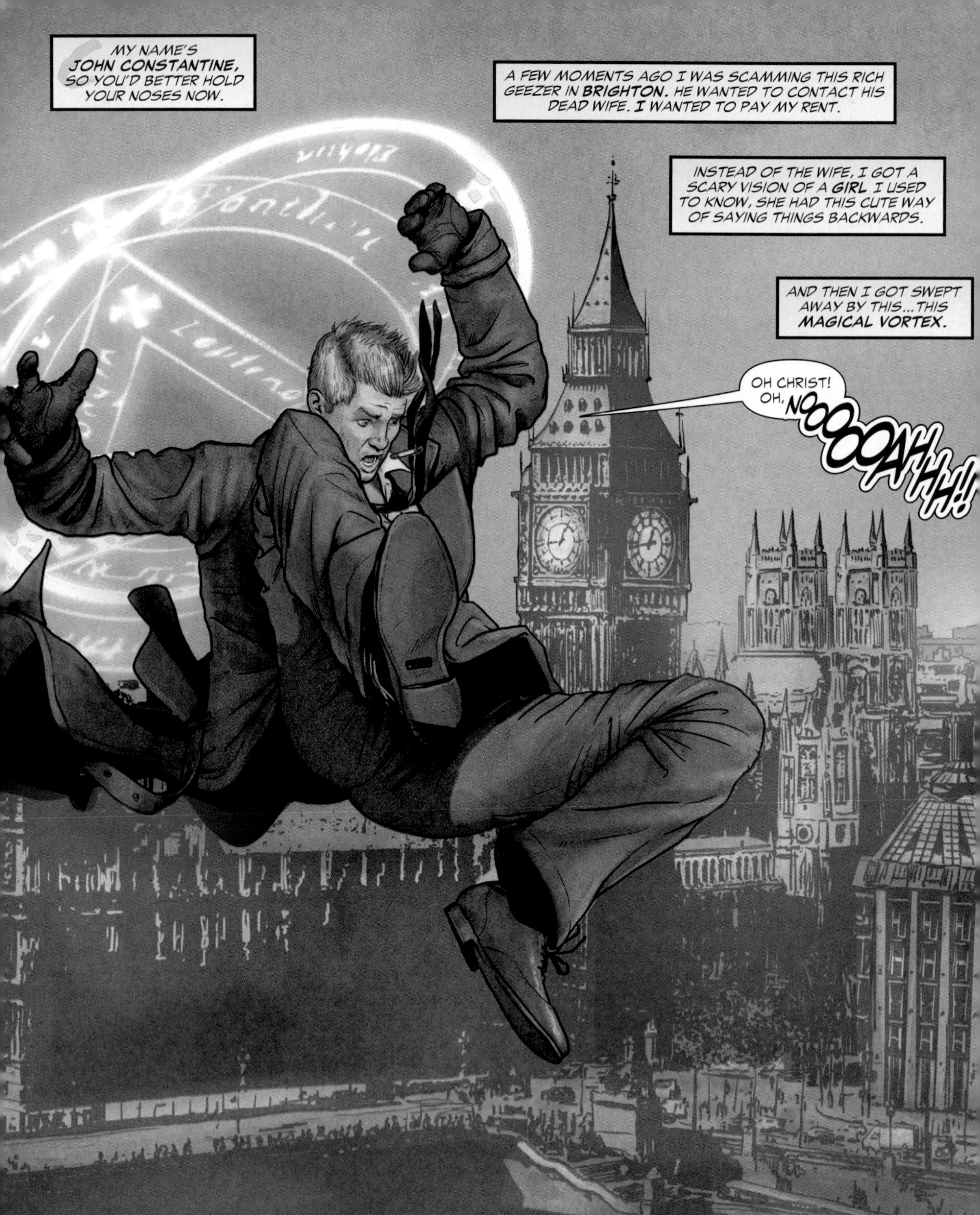
MY NAME'S JOHN CONSTANTINE, SO YOU'D BETTER HOLD YOUR NOSES NOW.
A FEW MOMENTS AGO I WAS SCAMMING THIS RICH GEEZER IN BRIGHTON. HE WANTED TO CONTACT HIS DEAD WIFE. I WANTED TO PAY MY RENT.
INSTEAD OF THE WIFE, I GOT A SCARY VISION OF A GIRL I USED TO KNOW, SHE HAD THIS CUTE WAY OF SAYING THINGS BACKWARDS.
AND THEN I GOT SWEPT AWAY BY THIS...THIS MAGICAL VORTEX.
OH CHRIST! OH, NOOOOOAHHH!!

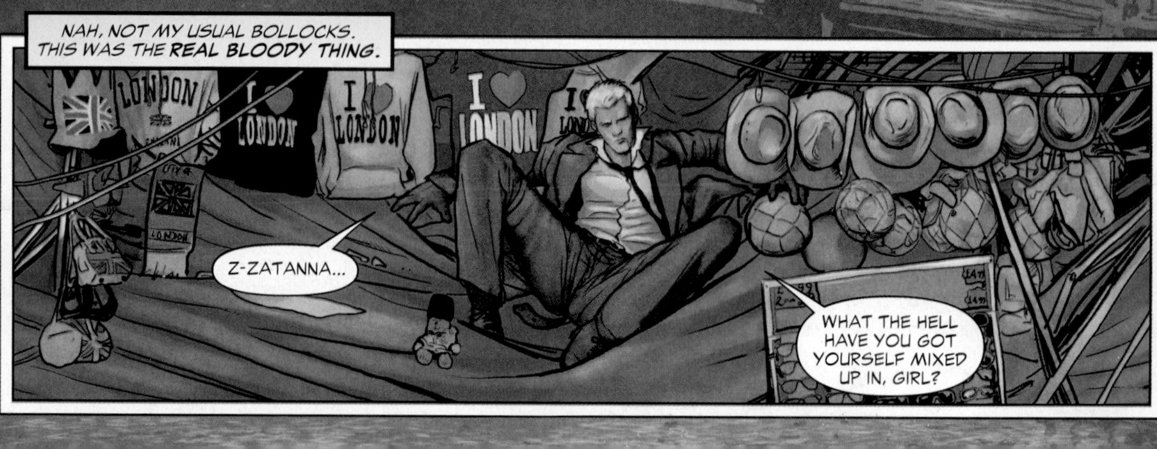
NAH, NOT MY USUAL BOLLOCKS. THIS WAS THE REAL BLOODY THING.
LONDON
I LONDON
I LONDON
I LONDON
Z-ZATANNA...
WHAT THE HELL HAVE YOU GOT YOURSELF MIXED UP IN, GIRL?

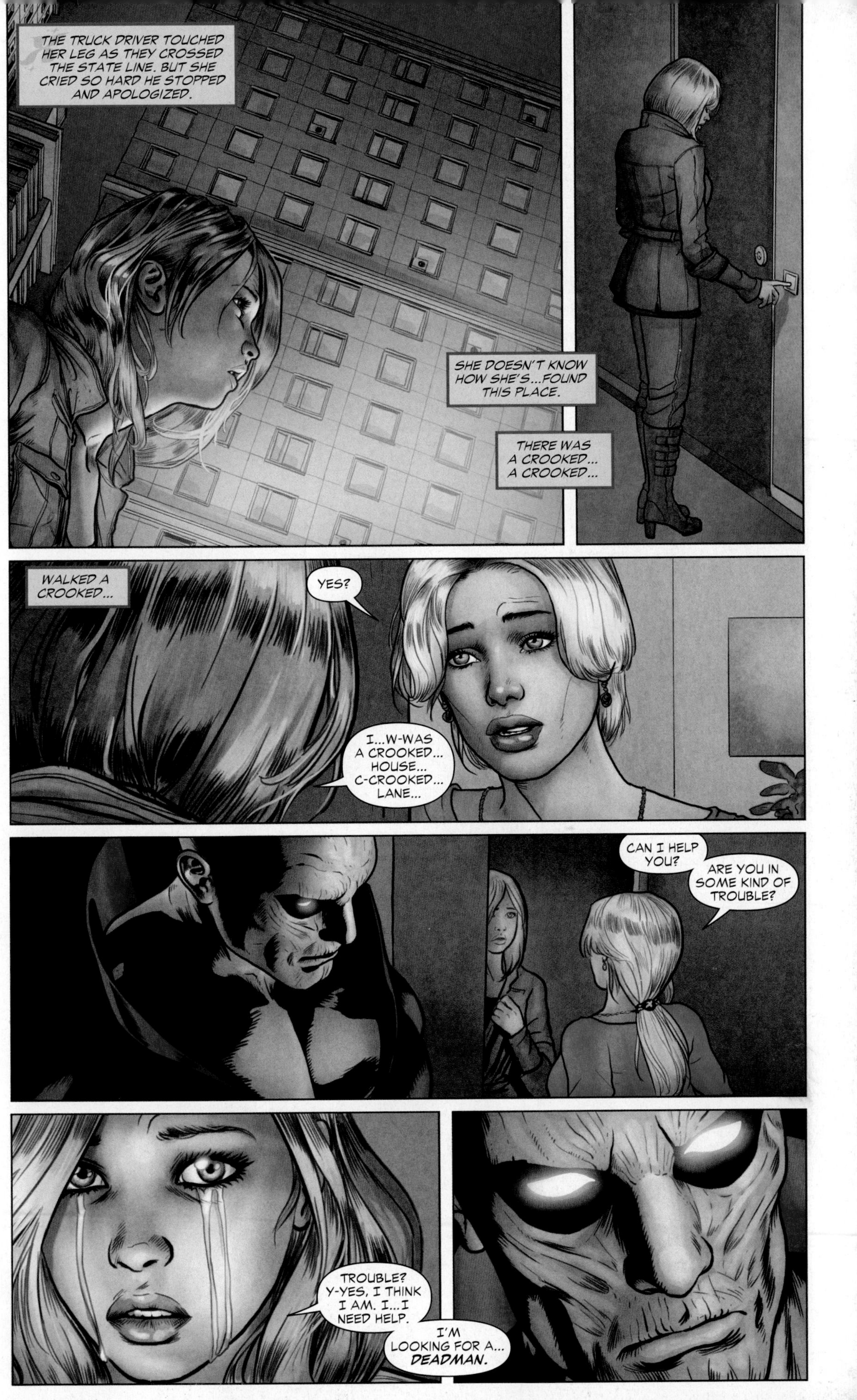
THE TRUCK DRIVER TOUCHED HER LEG AS THEY CROSSED THE STATE LINE. BUT SHE CRIED SO HARD HE STOPPED AND APOLOGIZED.
SHE DOESN'T KNOW HOW SHE'S...FOUND THIS PLACE.
THERE WAS A CROOKED... A CROOKED...
WALKED A CROOKED...
YES?
I...W-WAS A CROOKED... HOUSE... C-CROOKED... LANE...
CAN I HELP YOU?
ARE YOU IN SOME KIND OF TROUBLE?
TROUBLE? Y-YES, I THINK I AM. I...I NEED HELP.
I'M LOOKING FOR A... DEADMAN.

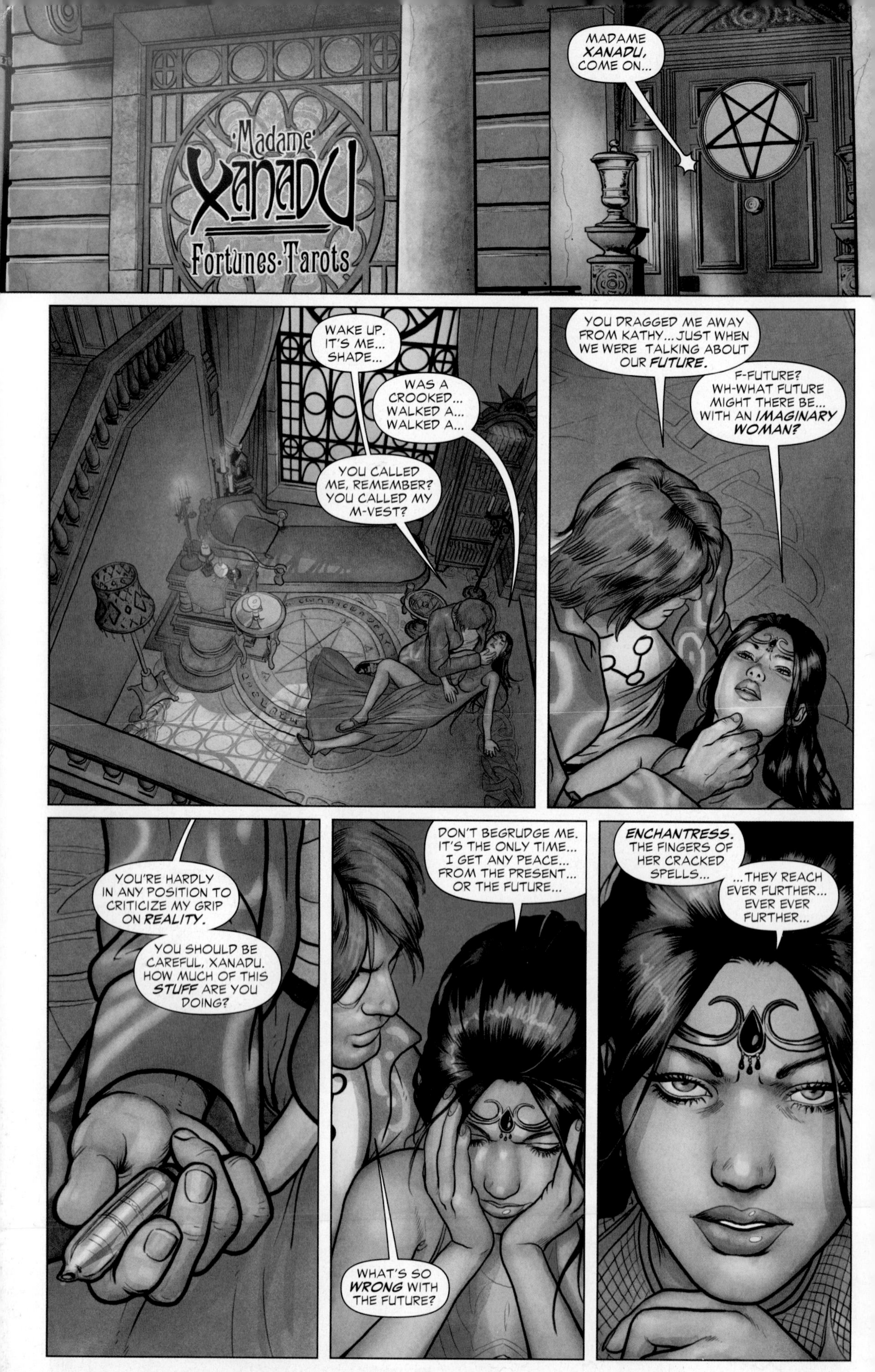
Madame Xanadu
Fortunes · Tarots
MADAME XANADU, COME ON...
WAKE UP. IT'S ME... SHADE...
WAS A CROOKED... WALKED A... WALKED A...
YOU CALLED ME, REMEMBER? YOU CALLED MY M-VEST?
YOU DRAGGED ME AWAY FROM KATHY... JUST WHEN WE WERE TALKING ABOUT OUR FUTURE.
F-FUTURE? WH-WHAT FUTURE MIGHT THERE BE... WITH AN IMAGINARY WOMAN?
YOU'RE HARDLY IN ANY POSITION TO CRITICIZE MY GRIP ON REALITY.
YOU SHOULD BE CAREFUL, XANADU. HOW MUCH OF THIS STUFF ARE YOU DOING?
DON'T BEGRUDGE ME. IT'S THE ONLY TIME... I GET ANY PEACE... FROM THE PRESENT... OR THE FUTURE...
WHAT'S SO WRONG WITH THE FUTURE?
ENCHANTRESS. THE FINGERS OF HER CRACKED SPELLS...
...THEY REACH EVER FURTHER... EVER EVER FURTHER...

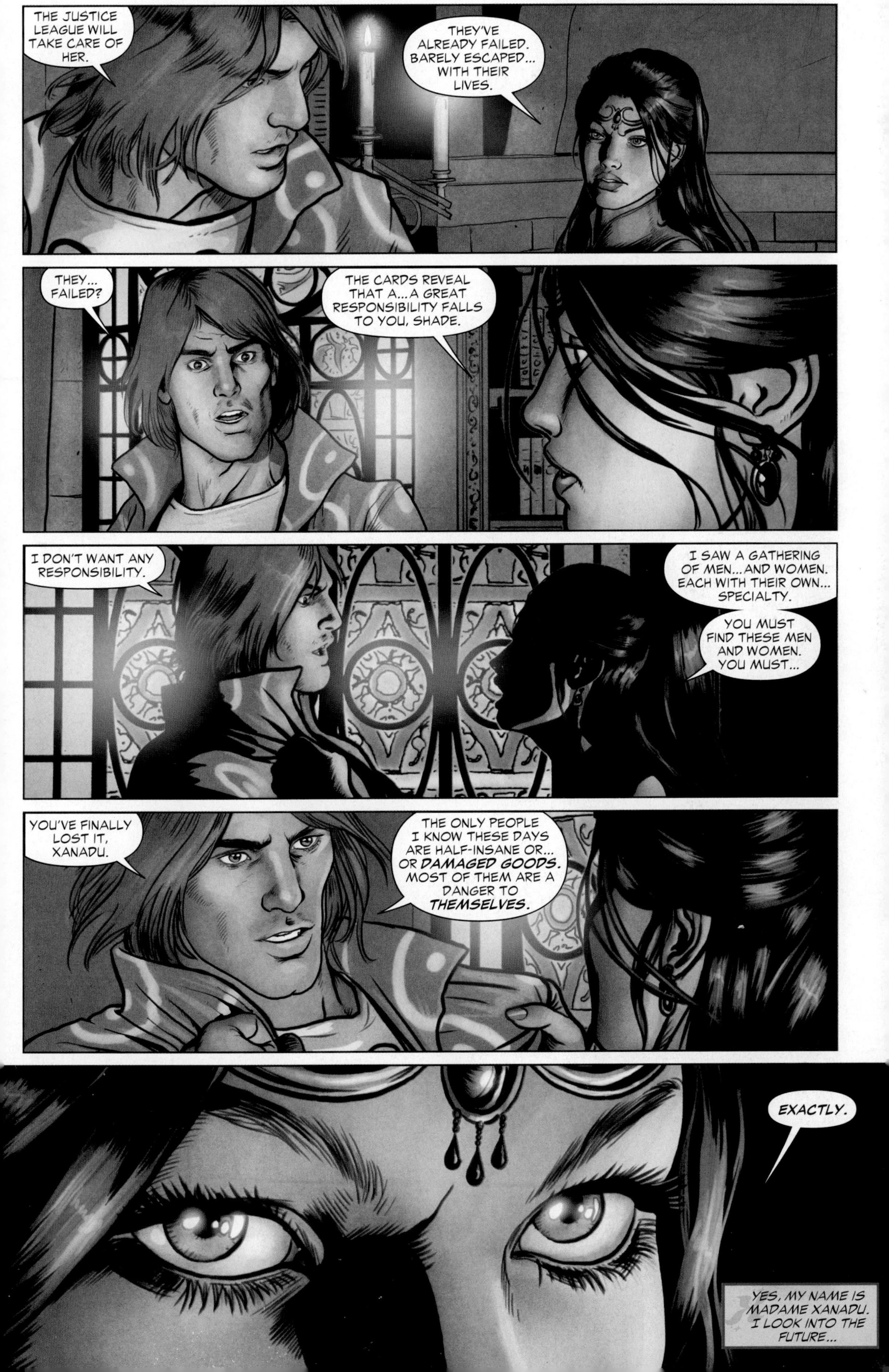
THE JUSTICE LEAGUE WILL TAKE CARE OF HER.
THEY'VE ALREADY FAILED. BARELY ESCAPED... WITH THEIR LIVES.
THEY... FAILED?
THE CARDS REVEAL THAT A... A GREAT RESPONSIBILITY FALLS TO YOU, SHADE.
I DON'T WANT ANY RESPONSIBILITY.
I SAW A GATHERING OF MEN... AND WOMEN. EACH WITH THEIR OWN... SPECIALTY.
YOU MUST FIND THESE MEN AND WOMEN. YOU MUST...
YOU'VE FINALLY LOST IT, XANADU.
THE ONLY PEOPLE I KNOW THESE DAYS ARE HALF-INSANE OR... OR *DAMAGED GOODS*. MOST OF THEM ARE A DANGER TO *THEMSELVES*.
EXACTLY.
YES, MY NAME IS MADAME XANADU. I LOOK INTO THE FUTURE...

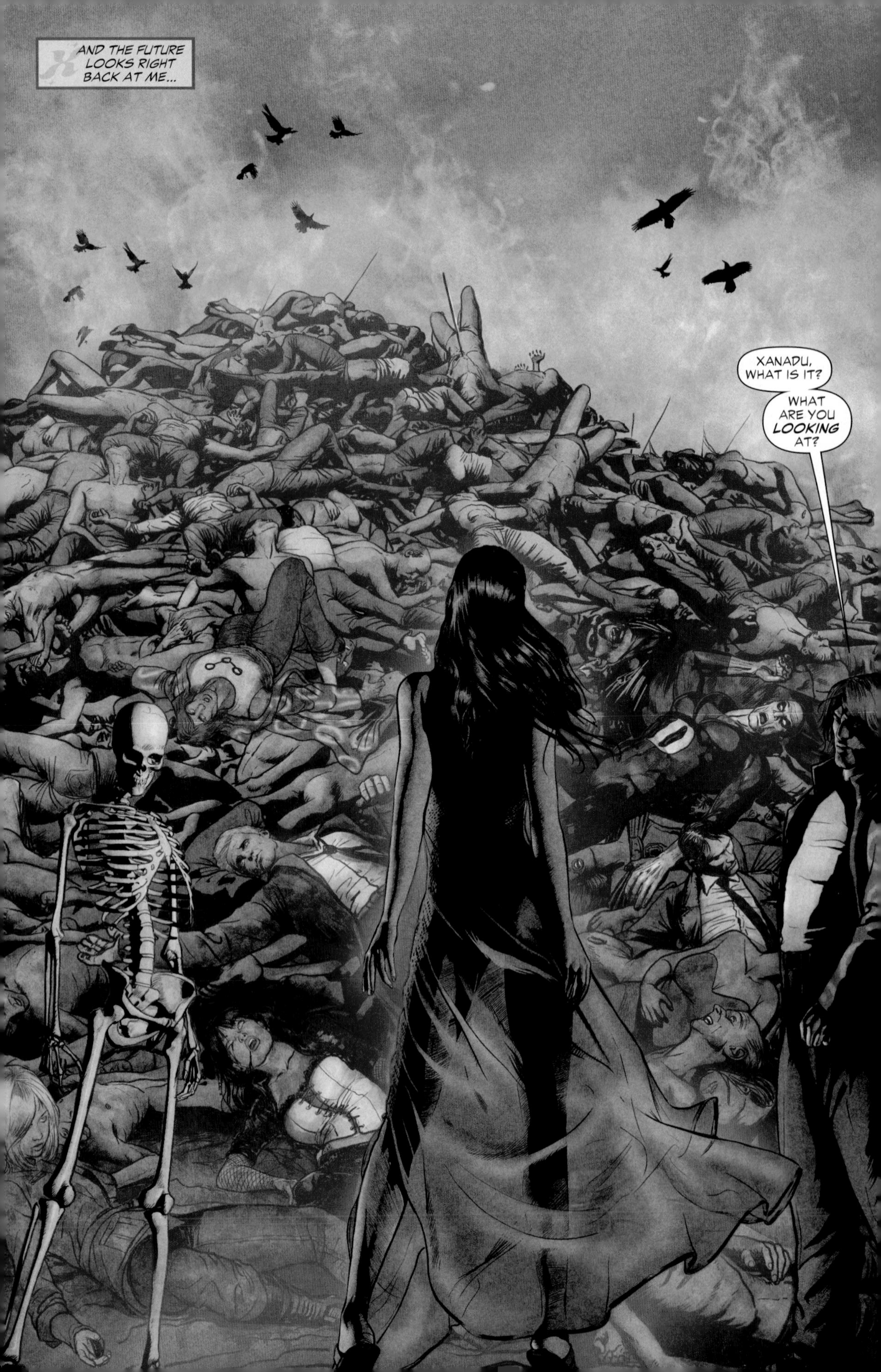
AND THE FUTURE LOOKS RIGHT BACK AT ME...
XANADU, WHAT IS IT?
WHAT ARE YOU LOOKING AT?

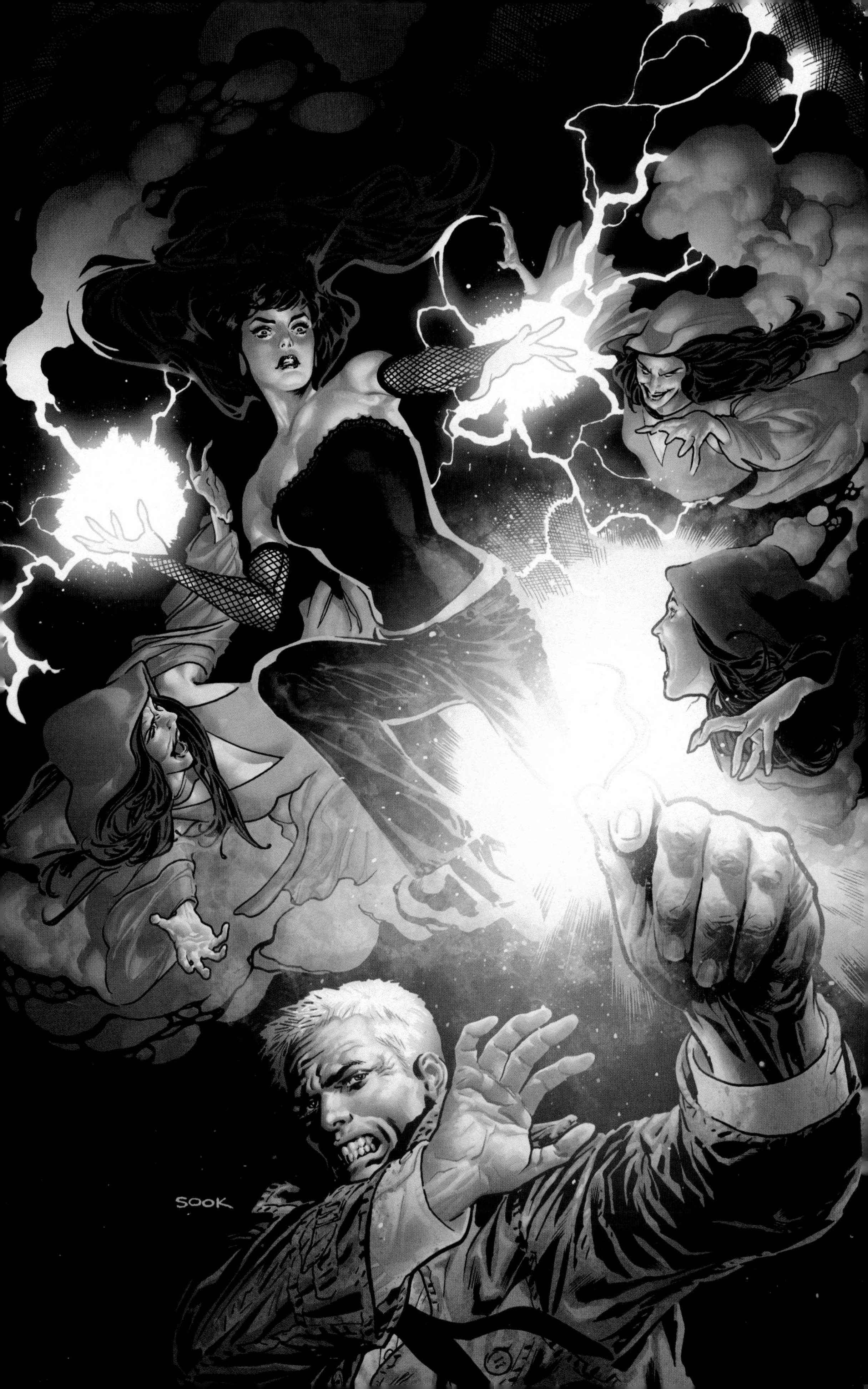
SOOK

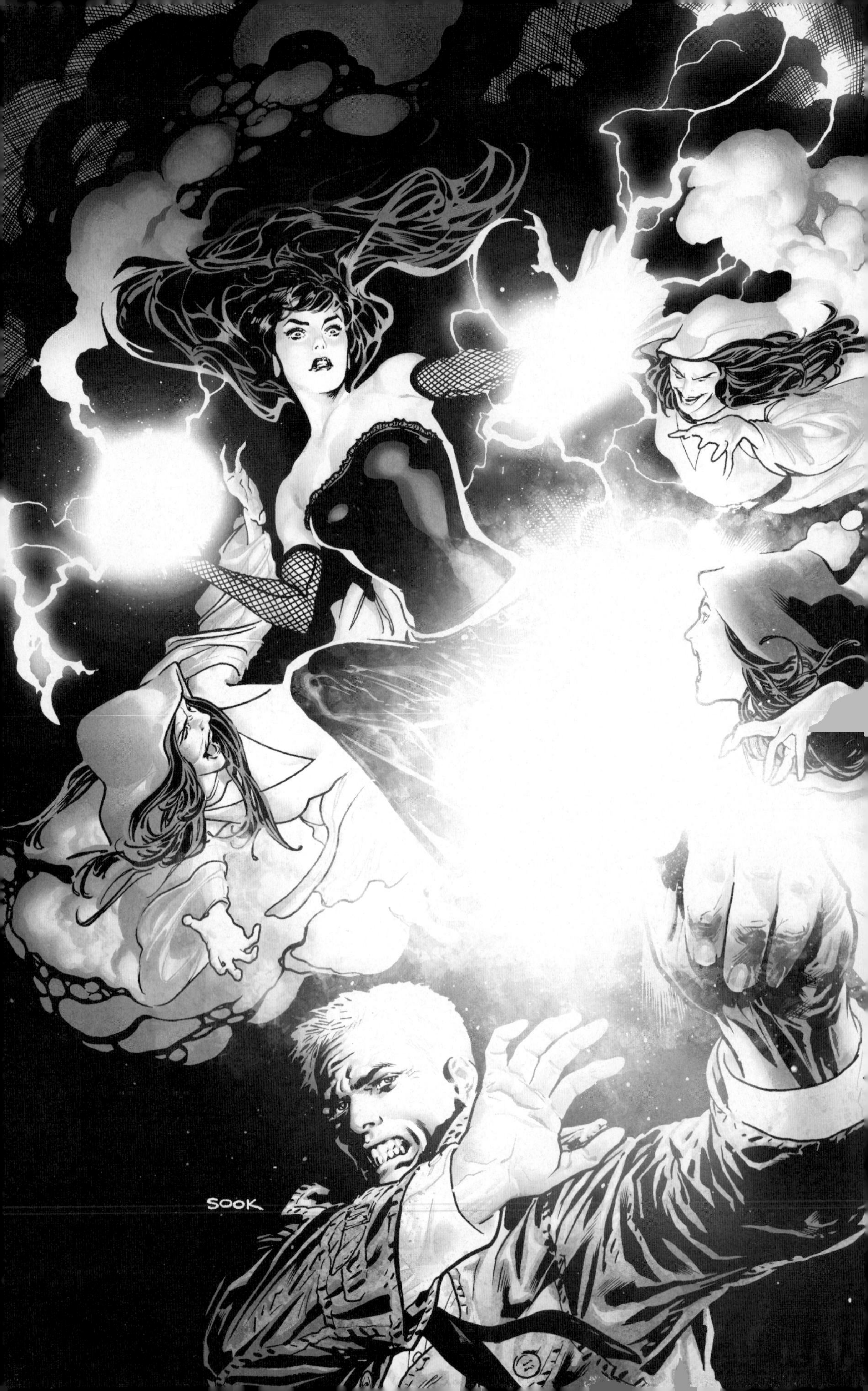
SOOK

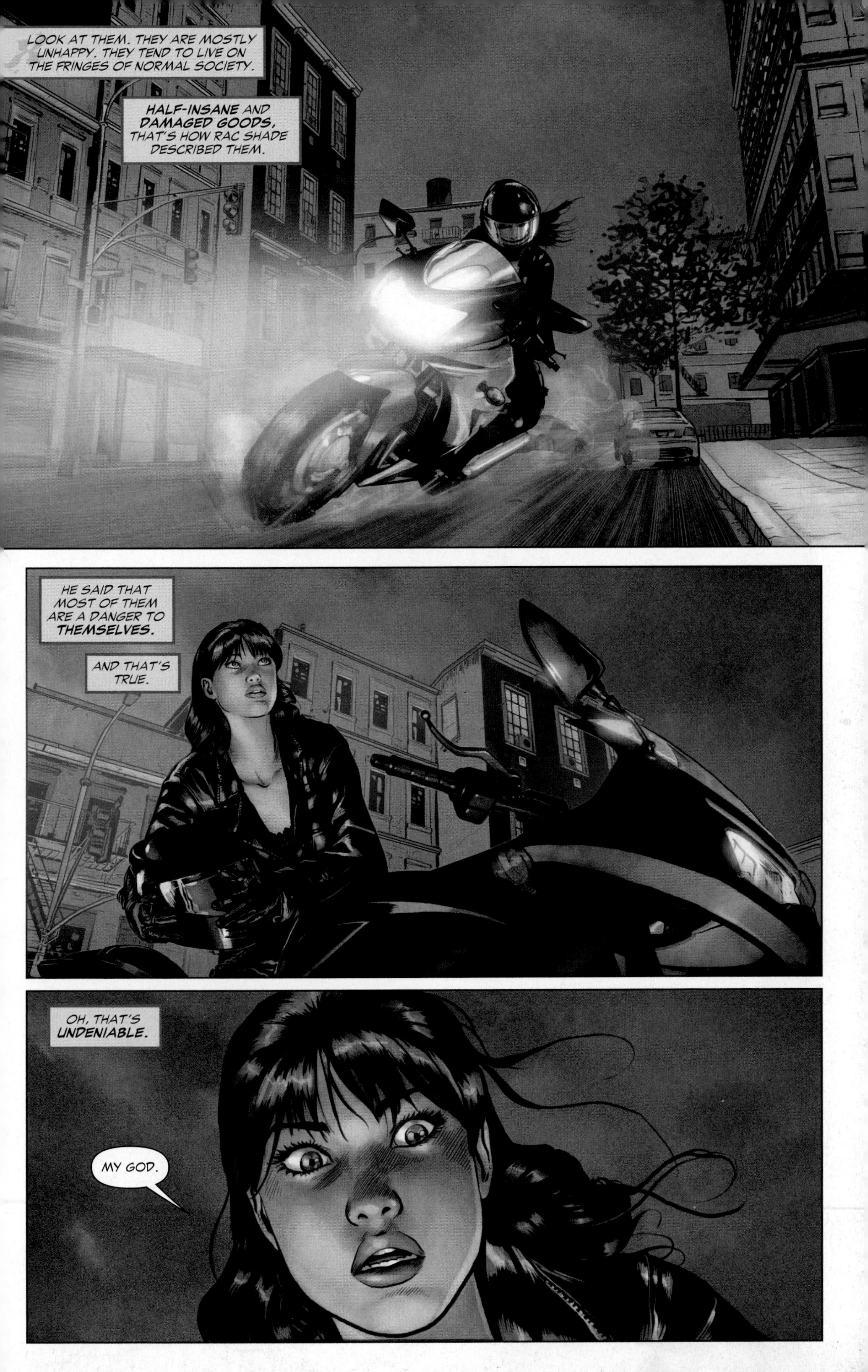
LOOK AT THEM. THEY ARE MOSTLY UNHAPPY. THEY TEND TO LIVE ON THE FRINGES OF NORMAL SOCIETY.
HALF-INSANE AND DAMAGED GOODS, THAT'S HOW RAC SHADE DESCRIBED THEM.
HE SAID THAT MOST OF THEM ARE A DANGER TO THEMSELVES.
AND THAT'S TRUE.
OH, THAT'S UNDENIABLE.
MY GOD.

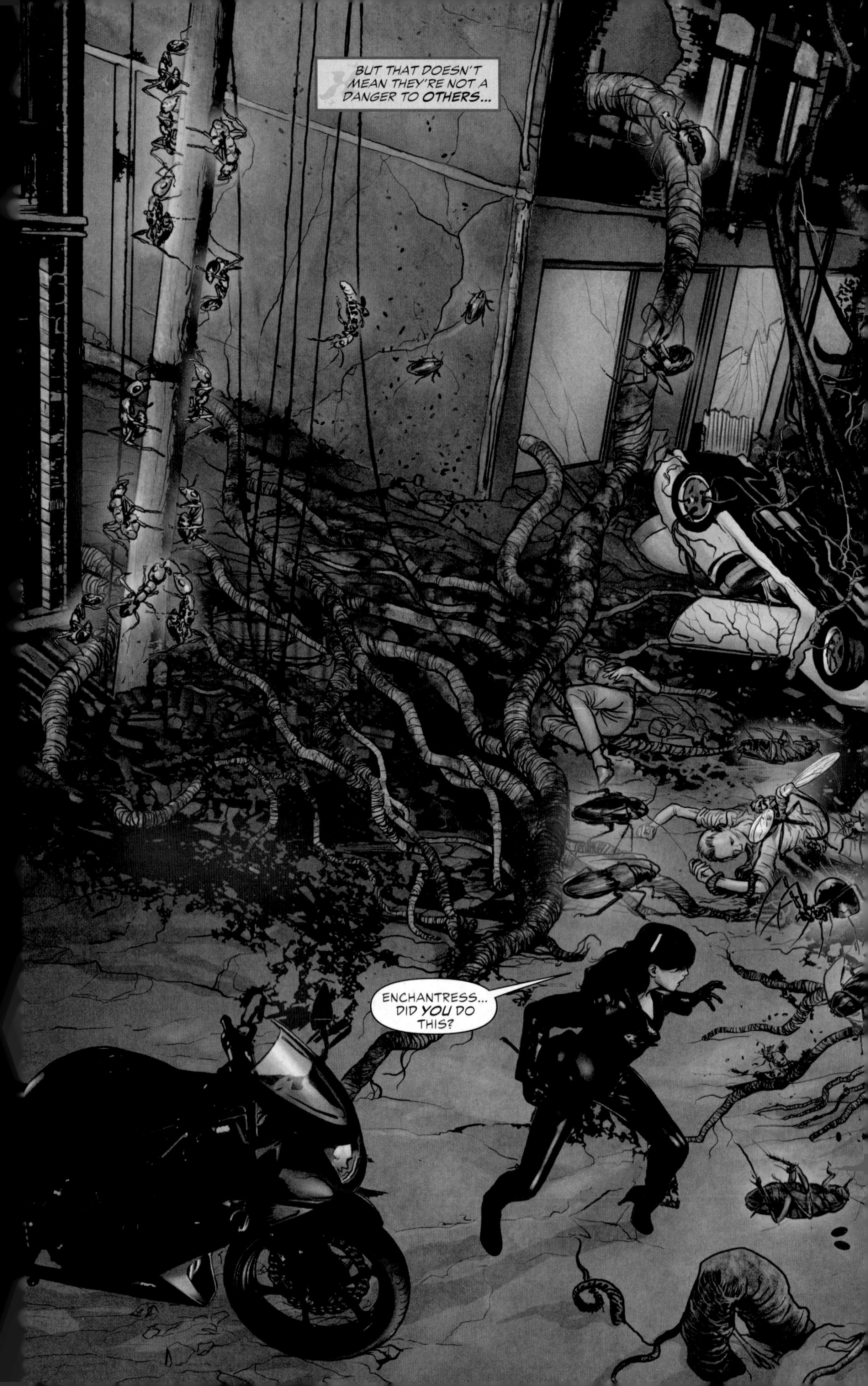
BUT THAT DOESN'T MEAN THEY'RE NOT A DANGER TO OTHERS...
ENCHANTRESS... DID YOU DO THIS?

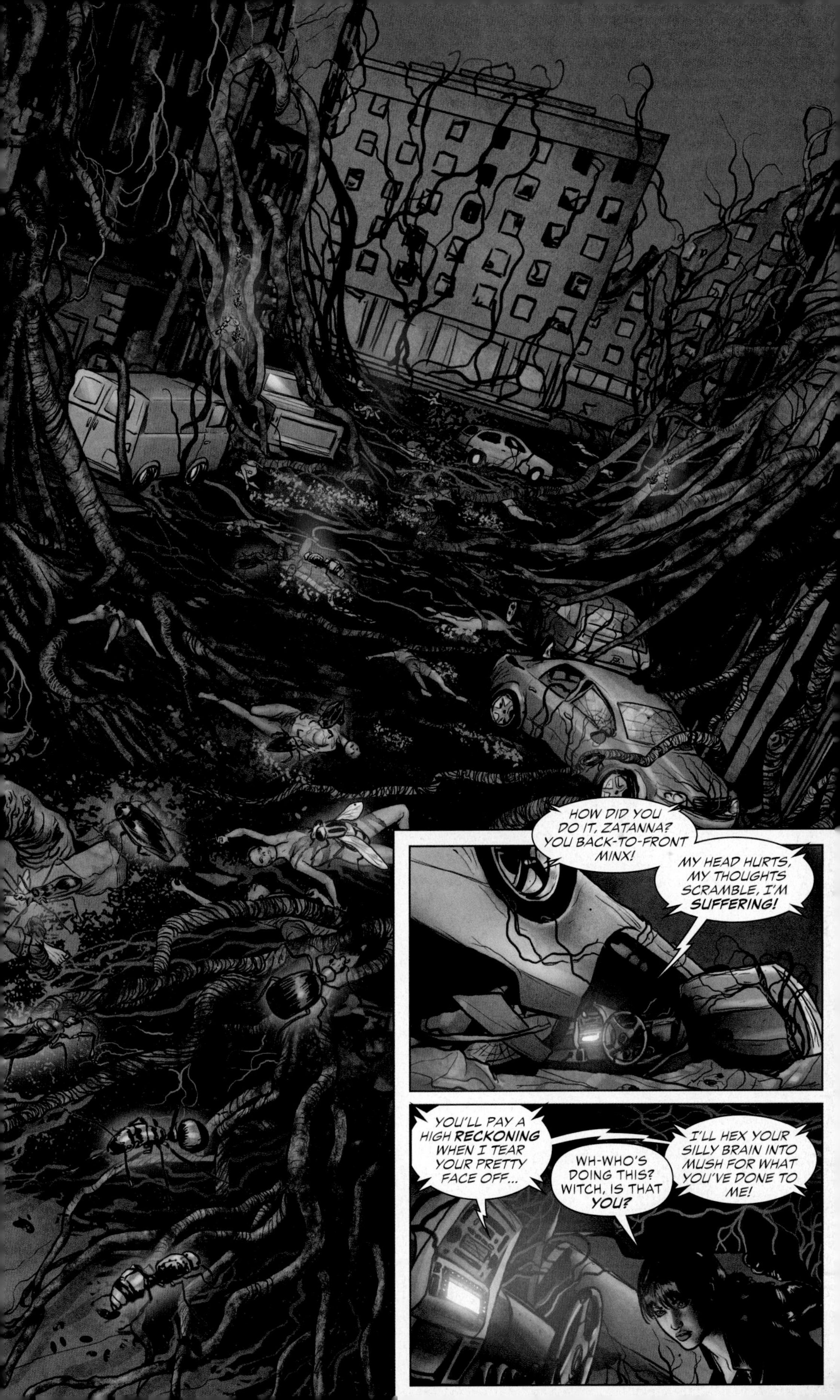
HOW DID YOU DO IT, ZATANNA? YOU BACK-TO-FRONT MINX!
MY HEAD HURTS, MY THOUGHTS SCRAMBLE, I'M SUFFERING!
YOU'LL PAY A HIGH RECKONING WHEN I TEAR YOUR PRETTY FACE OFF...
I'LL HEX YOUR SILLY BRAIN INTO MUSH FOR WHAT YOU'VE DONE TO ME!
WH-WHO'S DOING THIS? WITCH, IS THAT YOU?

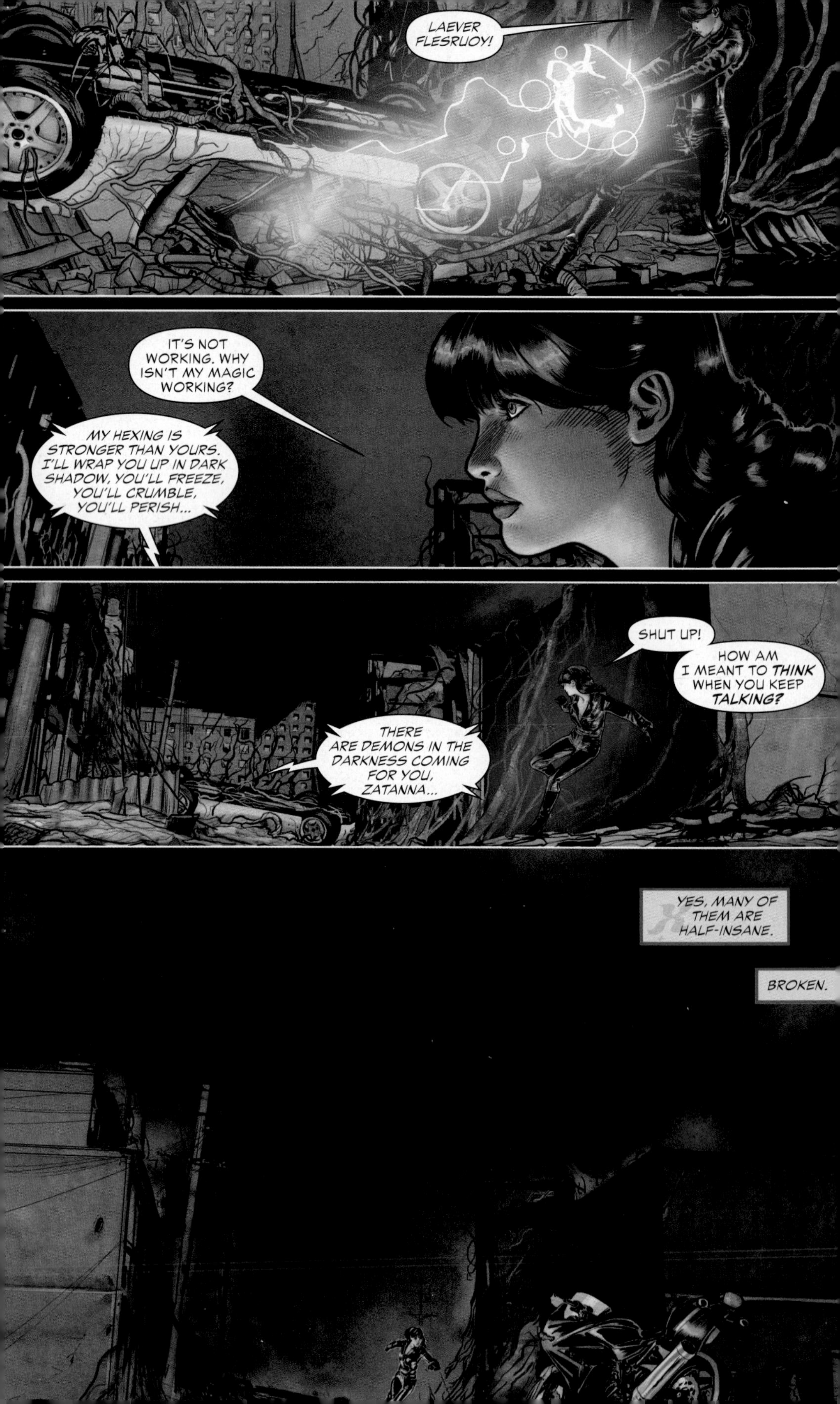
LAEVER FLESRUOY!
IT'S NOT WORKING. WHY ISN'T MY MAGIC WORKING?
MY HEXING IS STRONGER THAN YOURS. I'LL WRAP YOU UP IN DARK SHADOW, YOU'LL FREEZE, YOU'LL CRUMBLE, YOU'LL PERISH...
SHUT UP!
HOW AM I MEANT TO THINK WHEN YOU KEEP TALKING?
THERE ARE DEMONS IN THE DARKNESS COMING FOR YOU, ZATANNA...
YES, MANY OF THEM ARE HALF-INSANE.
BROKEN.

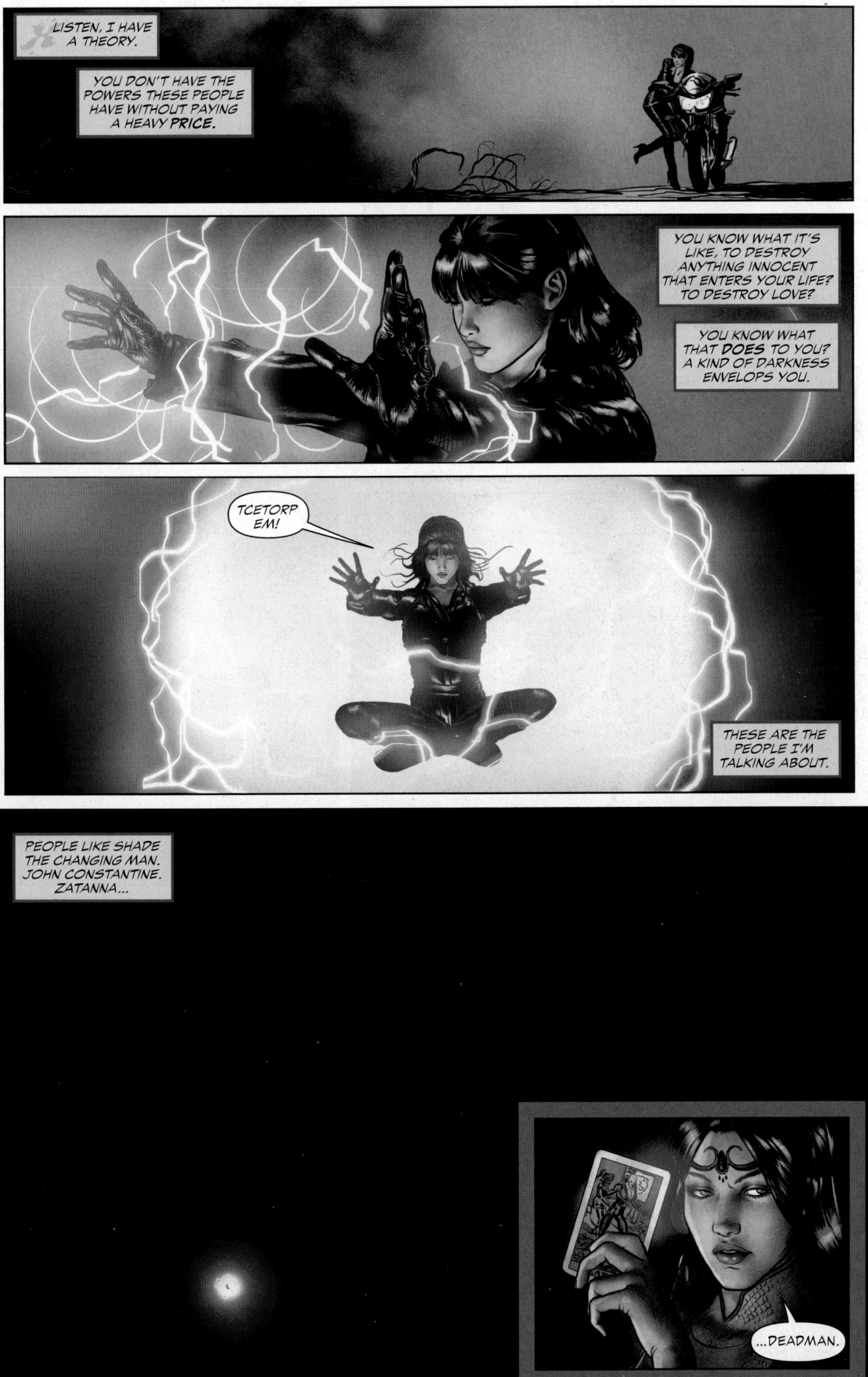

LISTEN, I HAVE A THEORY.
YOU DON'T HAVE THE POWERS THESE PEOPLE HAVE WITHOUT PAYING A HEAVY PRICE.
YOU KNOW WHAT IT'S LIKE, TO DESTROY ANYTHING INNOCENT THAT ENTERS YOUR LIFE? TO DESTROY LOVE?
YOU KNOW WHAT THAT DOES TO YOU? A KIND OF DARKNESS ENVELOPS YOU.
TCETORP EM!
THESE ARE THE PEOPLE I'M TALKING ABOUT.
PEOPLE LIKE SHADE THE CHANGING MAN. JOHN CONSTANTINE. ZATANNA...
...DEADMAN.

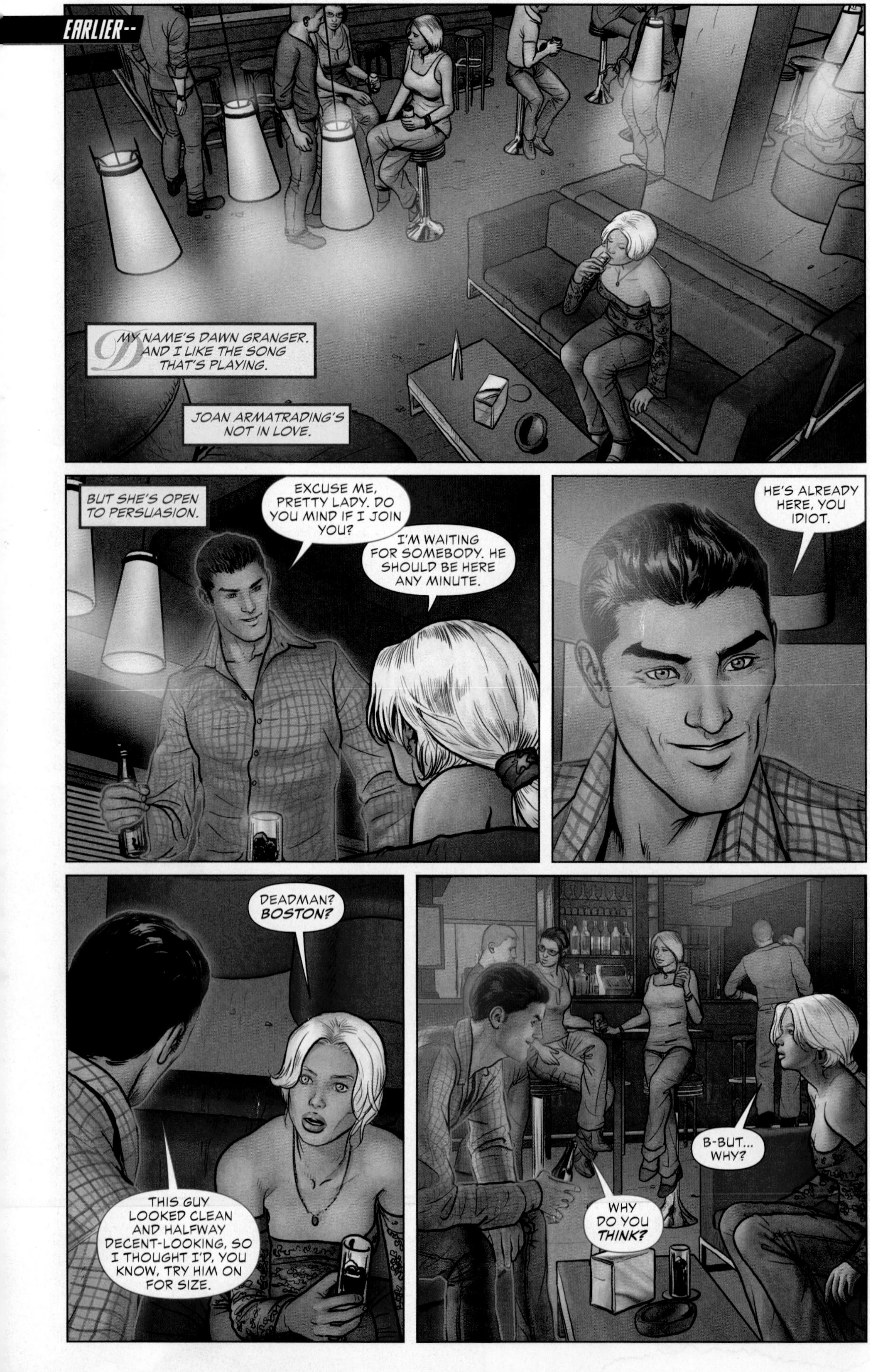
EARLIER--
MY NAME'S DAWN GRANGER. AND I LIKE THE SONG THAT'S PLAYING.
JOAN ARMATRADING'S NOT IN LOVE.
BUT SHE'S OPEN TO PERSUASION.
EXCUSE ME, PRETTY LADY. DO YOU MIND IF I JOIN YOU?
I'M WAITING FOR SOMEBODY. HE SHOULD BE HERE ANY MINUTE.
HE'S ALREADY HERE, YOU IDIOT.
DEADMAN? BOSTON?
THIS GUY LOOKED CLEAN AND HALFWAY DECENT-LOOKING, SO I THOUGHT I'D, YOU KNOW, TRY HIM ON FOR SIZE.
B-BUT... WHY?
WHY DO YOU THINK?

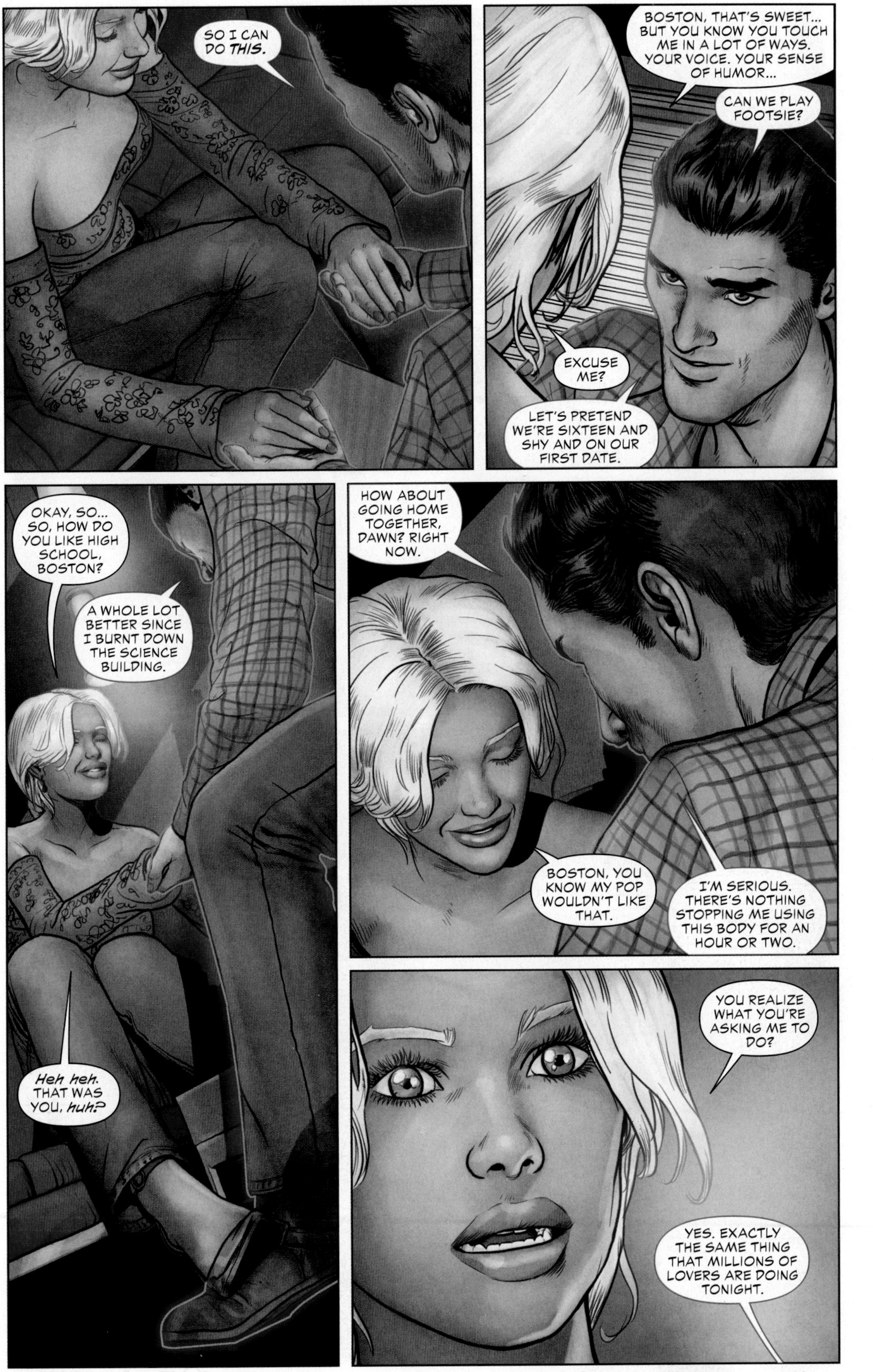
SO I CAN DO *THIS.*
BOSTON, THAT'S SWEET... BUT YOU KNOW YOU TOUCH ME IN A LOT OF WAYS. YOUR VOICE. YOUR SENSE OF HUMOR...
CAN WE PLAY FOOTSIE?
EXCUSE ME?
LET'S PRETEND WE'RE SIXTEEN AND SHY AND ON OUR FIRST DATE.
OKAY, SO... SO, HOW DO YOU LIKE HIGH SCHOOL, BOSTON?
A WHOLE LOT BETTER SINCE I BURNT DOWN THE SCIENCE BUILDING.
Heh heh. THAT WAS YOU, *huh?*
HOW ABOUT GOING HOME TOGETHER, DAWN? RIGHT NOW.
BOSTON, YOU KNOW MY POP WOULDN'T LIKE THAT.
I'M SERIOUS. THERE'S NOTHING STOPPING ME USING THIS BODY FOR AN HOUR OR TWO.
YOU REALIZE WHAT YOU'RE ASKING ME TO DO?
YES. EXACTLY THE SAME THING THAT MILLIONS OF LOVERS ARE DOING TONIGHT.

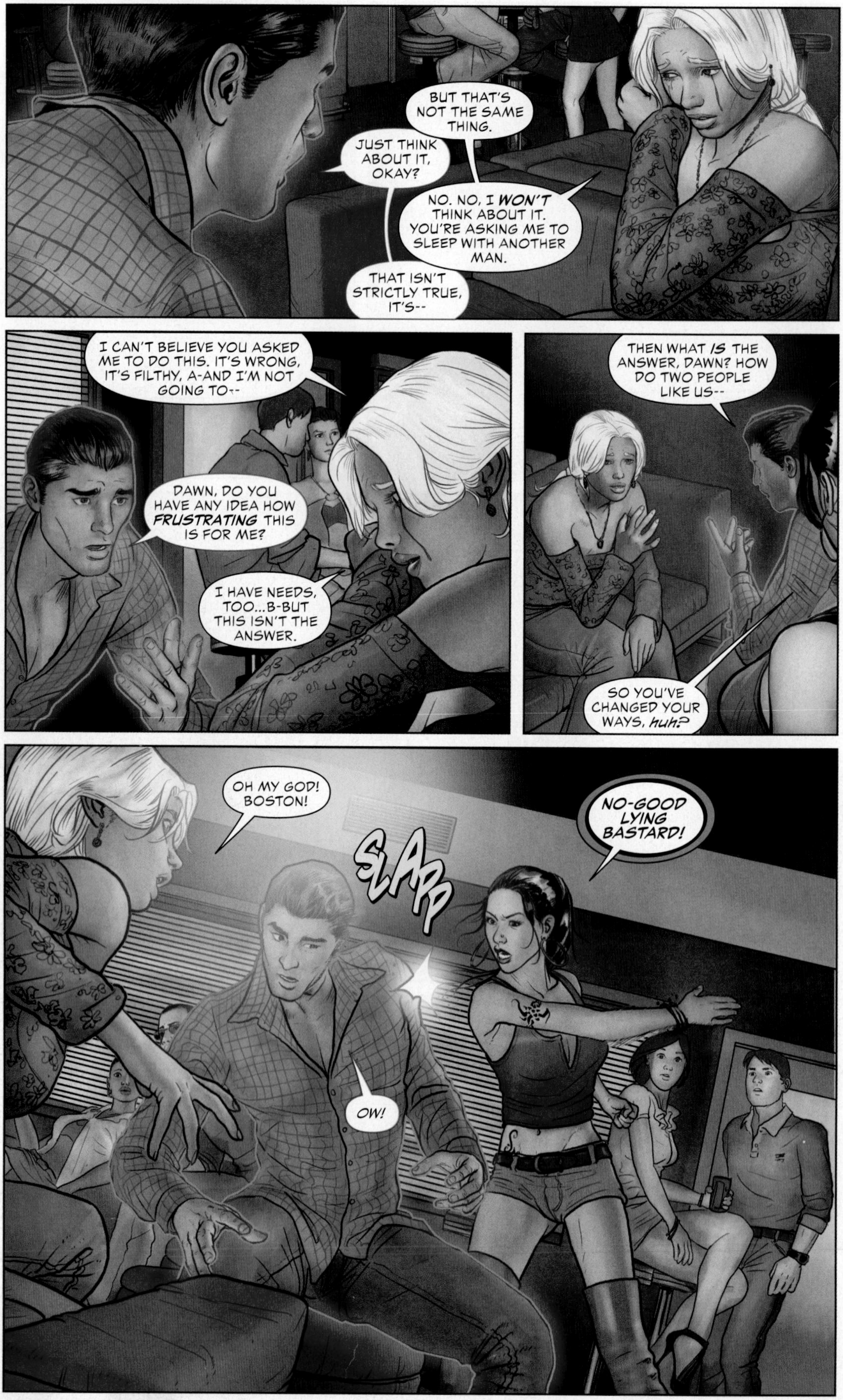
BUT THAT'S NOT THE SAME THING.
JUST THINK ABOUT IT, OKAY?
NO. NO, I WON'T THINK ABOUT IT. YOU'RE ASKING ME TO SLEEP WITH ANOTHER MAN.
THAT ISN'T STRICTLY TRUE, IT'S--
I CAN'T BELIEVE YOU ASKED ME TO DO THIS. IT'S WRONG, IT'S FILTHY, A-AND I'M NOT GOING TO--
DAWN, DO YOU HAVE ANY IDEA HOW FRUSTRATING THIS IS FOR ME?
I HAVE NEEDS, TOO...B-BUT THIS ISN'T THE ANSWER.
THEN WHAT IS THE ANSWER, DAWN? HOW DO TWO PEOPLE LIKE US--
SO YOU'VE CHANGED YOUR WAYS, huh?
OH MY GOD! BOSTON!
SLAPP
NO-GOOD LYING BASTARD!
OW!

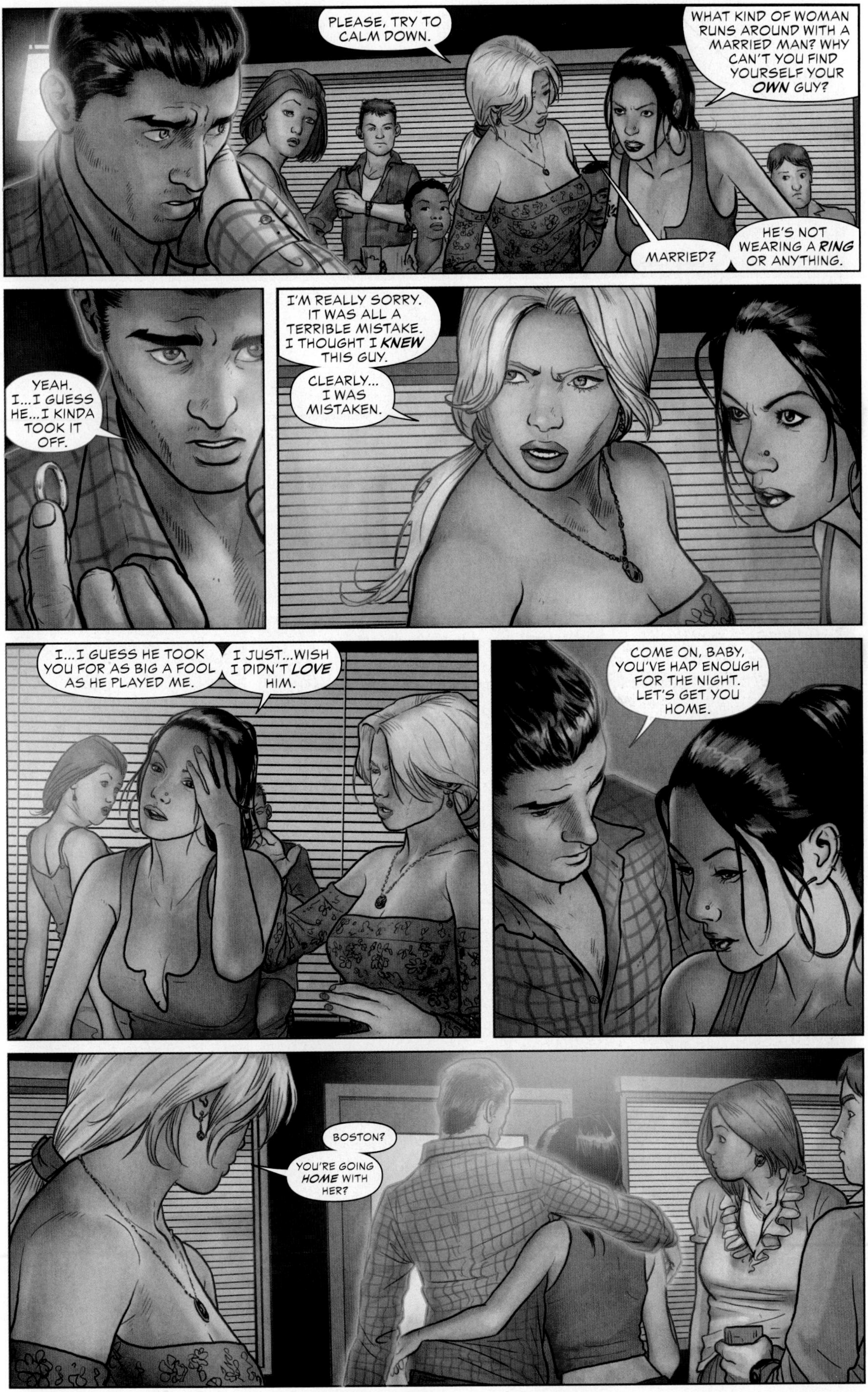
PLEASE, TRY TO CALM DOWN.
WHAT KIND OF WOMAN RUNS AROUND WITH A MARRIED MAN? WHY CAN'T YOU FIND YOURSELF YOUR OWN GUY?
MARRIED?
HE'S NOT WEARING A RING OR ANYTHING.
YEAH. I...I GUESS HE...I KINDA TOOK IT OFF.
I'M REALLY SORRY. IT WAS ALL A TERRIBLE MISTAKE. I THOUGHT I KNEW THIS GUY.
CLEARLY... I WAS MISTAKEN.
I...I GUESS HE TOOK YOU FOR AS BIG A FOOL AS HE PLAYED ME.
I JUST...WISH I DIDN'T LOVE HIM.
COME ON, BABY, YOU'VE HAD ENOUGH FOR THE NIGHT. LET'S GET YOU HOME.
BOSTON?
YOU'RE GOING HOME WITH HER?

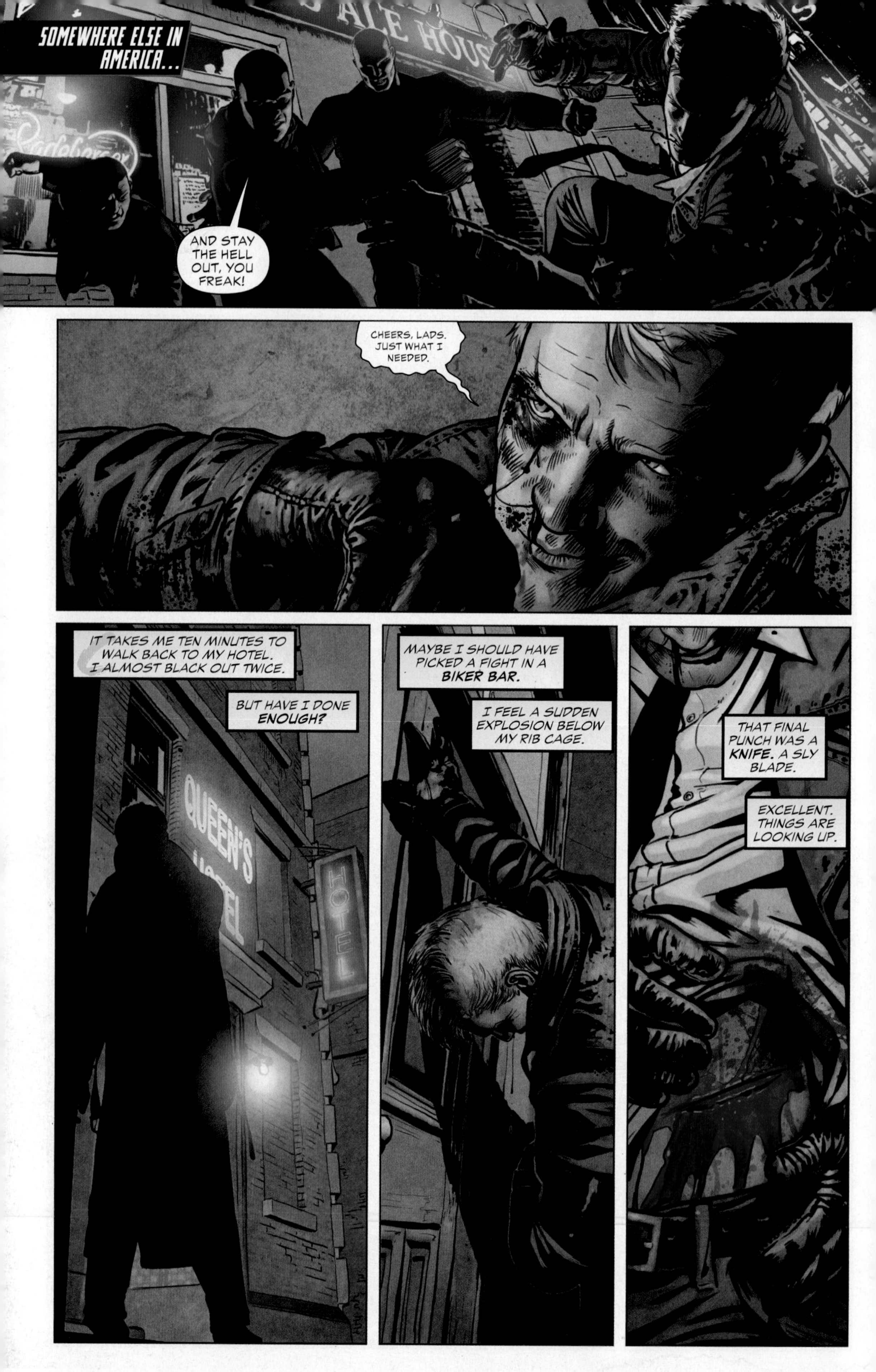
SOMEWHERE ELSE IN AMERICA...
AND STAY THE HELL OUT, YOU FREAK!
CHEERS, LADS. JUST WHAT I NEEDED.
IT TAKES ME TEN MINUTES TO WALK BACK TO MY HOTEL. I ALMOST BLACK OUT TWICE.
BUT HAVE I DONE ENOUGH?
QUEEN'S HOTEL
HOTEL
MAYBE I SHOULD HAVE PICKED A FIGHT IN A BIKER BAR.
I FEEL A SUDDEN EXPLOSION BELOW MY RIB CAGE.
THAT FINAL PUNCH WAS A KNIFE. A SLY BLADE.
EXCELLENT. THINGS ARE LOOKING UP.

THE IDEA ISN'T THAT I BLEED TO DEATH.

THE IDEA IS THAT PAIN AND DANGER, A SNIFF OF MORTALITY, OPENS UP THE CHANNELS. MAKES ME MORE *RECEPTIVE*.

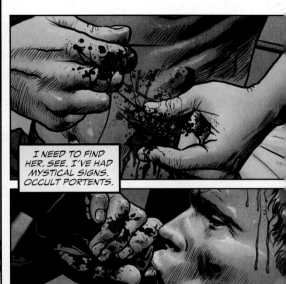

I NEED TO FIND HER, SEE. I'VE HAD MYSTICAL SIGNS. OCCULT PORTENTS.

I ALSO STUBBED MY BIG TOE, WHICH IS *ALWAYS* A BAD OMEN.

THE HAIR BELONGED TO ZATANNA. I ALSO HAVE ONE OF HER *EYELASHES*.

THIS IS WHERE THE SKILL COMES IN.

PAIN. SMOKE. DIVINATION.

ANOTHER DAY IN THE JOLLY LIFE OF JOHN CONSTANTINE.

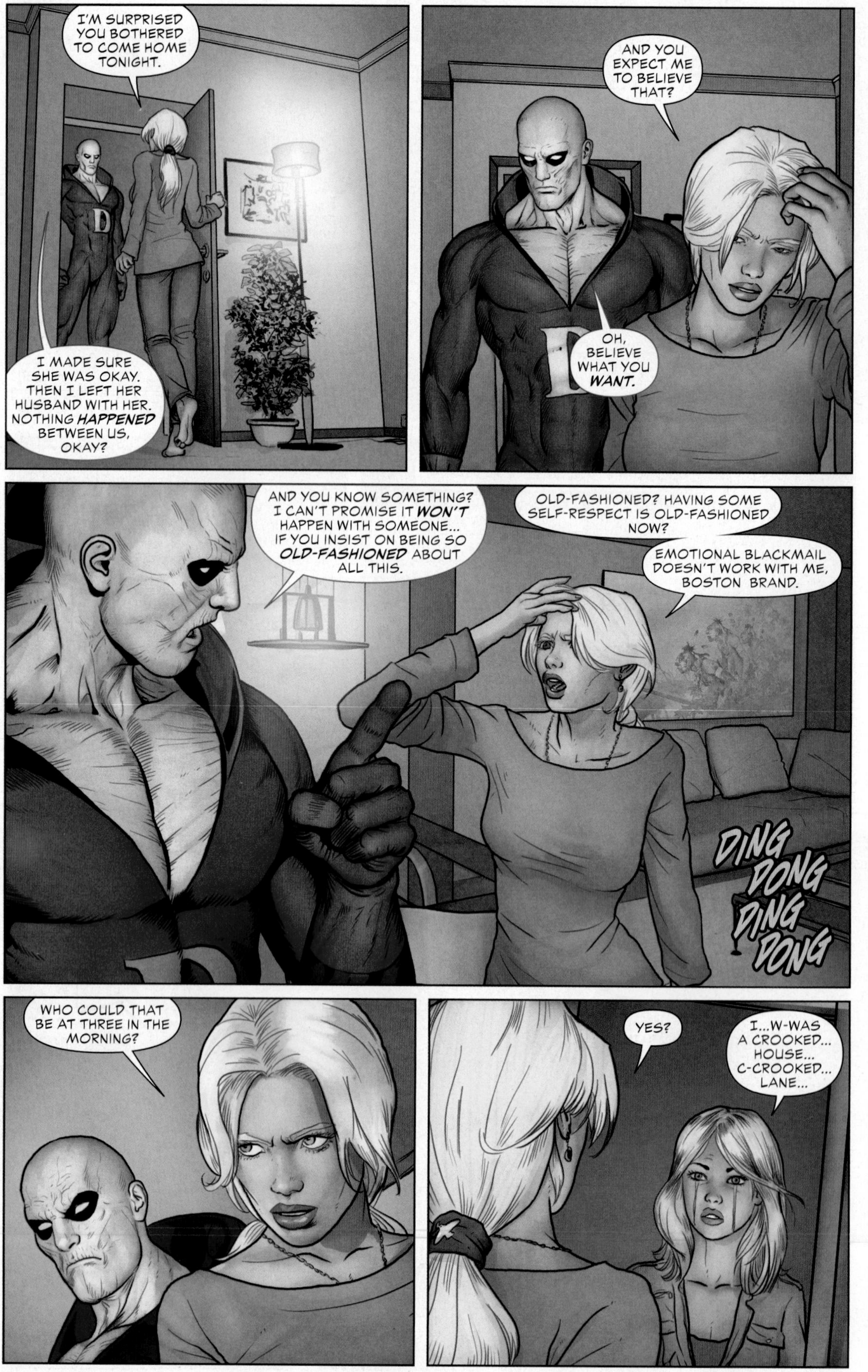
I'M SURPRISED YOU BOTHERED TO COME HOME TONIGHT.
I MADE SURE SHE WAS OKAY. THEN I LEFT HER HUSBAND WITH HER. NOTHING HAPPENED BETWEEN US, OKAY?
AND YOU EXPECT ME TO BELIEVE THAT?
OH, BELIEVE WHAT YOU WANT.
AND YOU KNOW SOMETHING? I CAN'T PROMISE IT WON'T HAPPEN WITH SOMEONE... IF YOU INSIST ON BEING SO OLD-FASHIONED ABOUT ALL THIS.
OLD-FASHIONED? HAVING SOME SELF-RESPECT IS OLD-FASHIONED NOW?
EMOTIONAL BLACKMAIL DOESN'T WORK WITH ME, BOSTON BRAND.
DING DONG DING DONG
WHO COULD THAT BE AT THREE IN THE MORNING?
YES?
I...W-WAS A CROOKED... HOUSE... C-CROOKED... LANE...

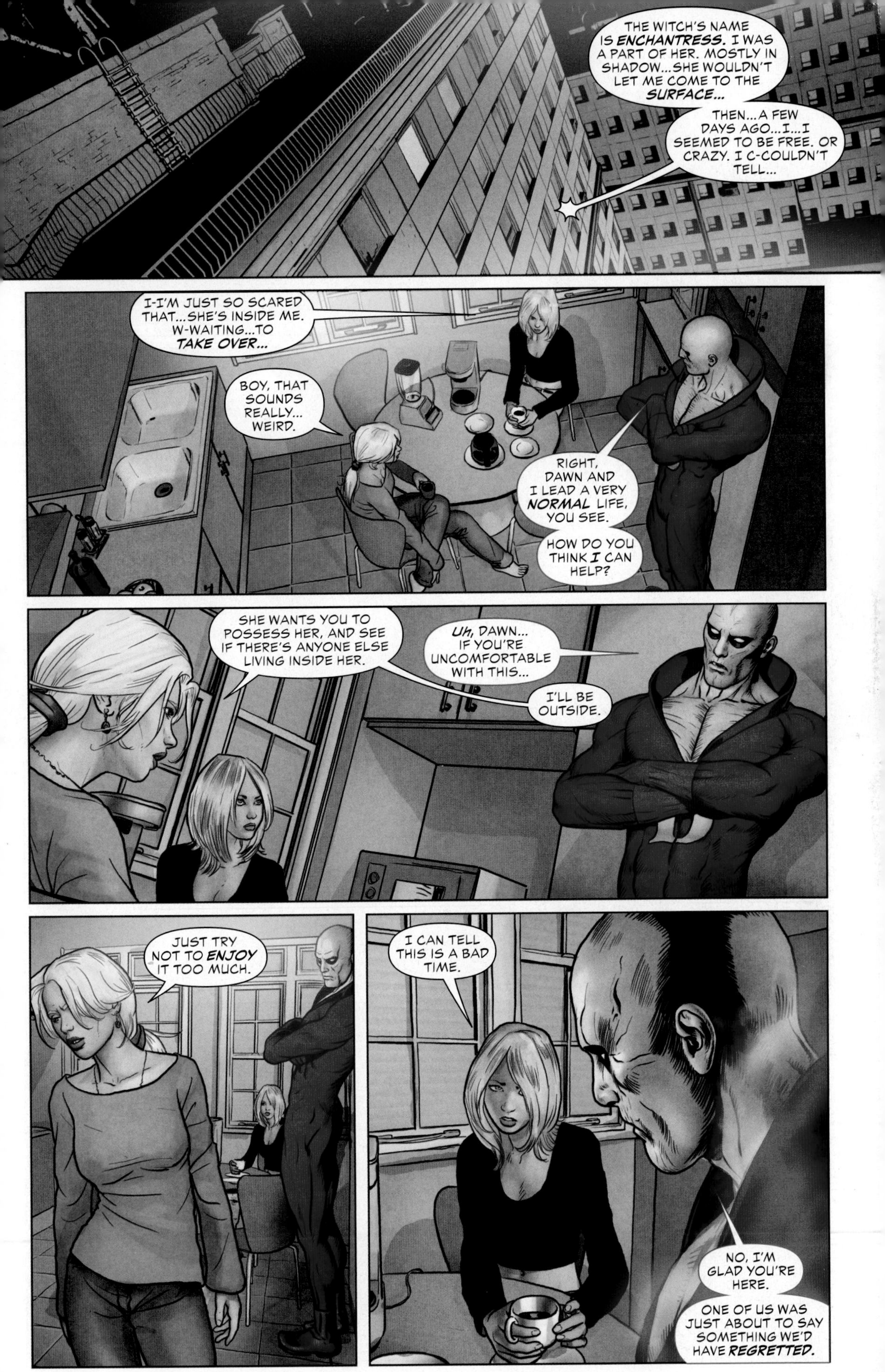
THE WITCH'S NAME IS ENCHANTRESS. I WAS A PART OF HER. MOSTLY IN SHADOW...SHE WOULDN'T LET ME COME TO THE SURFACE...
THEN...A FEW DAYS AGO...I...I SEEMED TO BE FREE. OR CRAZY. I C-COULDN'T TELL...
I-I'M JUST SO SCARED THAT...SHE'S INSIDE ME. W-WAITING...TO TAKE OVER...
BOY, THAT SOUNDS REALLY... WEIRD.
RIGHT, DAWN AND I LEAD A VERY NORMAL LIFE, YOU SEE.
HOW DO YOU THINK I CAN HELP?
SHE WANTS YOU TO POSSESS HER, AND SEE IF THERE'S ANYONE ELSE LIVING INSIDE HER.
Uh, DAWN... IF YOU'RE UNCOMFORTABLE WITH THIS...
I'LL BE OUTSIDE.
JUST TRY NOT TO ENJOY IT TOO MUCH.
I CAN TELL THIS IS A BAD TIME.
NO, I'M GLAD YOU'RE HERE.
ONE OF US WAS JUST ABOUT TO SAY SOMETHING WE'D HAVE REGRETTED.

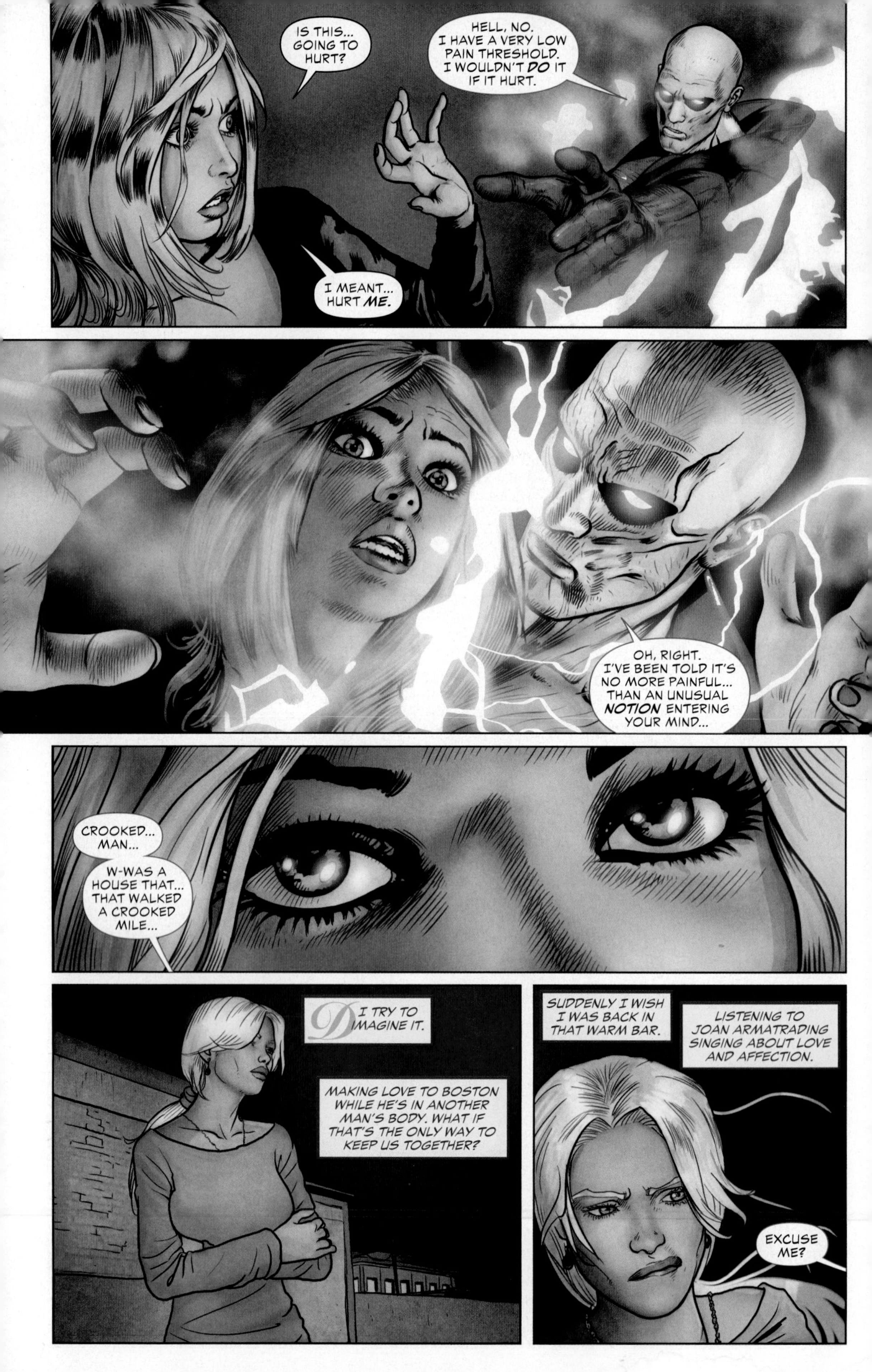
IS THIS... GOING TO HURT?
HELL, NO. I HAVE A VERY LOW PAIN THRESHOLD. I WOULDN'T *DO* IT IF IT HURT.
I MEANT... HURT *ME.*
OH, RIGHT. I'VE BEEN TOLD IT'S NO MORE PAINFUL... THAN AN UNUSUAL *NOTION* ENTERING YOUR MIND...
CROOKED... MAN...
W-WAS A HOUSE THAT... THAT WALKED A CROOKED MILE...
I TRY TO IMAGINE IT.
MAKING LOVE TO BOSTON WHILE HE'S IN ANOTHER MAN'S BODY. WHAT IF THAT'S THE ONLY WAY TO KEEP US TOGETHER?
SUDDENLY I WISH I WAS BACK IN THAT WARM BAR.
LISTENING TO JOAN ARMATRADING SINGING ABOUT LOVE AND AFFECTION.
EXCUSE ME?

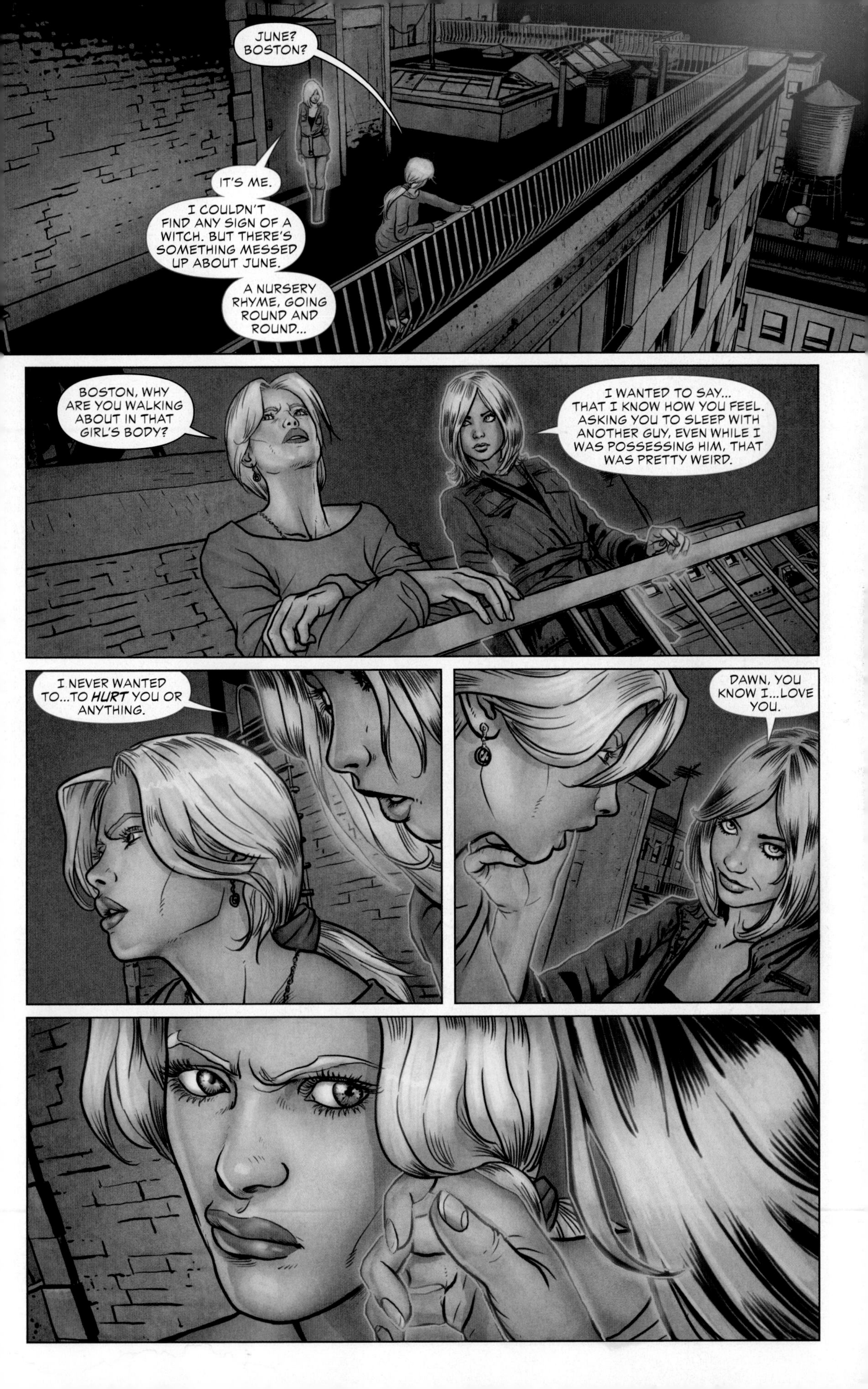
JUNE? BOSTON?
IT'S ME.
I COULDN'T FIND ANY SIGN OF A WITCH. BUT THERE'S SOMETHING MESSED UP ABOUT JUNE.
A NURSERY RHYME, GOING ROUND AND ROUND...
BOSTON, WHY ARE YOU WALKING ABOUT IN THAT GIRL'S BODY?
I WANTED TO SAY... THAT I KNOW HOW YOU FEEL. ASKING YOU TO SLEEP WITH ANOTHER GUY, EVEN WHILE I WAS POSSESSING HIM, THAT WAS PRETTY WEIRD.
I NEVER WANTED TO...TO HURT YOU OR ANYTHING.
DAWN, YOU KNOW I...LOVE YOU.

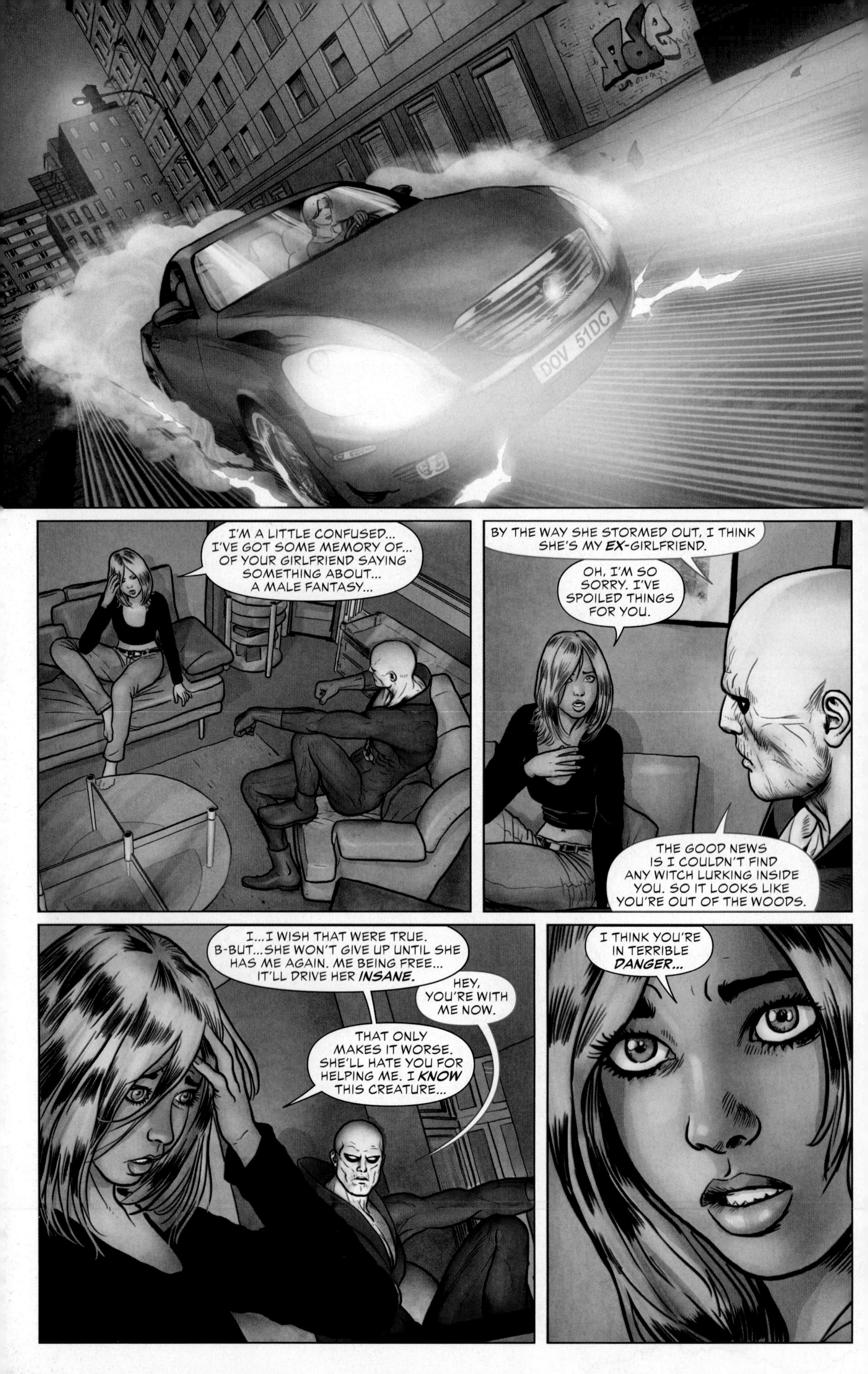
DOV 51DC
I'M A LITTLE CONFUSED... I'VE GOT SOME MEMORY OF... OF YOUR GIRLFRIEND SAYING SOMETHING ABOUT... A MALE FANTASY...
BY THE WAY SHE STORMED OUT, I THINK SHE'S MY EX-GIRLFRIEND.
OH, I'M SO SORRY. I'VE SPOILED THINGS FOR YOU.
THE GOOD NEWS IS I COULDN'T FIND ANY WITCH LURKING INSIDE YOU. SO IT LOOKS LIKE YOU'RE OUT OF THE WOODS.
I...I WISH THAT WERE TRUE. B-BUT...SHE WON'T GIVE UP UNTIL SHE HAS ME AGAIN. ME BEING FREE... IT'LL DRIVE HER INSANE.
HEY, YOU'RE WITH ME NOW.
THAT ONLY MAKES IT WORSE. SHE'LL HATE YOU FOR HELPING ME. I KNOW THIS CREATURE...
I THINK YOU'RE IN TERRIBLE DANGER...

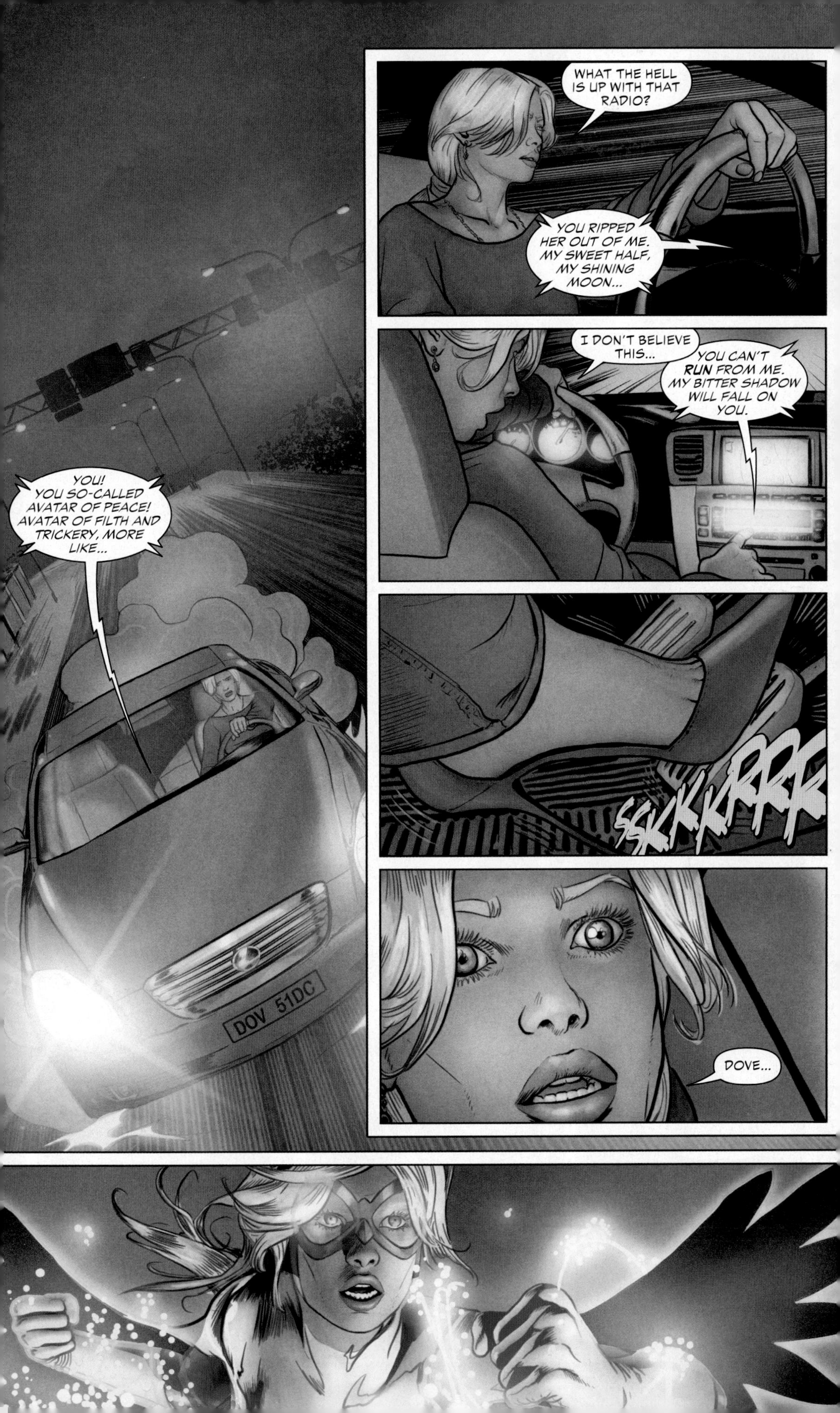
WHAT THE HELL IS UP WITH THAT RADIO?
YOU RIPPED HER OUT OF ME. MY SWEET HALF, MY SHINING MOON...
I DON'T BELIEVE THIS...
YOU CAN'T RUN FROM ME. MY BITTER SHADOW WILL FALL ON YOU.
SSKKKRRRK
DOVE...
YOU! YOU SO-CALLED AVATAR OF PEACE! AVATAR OF FILTH AND TRICKERY, MORE LIKE...
DOV 51DC

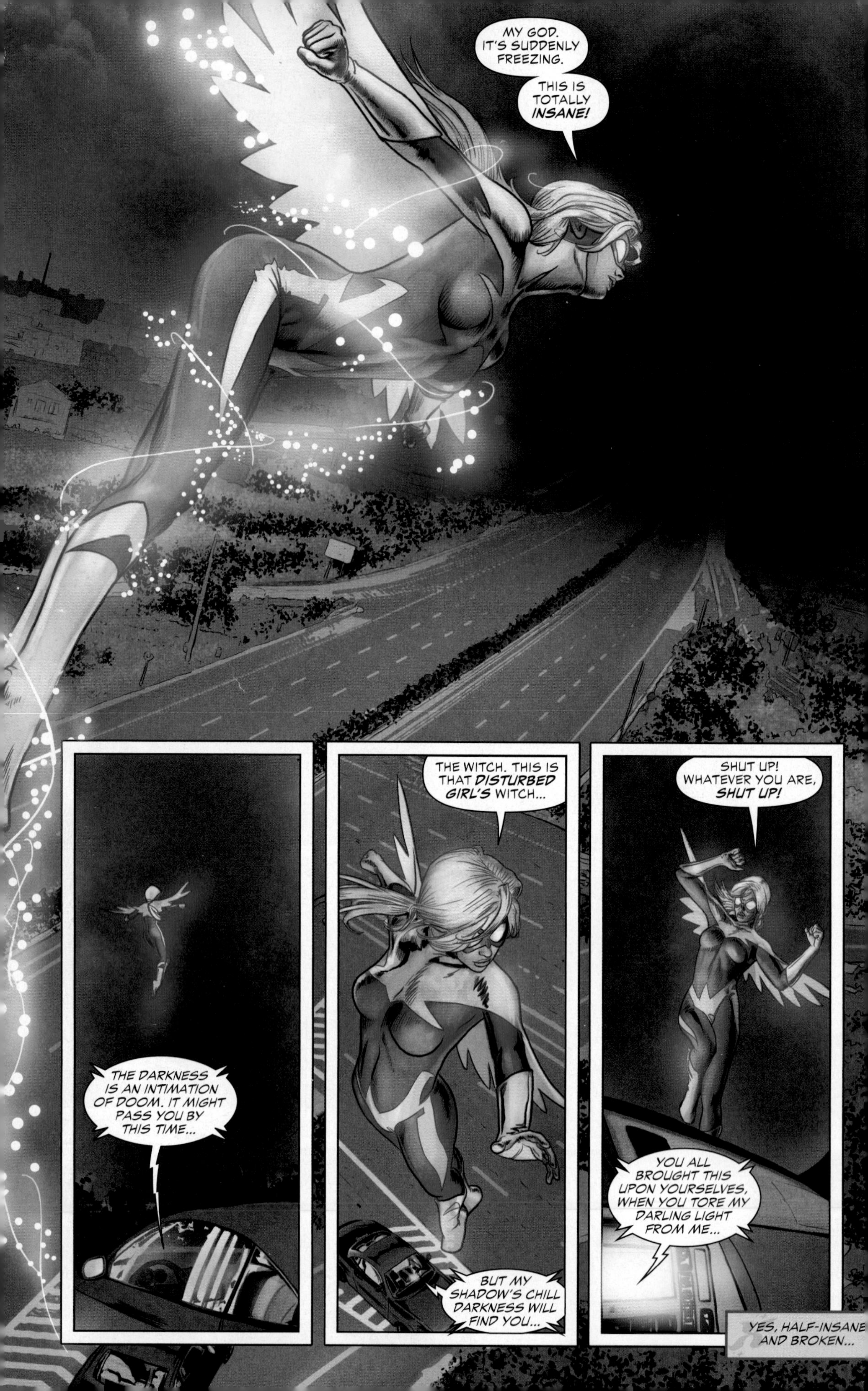
MY GOD. IT'S SUDDENLY FREEZING.
THIS IS TOTALLY INSANE!
THE DARKNESS IS AN INTIMATION OF DOOM. IT MIGHT PASS YOU BY THIS TIME...
THE WITCH. THIS IS THAT DISTURBED GIRL'S WITCH...
BUT MY SHADOW'S CHILL DARKNESS WILL FIND YOU...
SHUT UP! WHATEVER YOU ARE, SHUT UP!
YOU ALL BROUGHT THIS UPON YOURSELVES, WHEN YOU TORE MY DARLING LIGHT FROM ME...
YES, HALF-INSANE AND BROKEN...

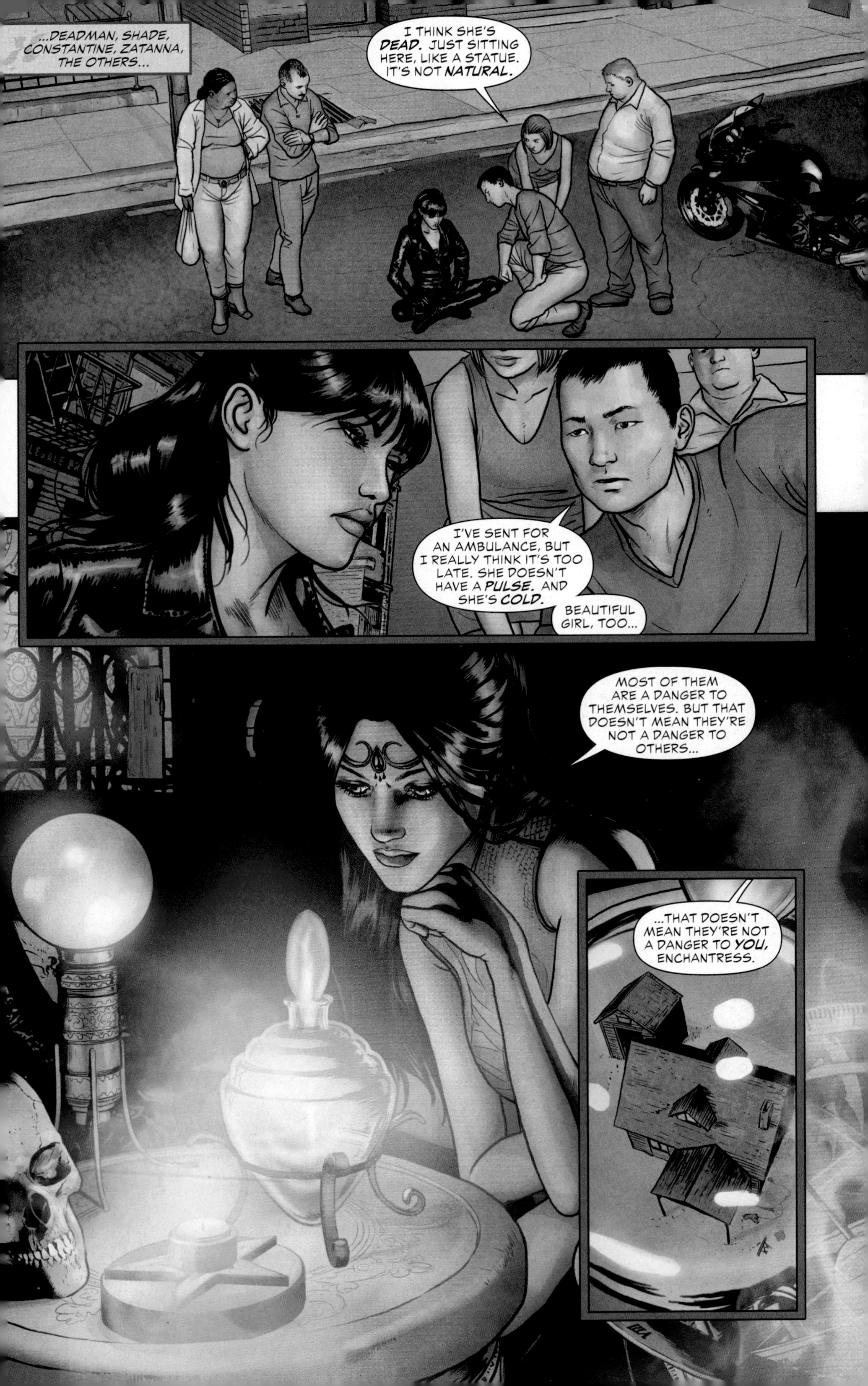
...DEADMAN, SHADE, CONSTANTINE, ZATANNA, THE OTHERS...
I THINK SHE'S DEAD. JUST SITTING HERE, LIKE A STATUE. IT'S NOT NATURAL.
I'VE SENT FOR AN AMBULANCE, BUT I REALLY THINK IT'S TOO LATE. SHE DOESN'T HAVE A PULSE. AND SHE'S COLD.
BEAUTIFUL GIRL, TOO...
MOST OF THEM ARE A DANGER TO THEMSELVES. BUT THAT DOESN'T MEAN THEY'RE NOT A DANGER TO OTHERS...
...THAT DOESN'T MEAN THEY'RE NOT A DANGER TO YOU, ENCHANTRESS.

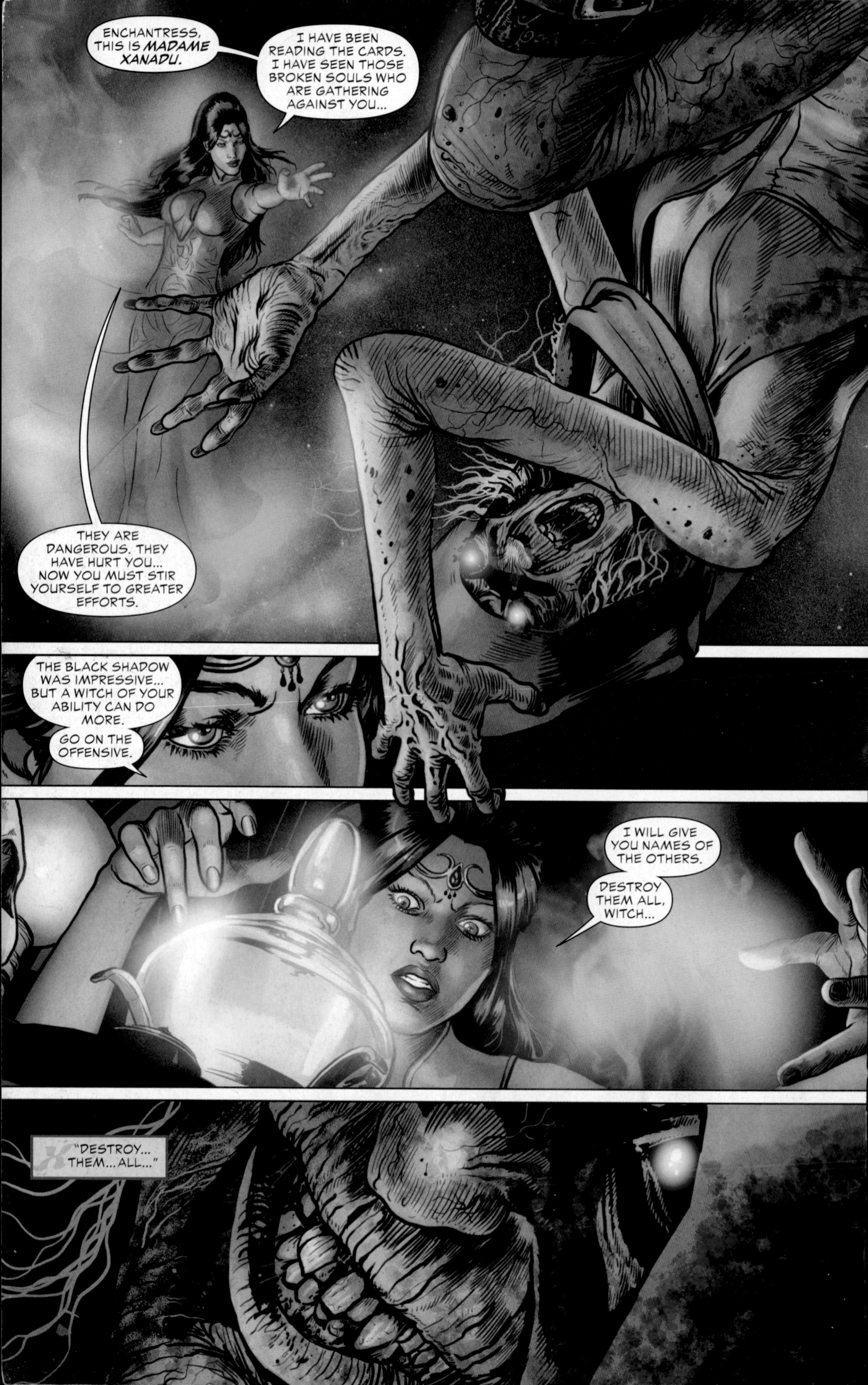
ENCHANTRESS, THIS IS MADAME XANADU.
I HAVE BEEN READING THE CARDS. I HAVE SEEN THOSE BROKEN SOULS WHO ARE GATHERING AGAINST YOU...
THEY ARE DANGEROUS. THEY HAVE HURT YOU... NOW YOU MUST STIR YOURSELF TO GREATER EFFORTS.
THE BLACK SHADOW WAS IMPRESSIVE... BUT A WITCH OF YOUR ABILITY CAN DO MORE.
GO ON THE OFFENSIVE.
I WILL GIVE YOU NAMES OF THE OTHERS.
DESTROY THEM ALL, WITCH...
"DESTROY... THEM... ALL..."

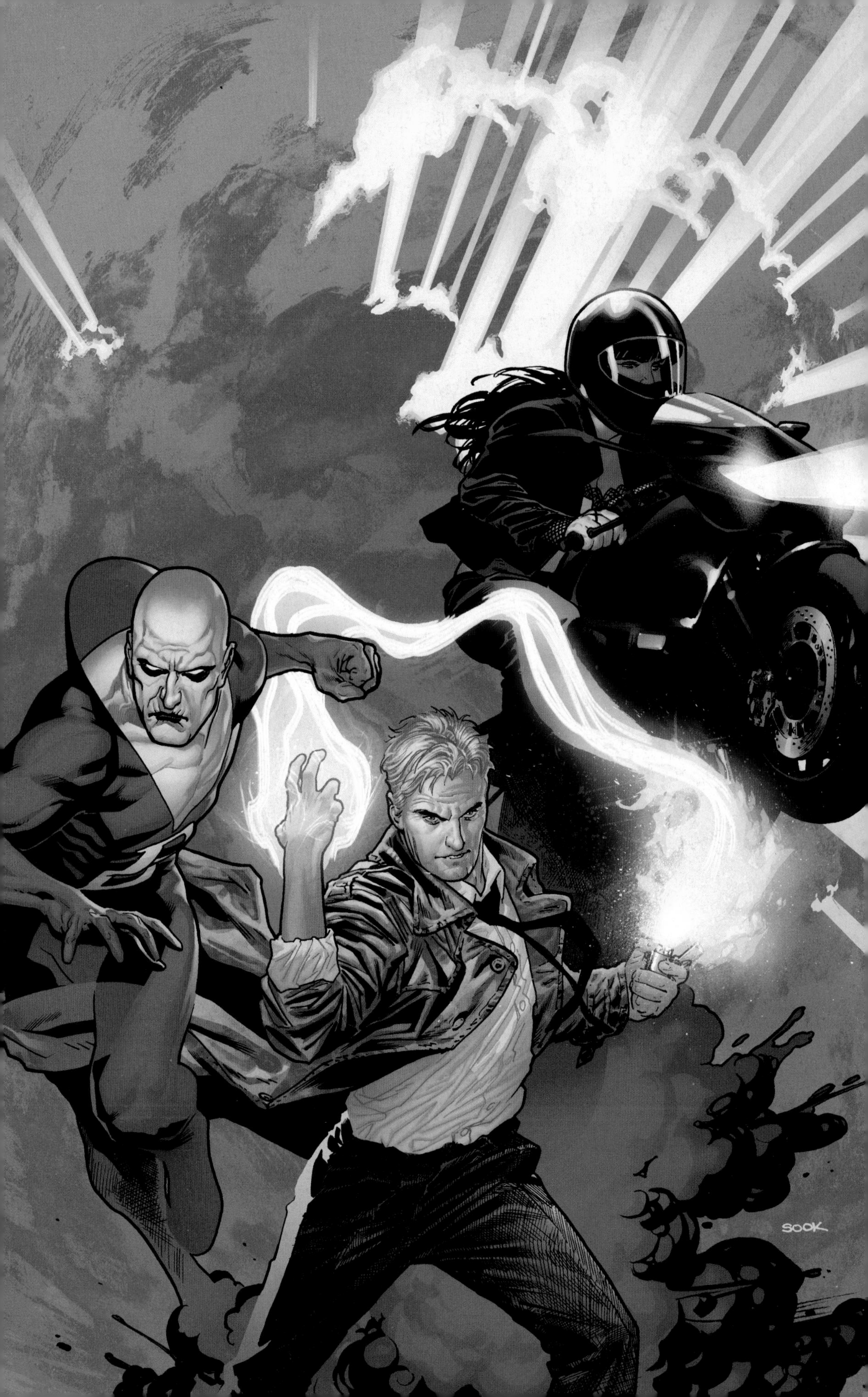
SOOK

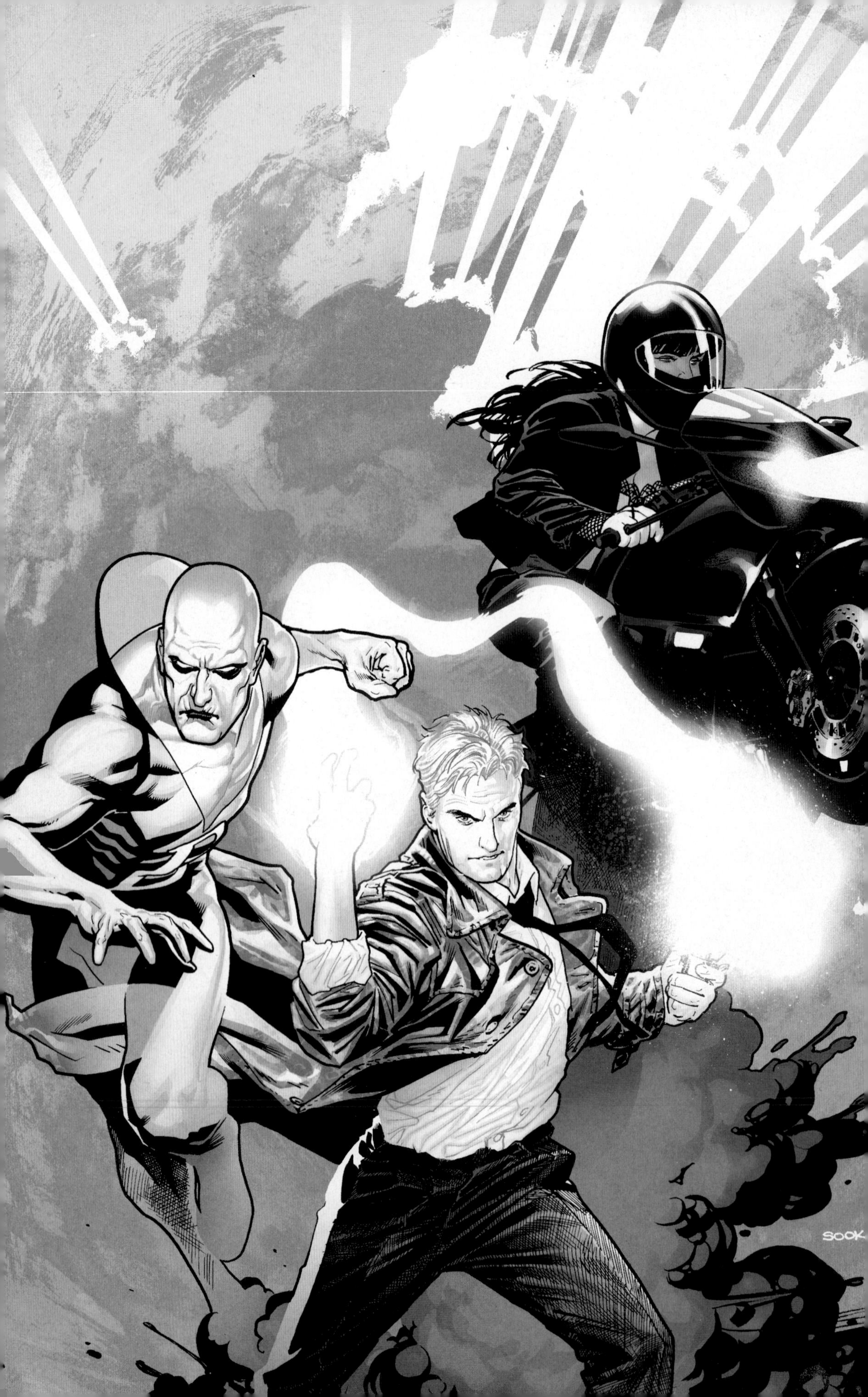
SOOK

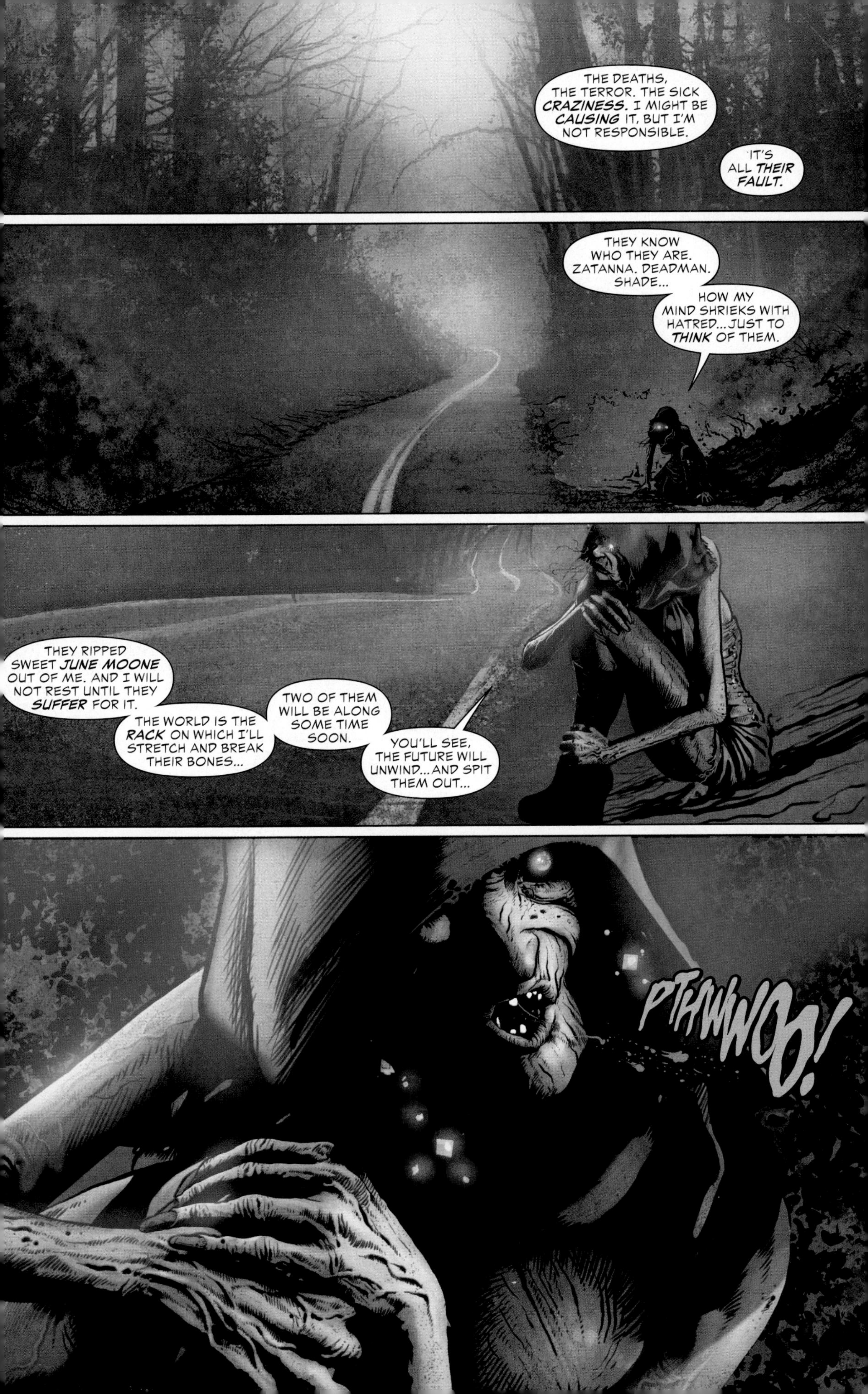
THE DEATHS, THE TERROR. THE SICK CRAZINESS. I MIGHT BE CAUSING IT, BUT I'M NOT RESPONSIBLE.
IT'S ALL THEIR FAULT.
THEY KNOW WHO THEY ARE. ZATANNA. DEADMAN. SHADE...
HOW MY MIND SHRIEKS WITH HATRED... JUST TO THINK OF THEM.
THEY RIPPED SWEET JUNE MOONE OUT OF ME. AND I WILL NOT REST UNTIL THEY SUFFER FOR IT.
THE WORLD IS THE RACK ON WHICH I'LL STRETCH AND BREAK THEIR BONES...
TWO OF THEM WILL BE ALONG SOME TIME SOON.
YOU'LL SEE, THE FUTURE WILL UNWIND... AND SPIT THEM OUT...
PTHWWOO!

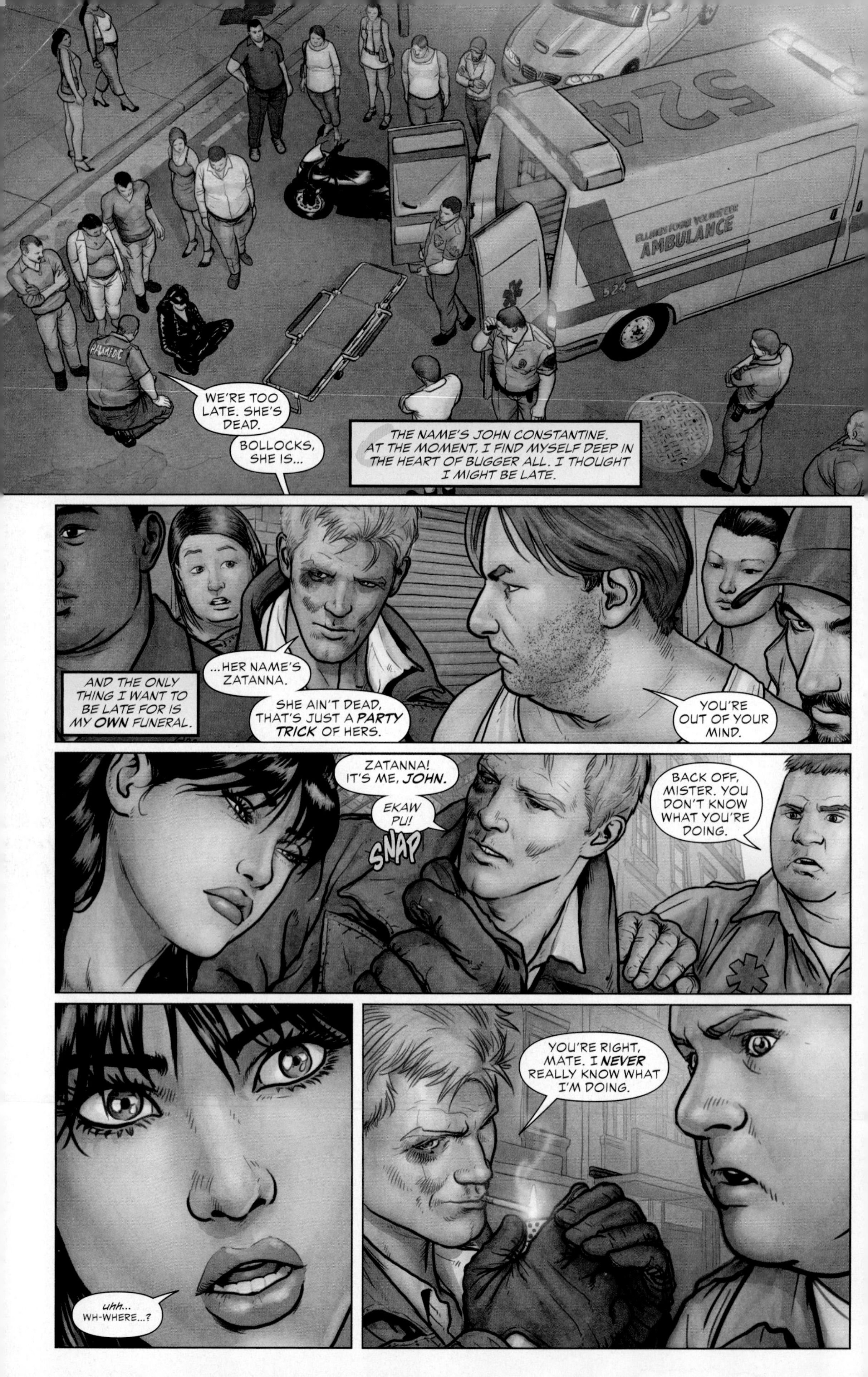

WE'RE TOO LATE. SHE'S DEAD.
BOLLOCKS, SHE IS...
THE NAME'S JOHN CONSTANTINE. AT THE MOMENT, I FIND MYSELF DEEP IN THE HEART OF BUGGER ALL. I THOUGHT I MIGHT BE LATE.
AMBULANCE
524
AND THE ONLY THING I WANT TO BE LATE FOR IS MY OWN FUNERAL.
...HER NAME'S ZATANNA.
SHE AIN'T DEAD, THAT'S JUST A PARTY TRICK OF HERS.
YOU'RE OUT OF YOUR MIND.
ZATANNA! IT'S ME, JOHN.
EKAW PU!
SNAP
BACK OFF, MISTER. YOU DON'T KNOW WHAT YOU'RE DOING.
uhh... WH-WHERE...?
YOU'RE RIGHT, MATE. I NEVER REALLY KNOW WHAT I'M DOING.

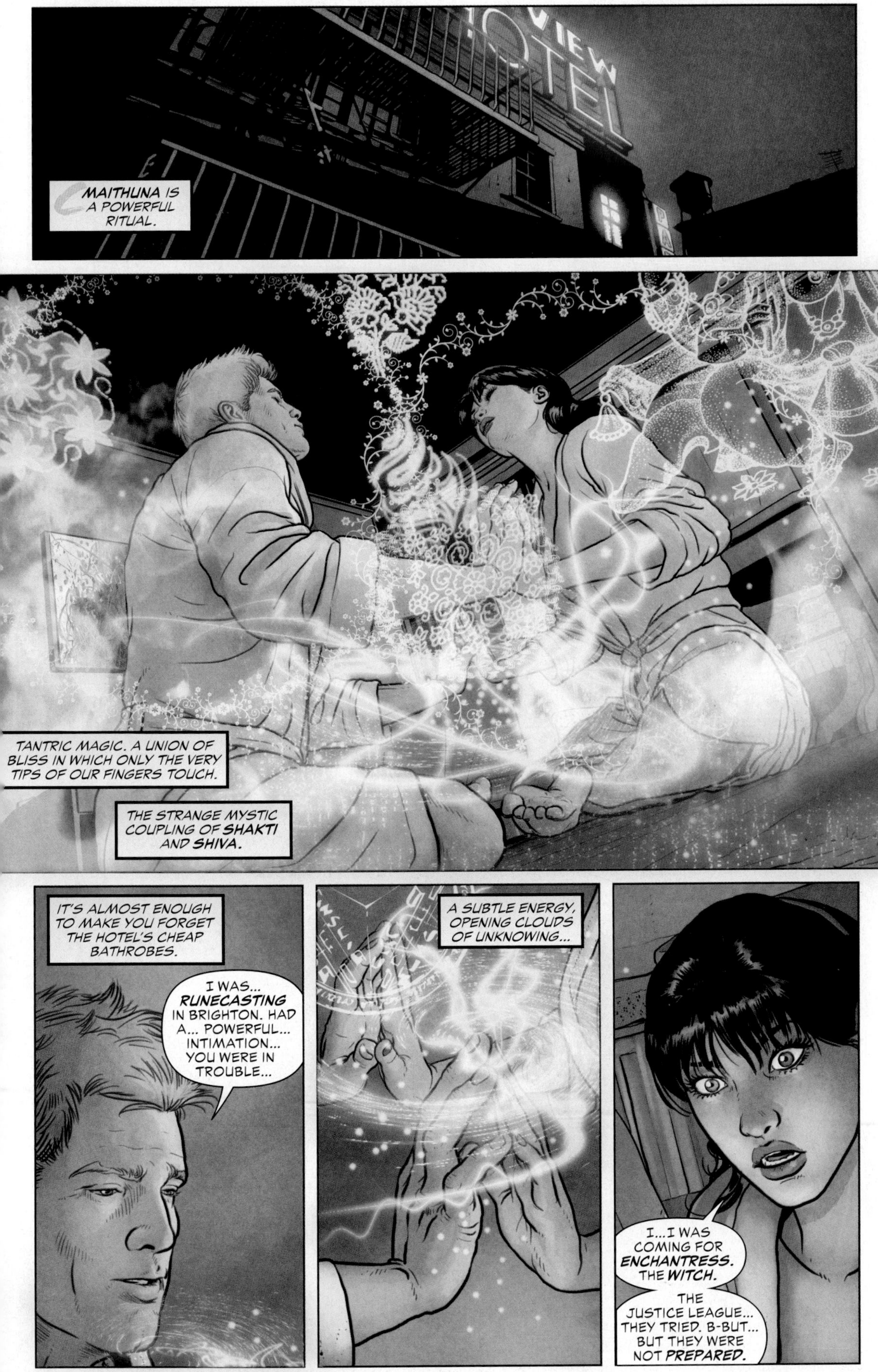
VIEW HOTEL
MAITHUNA IS A POWERFUL RITUAL.
TANTRIC MAGIC. A UNION OF BLISS IN WHICH ONLY THE VERY TIPS OF OUR FINGERS TOUCH.
THE STRANGE MYSTIC COUPLING OF SHAKTI AND SHIVA.
IT'S ALMOST ENOUGH TO MAKE YOU FORGET THE HOTEL'S CHEAP BATHROBES.
I WAS... RUNECASTING IN BRIGHTON. HAD A... POWERFUL... INTIMATION... YOU WERE IN TROUBLE...
A SUBTLE ENERGY, OPENING CLOUDS OF UNKNOWING...
I...I WAS COMING FOR ENCHANTRESS. THE WITCH.
THE JUSTICE LEAGUE... THEY TRIED. B-BUT... BUT THEY WERE NOT PREPARED.

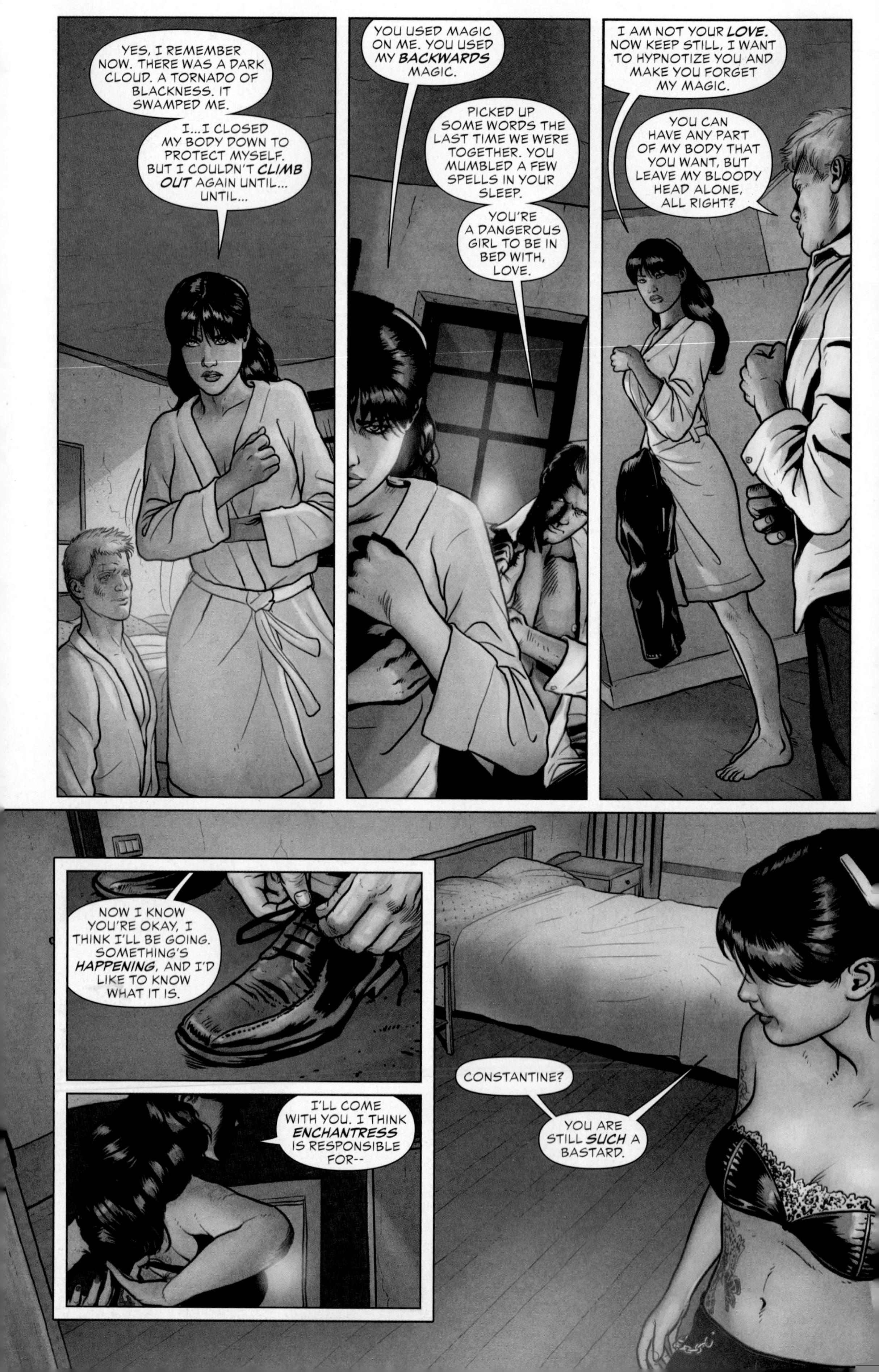
YES, I REMEMBER NOW. THERE WAS A DARK CLOUD. A TORNADO OF BLACKNESS. IT SWAMPED ME.
I...I CLOSED MY BODY DOWN TO PROTECT MYSELF. BUT I COULDN'T *CLIMB OUT* AGAIN UNTIL... UNTIL...
YOU USED MAGIC ON ME. YOU USED MY *BACKWARDS* MAGIC.
PICKED UP SOME WORDS THE LAST TIME WE WERE TOGETHER. YOU MUMBLED A FEW SPELLS IN YOUR SLEEP.
YOU'RE A DANGEROUS GIRL TO BE IN BED WITH, LOVE.
I AM NOT YOUR *LOVE.* NOW KEEP STILL, I WANT TO HYPNOTIZE YOU AND MAKE YOU FORGET MY MAGIC.
YOU CAN HAVE ANY PART OF MY BODY THAT YOU WANT, BUT LEAVE MY BLOODY HEAD ALONE, ALL RIGHT?
NOW I KNOW YOU'RE OKAY, I THINK I'LL BE GOING. SOMETHING'S *HAPPENING*, AND I'D LIKE TO KNOW WHAT IT IS.
I'LL COME WITH YOU. I THINK *ENCHANTRESS* IS RESPONSIBLE FOR--
CONSTANTINE?
YOU ARE STILL *SUCH* A BASTARD.

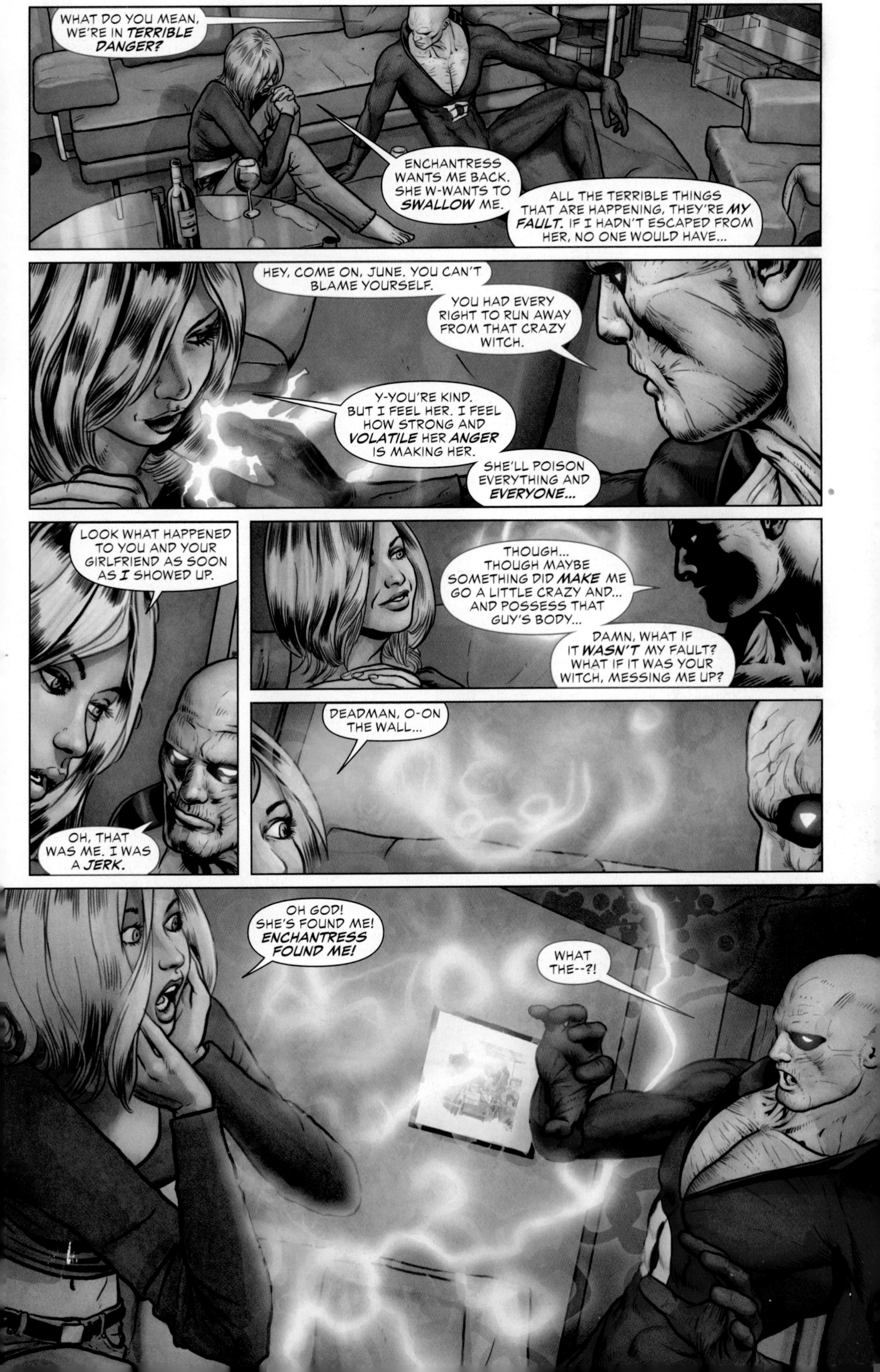
WHAT DO YOU MEAN, WE'RE IN TERRIBLE DANGER?
ENCHANTRESS WANTS ME BACK. SHE W-WANTS TO SWALLOW ME.
ALL THE TERRIBLE THINGS THAT ARE HAPPENING, THEY'RE MY FAULT. IF I HADN'T ESCAPED FROM HER, NO ONE WOULD HAVE...
HEY, COME ON, JUNE. YOU CAN'T BLAME YOURSELF.
YOU HAD EVERY RIGHT TO RUN AWAY FROM THAT CRAZY WITCH.
Y-YOU'RE KIND. BUT I FEEL HER. I FEEL HOW STRONG AND VOLATILE HER ANGER IS MAKING HER.
SHE'LL POISON EVERYTHING AND EVERYONE...
LOOK WHAT HAPPENED TO YOU AND YOUR GIRLFRIEND AS SOON AS I SHOWED UP.
OH, THAT WAS ME. I WAS A JERK.
THOUGH... THOUGH MAYBE SOMETHING DID MAKE ME GO A LITTLE CRAZY AND... AND POSSESS THAT GUY'S BODY...
DAMN, WHAT IF IT WASN'T MY FAULT? WHAT IF IT WAS YOUR WITCH, MESSING ME UP?
DEADMAN, O-ON THE WALL...
OH GOD! SHE'S FOUND ME! ENCHANTRESS FOUND ME!
WHAT THE--?!

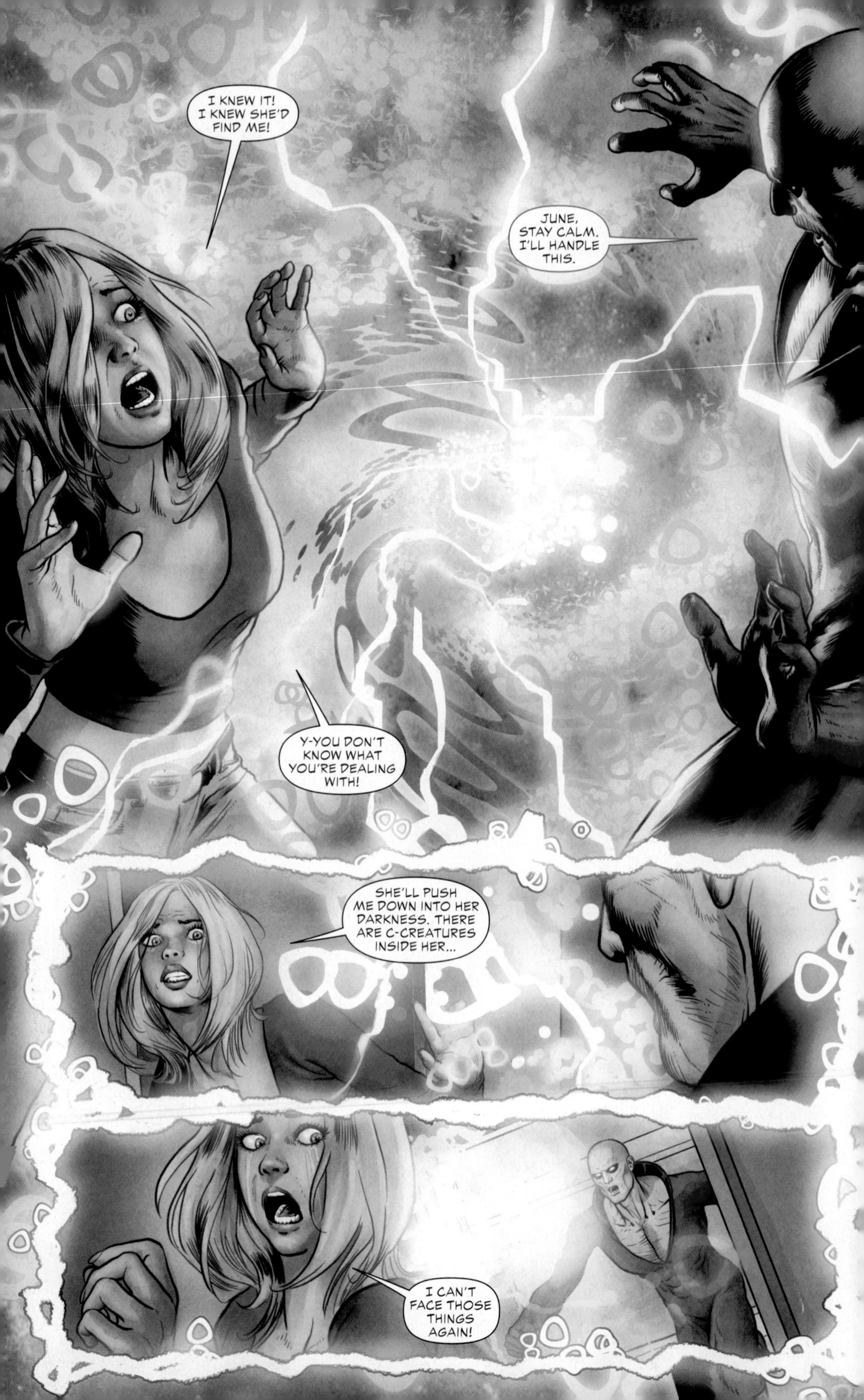
I KNEW IT! I KNEW SHE'D FIND ME!
JUNE, STAY CALM. I'LL HANDLE THIS.
Y-YOU DON'T KNOW WHAT YOU'RE DEALING WITH!
SHE'LL PUSH ME DOWN INTO HER DARKNESS. THERE ARE C-CREATURES INSIDE HER...
I CAN'T FACE THOSE THINGS AGAIN!

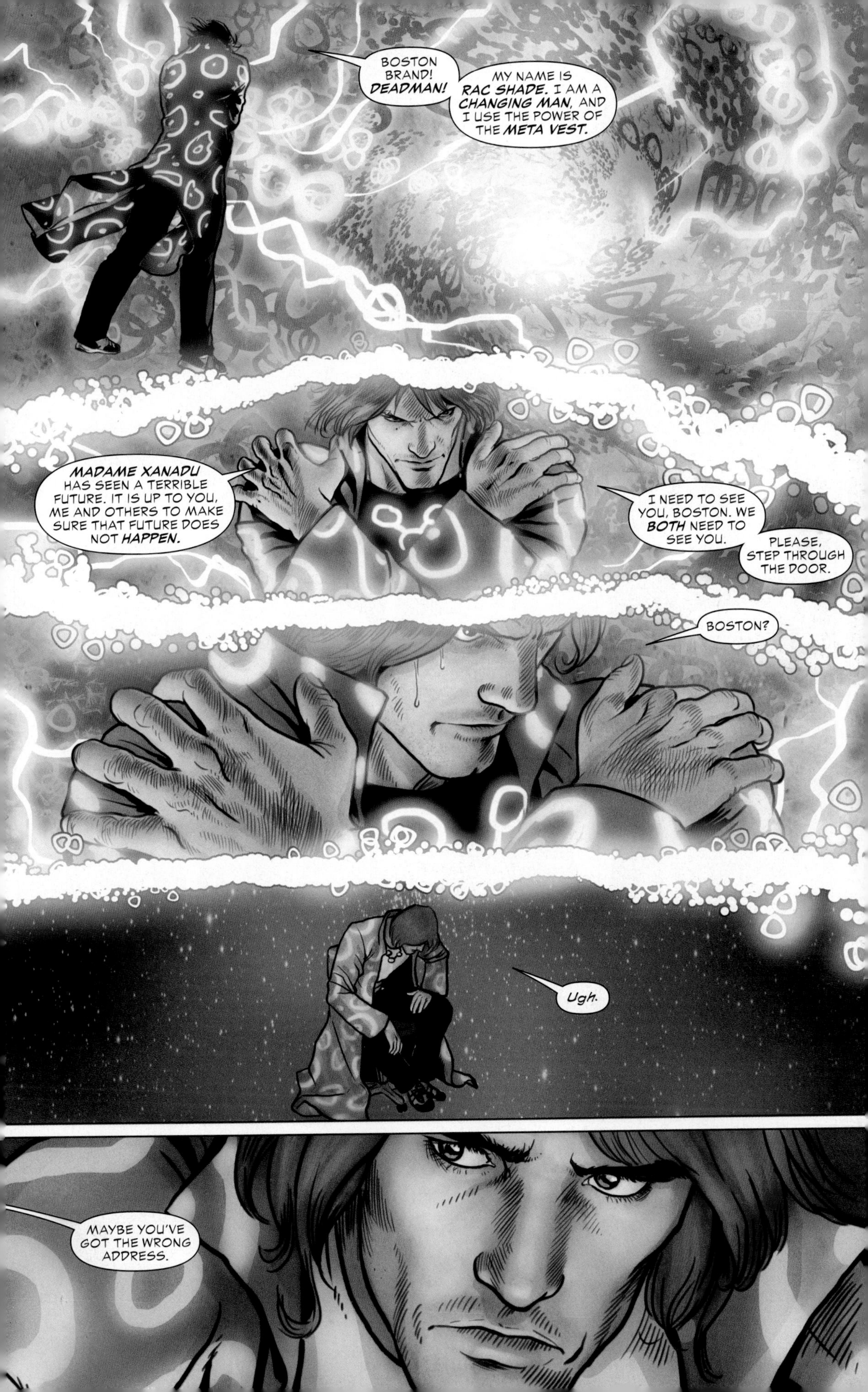
BOSTON BRAND! DEADMAN!
MY NAME IS RAC SHADE. I AM A CHANGING MAN, AND I USE THE POWER OF THE META VEST.
MADAME XANADU HAS SEEN A TERRIBLE FUTURE. IT IS UP TO YOU, ME AND OTHERS TO MAKE SURE THAT FUTURE DOES NOT HAPPEN.
I NEED TO SEE YOU, BOSTON. WE BOTH NEED TO SEE YOU.
PLEASE, STEP THROUGH THE DOOR.
BOSTON?
Ugh.
MAYBE YOU'VE GOT THE WRONG ADDRESS.

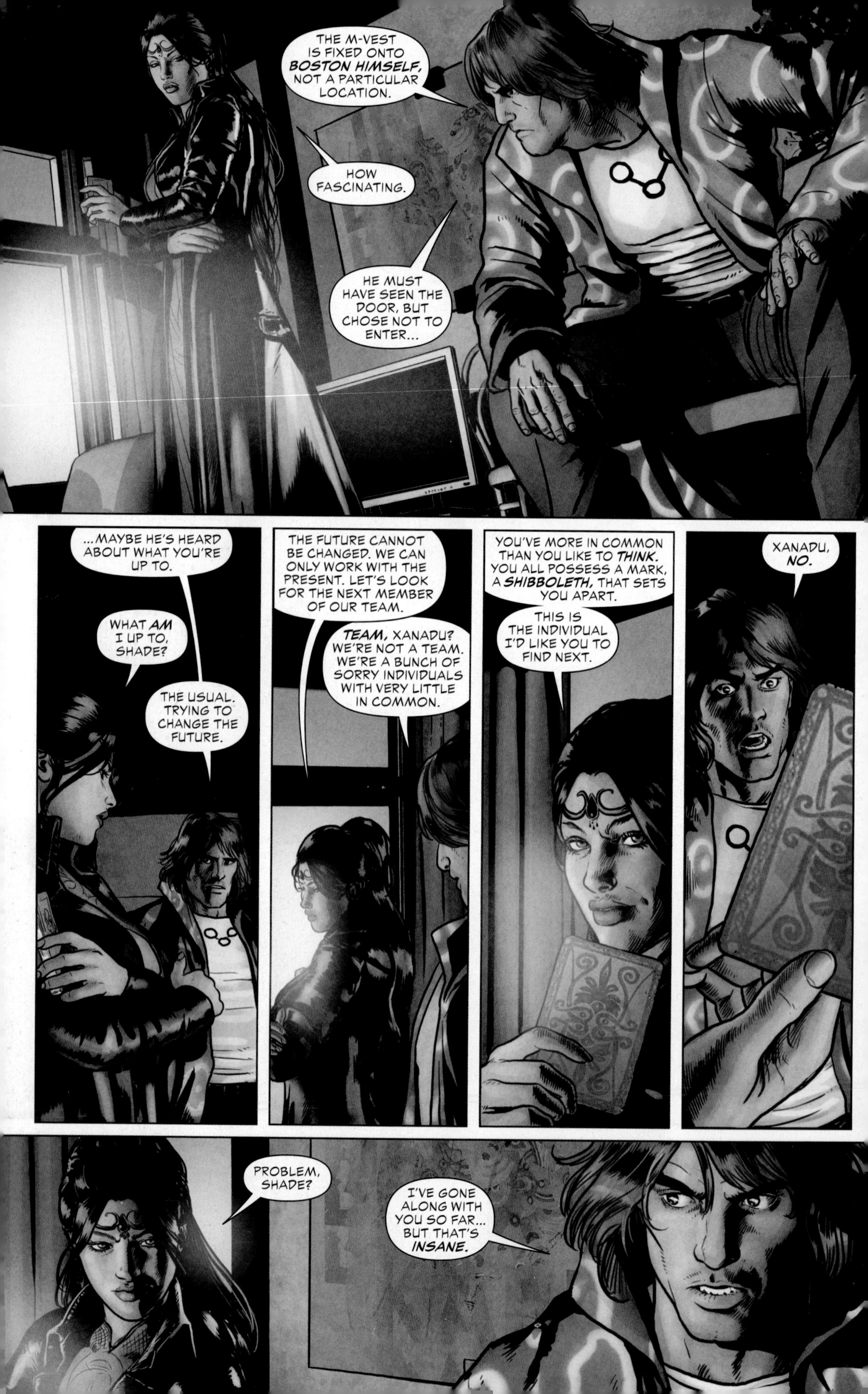
THE M-VEST IS FIXED ONTO *BOSTON HIMSELF,* NOT A PARTICULAR LOCATION.
HOW FASCINATING.
HE MUST HAVE SEEN THE DOOR, BUT CHOSE NOT TO ENTER...
...MAYBE HE'S HEARD ABOUT WHAT YOU'RE UP TO.
WHAT *AM* I UP TO, SHADE?
THE USUAL. TRYING TO CHANGE THE FUTURE.
THE FUTURE CANNOT BE CHANGED. WE CAN ONLY WORK WITH THE PRESENT. LET'S LOOK FOR THE NEXT MEMBER OF OUR TEAM.
TEAM, XANADU? WE'RE NOT A TEAM. WE'RE A BUNCH OF SORRY INDIVIDUALS WITH VERY LITTLE IN COMMON.
YOU'VE MORE IN COMMON THAN YOU LIKE TO *THINK.* YOU ALL POSSESS A MARK, A *SHIBBOLETH,* THAT SETS YOU APART.
THIS IS THE INDIVIDUAL I'D LIKE YOU TO FIND NEXT.
XANADU, *NO.*
PROBLEM, SHADE?
I'VE GONE ALONG WITH YOU SO FAR... BUT THAT'S *INSANE.*

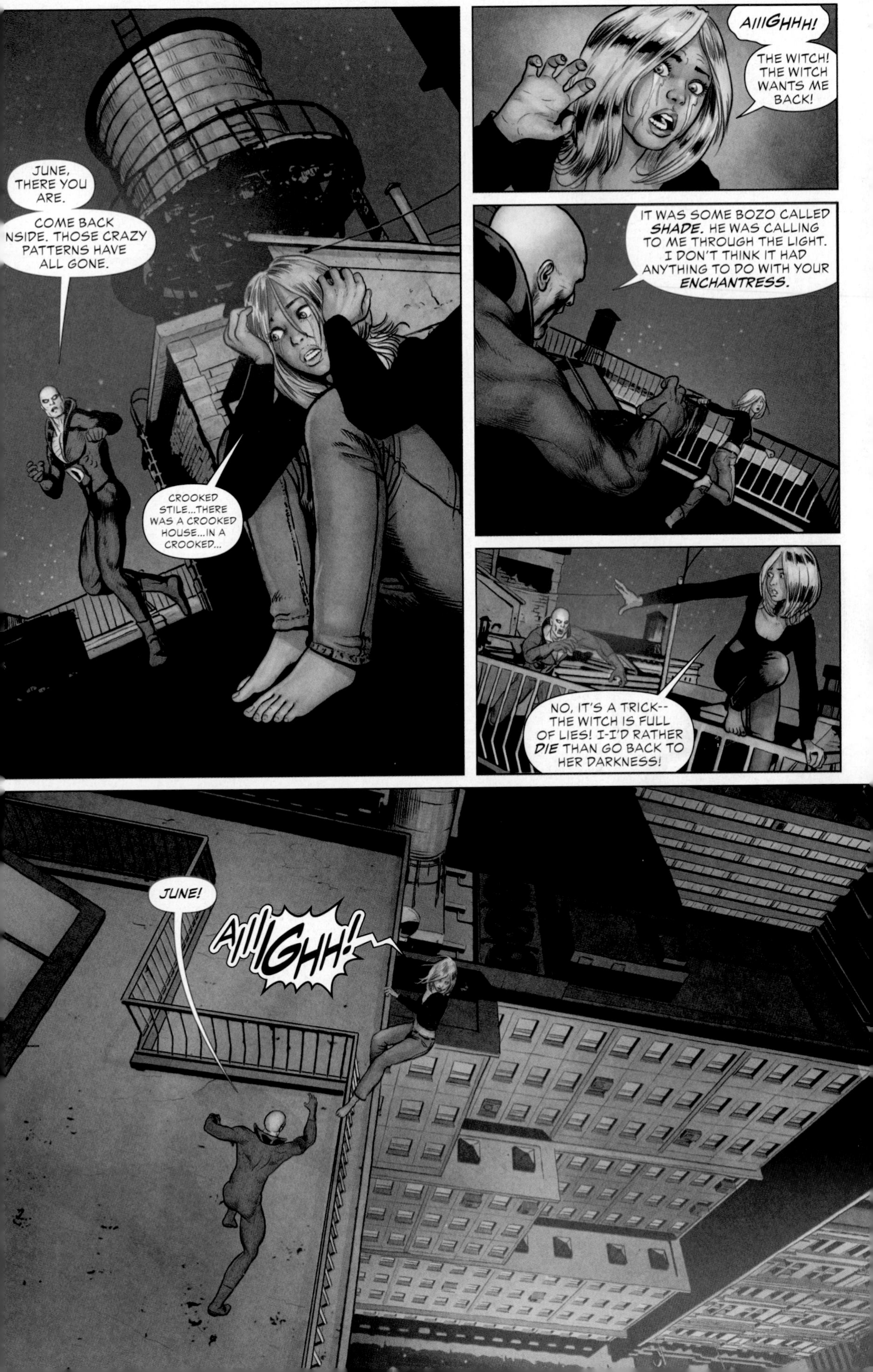

JUNE, THERE YOU ARE.
COME BACK NSIDE. THOSE CRAZY PATTERNS HAVE ALL GONE.
CROOKED STILE...THERE WAS A CROOKED HOUSE...IN A CROOKED...
AIIIGHHH!
THE WITCH! THE WITCH WANTS ME BACK!
IT WAS SOME BOZO CALLED SHADE. HE WAS CALLING TO ME THROUGH THE LIGHT. I DON'T THINK IT HAD ANYTHING TO DO WITH YOUR ENCHANTRESS.
NO, IT'S A TRICK-- THE WITCH IS FULL OF LIES! I-I'D RATHER DIE THAN GO BACK TO HER DARKNESS!
JUNE!
AIIIGHH!

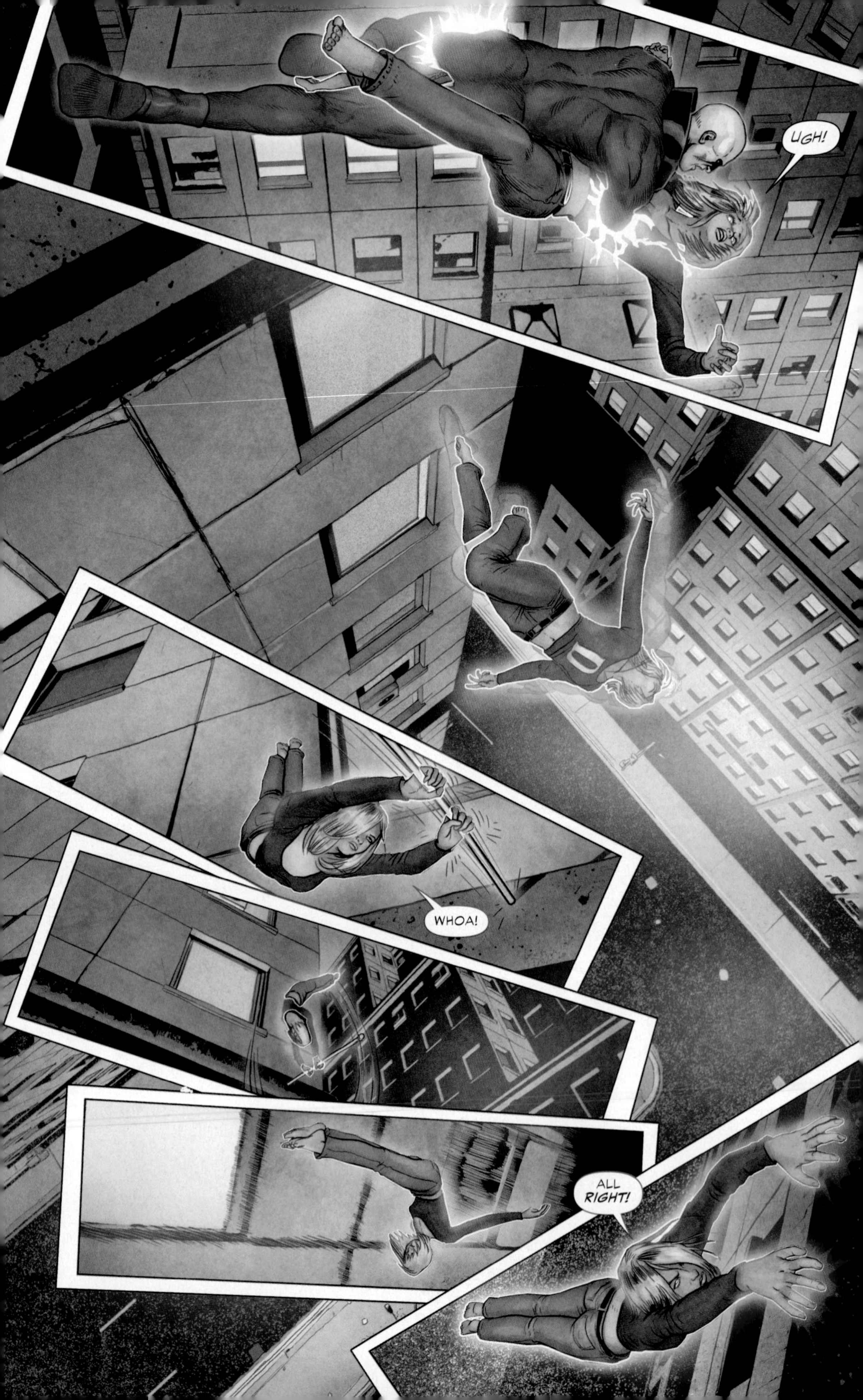
UGH!
WHOA!
ALL RIGHT!

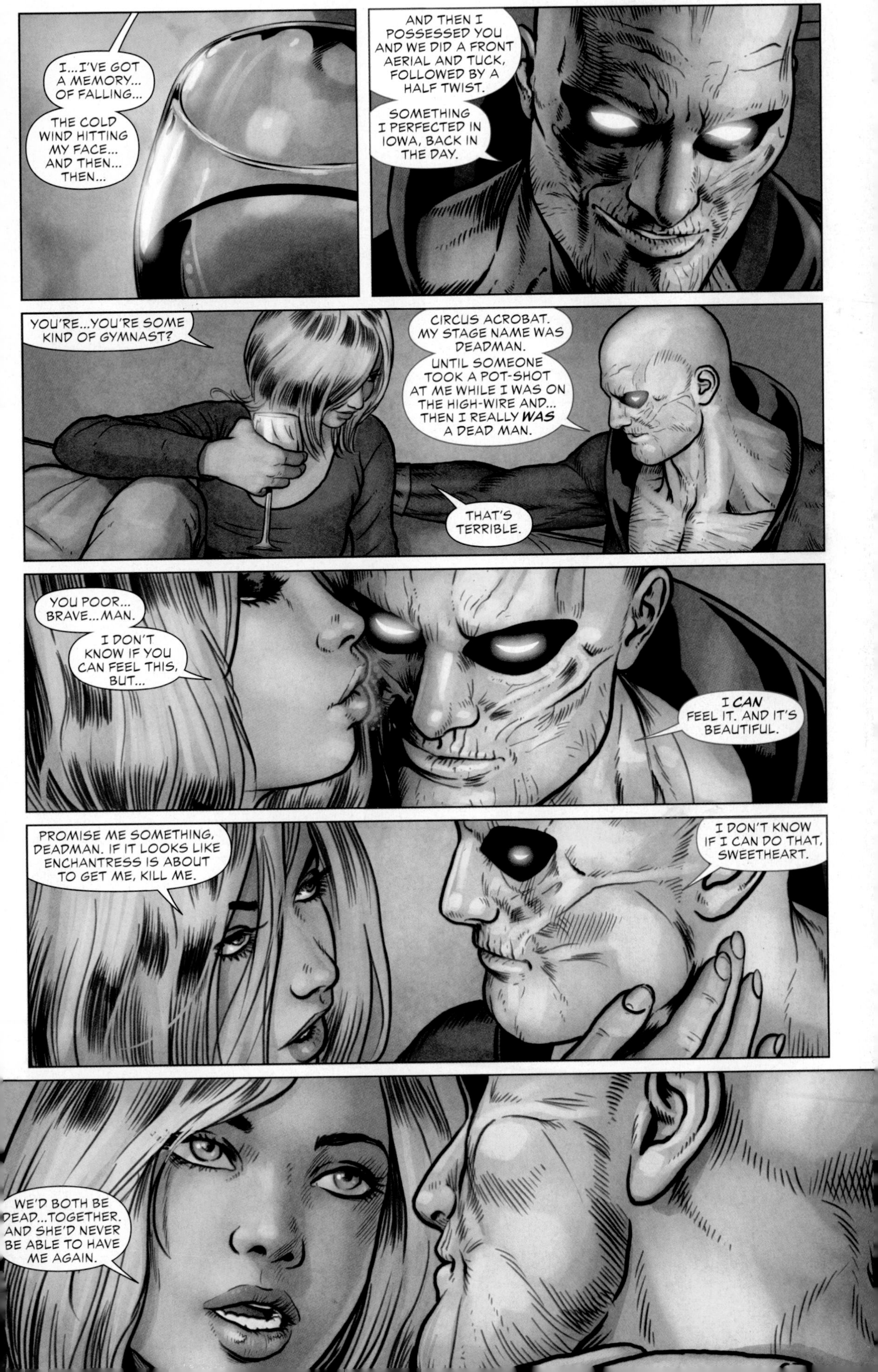
I...I'VE GOT A MEMORY... OF FALLING...
THE COLD WIND HITTING MY FACE... AND THEN... THEN...
AND THEN I POSSESSED YOU AND WE DID A FRONT AERIAL AND TUCK, FOLLOWED BY A HALF TWIST.
SOMETHING I PERFECTED IN IOWA, BACK IN THE DAY.
YOU'RE...YOU'RE SOME KIND OF GYMNAST?
CIRCUS ACROBAT. MY STAGE NAME WAS DEADMAN.
UNTIL SOMEONE TOOK A POT-SHOT AT ME WHILE I WAS ON THE HIGH-WIRE AND... THEN I REALLY **WAS** A DEAD MAN.
THAT'S TERRIBLE.
YOU POOR... BRAVE...MAN.
I DON'T KNOW IF YOU CAN FEEL THIS, BUT...
I **CAN** FEEL IT. AND IT'S BEAUTIFUL.
PROMISE ME SOMETHING, DEADMAN. IF IT LOOKS LIKE ENCHANTRESS IS ABOUT TO GET ME, KILL ME.
I DON'T KNOW IF I CAN DO THAT, SWEETHEART.
WE'D BOTH BE DEAD...TOGETHER. AND SHE'D NEVER BE ABLE TO HAVE ME AGAIN.

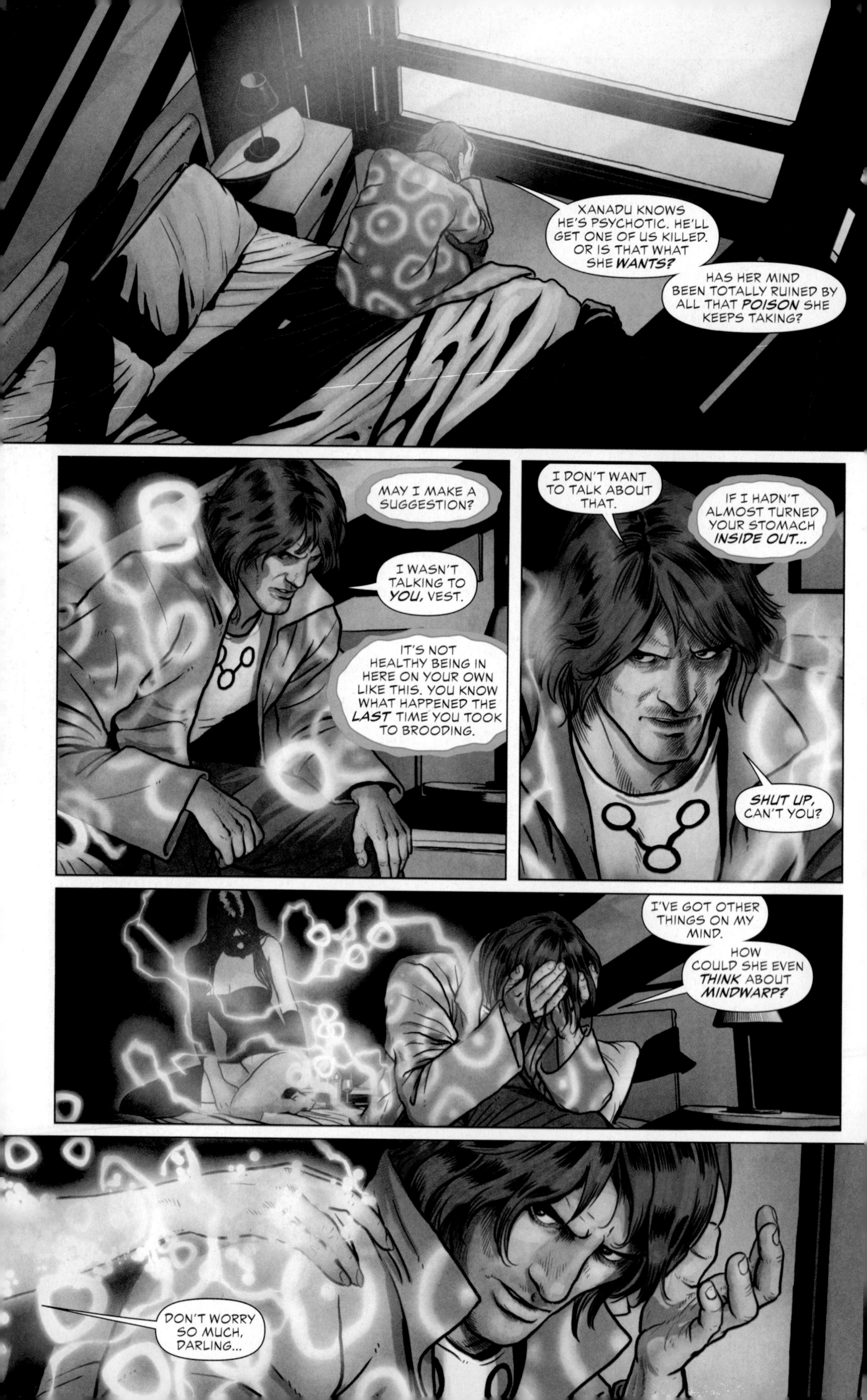
XANADU KNOWS HE'S PSYCHOTIC. HE'LL GET ONE OF US KILLED. OR IS THAT WHAT SHE WANTS?
HAS HER MIND BEEN TOTALLY RUINED BY ALL THAT POISON SHE KEEPS TAKING?
MAY I MAKE A SUGGESTION?
I WASN'T TALKING TO YOU, VEST.
IT'S NOT HEALTHY BEING IN HERE ON YOUR OWN LIKE THIS. YOU KNOW WHAT HAPPENED THE LAST TIME YOU TOOK TO BROODING.
I DON'T WANT TO TALK ABOUT THAT.
IF I HADN'T ALMOST TURNED YOUR STOMACH INSIDE OUT...
SHUT UP, CAN'T YOU?
I'VE GOT OTHER THINGS ON MY MIND.
HOW COULD SHE EVEN THINK ABOUT MINDWARP?
DON'T WORRY SO MUCH, DARLING...

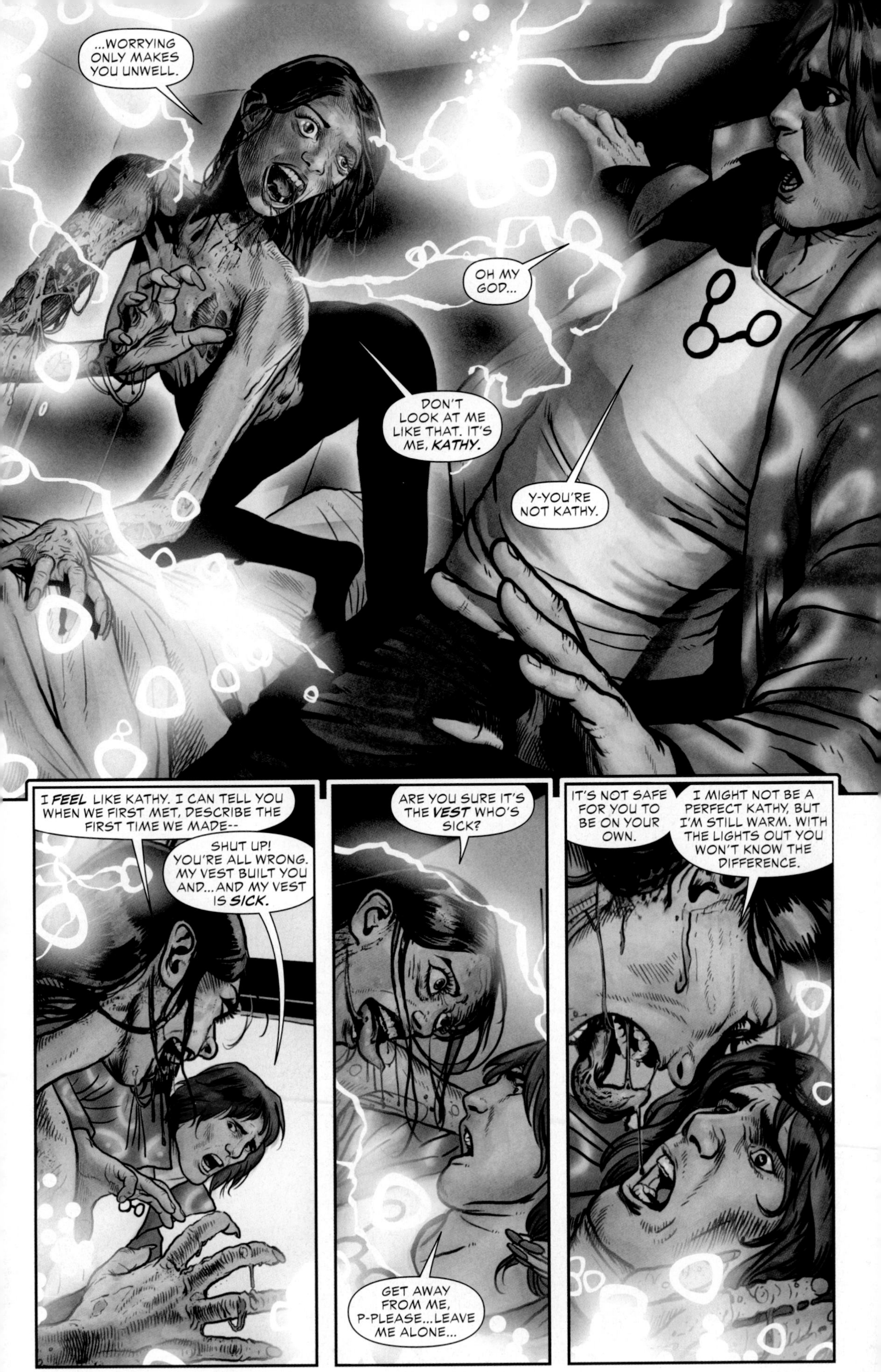
...WORRYING ONLY MAKES YOU UNWELL.
OH MY GOD...
DON'T LOOK AT ME LIKE THAT. IT'S ME, *KATHY.*
Y-YOU'RE NOT KATHY.
I *FEEL* LIKE KATHY. I CAN TELL YOU WHEN WE FIRST MET, DESCRIBE THE FIRST TIME WE MADE--
SHUT UP! YOU'RE ALL WRONG. MY VEST BUILT YOU AND...AND MY VEST IS *SICK.*
ARE YOU SURE IT'S THE *VEST* WHO'S SICK?
GET AWAY FROM ME, P-PLEASE...LEAVE ME ALONE...
IT'S NOT SAFE FOR YOU TO BE ON YOUR OWN.
I MIGHT NOT BE A PERFECT KATHY, BUT I'M STILL WARM. WITH THE LIGHTS OUT YOU WON'T KNOW THE DIFFERENCE.

YOU'RE TRYING TO MAKE ME DISAPPEAR, BUT YOUR HEART'S NOT IN IT.

I DON'T WANT...

BUT YOU DO. SOME PART OF YOU...SOME WEAK *SICK* PART OF YOU...

SHE'S RIGHT. I WANT IT. I HATE IT. I WANT IT.

AIEEEEE..!!

GET OFF ME!

EVEN WHEN SHE'S GONE I CAN HEAR HER CRYING.

A PATHETIC, LONELY SOBBING.

AND THEN I REALIZE...

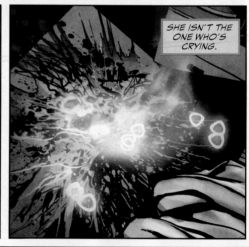

SHE ISN'T THE ONE WHO'S CRYING.

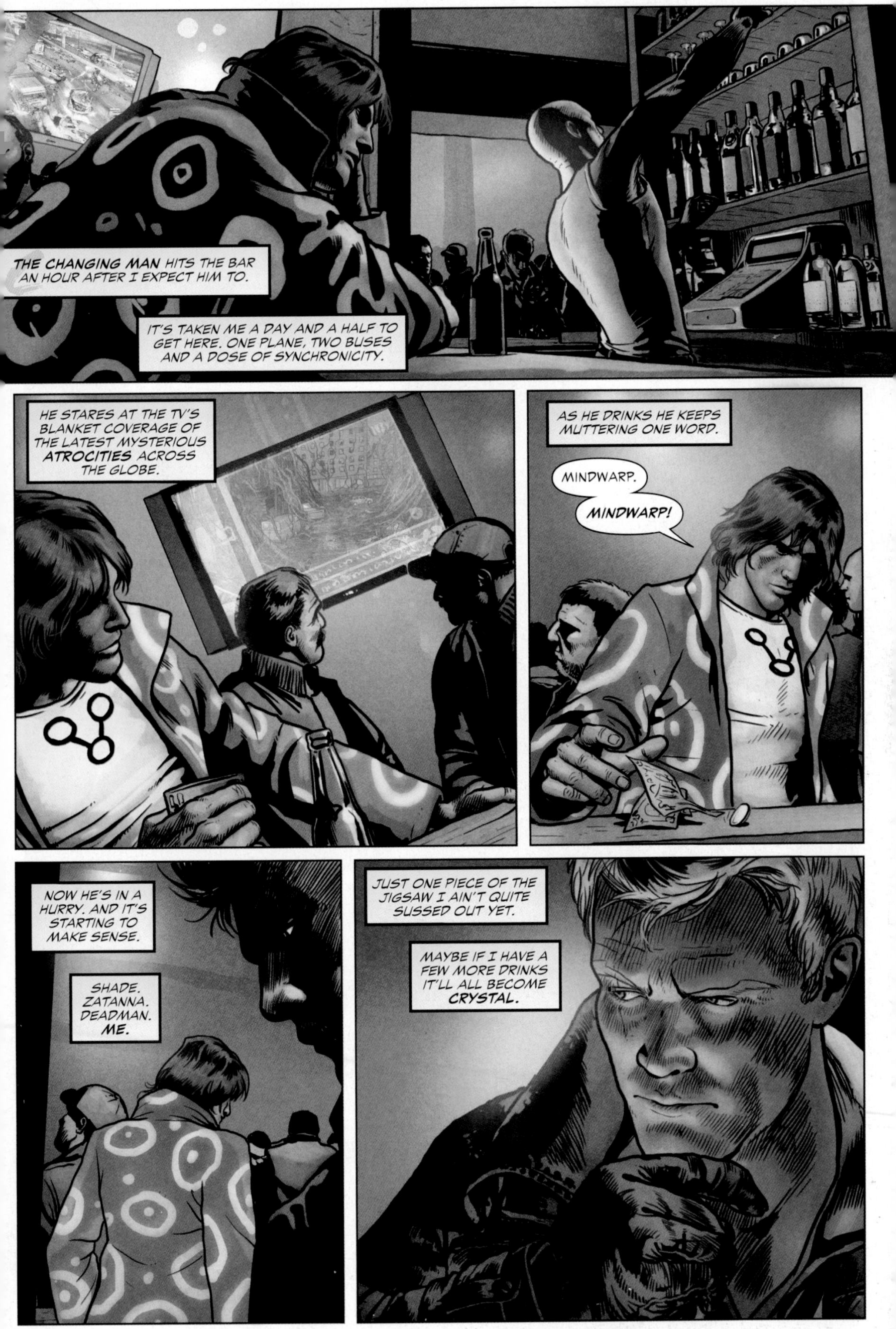
THE CHANGING MAN HITS THE BAR AN HOUR AFTER I EXPECT HIM TO.
IT'S TAKEN ME A DAY AND A HALF TO GET HERE. ONE PLANE, TWO BUSES AND A DOSE OF SYNCHRONICITY.
HE STARES AT THE TV'S BLANKET COVERAGE OF THE LATEST MYSTERIOUS ATROCITIES ACROSS THE GLOBE.
AS HE DRINKS HE KEEPS MUTTERING ONE WORD.
MINDWARP.
MINDWARP!
NOW HE'S IN A HURRY. AND IT'S STARTING TO MAKE SENSE.
SHADE. ZATANNA. DEADMAN. ME.
JUST ONE PIECE OF THE JIGSAW I AIN'T QUITE SUSSED OUT YET.
MAYBE IF I HAVE A FEW MORE DRINKS IT'LL ALL BECOME CRYSTAL.

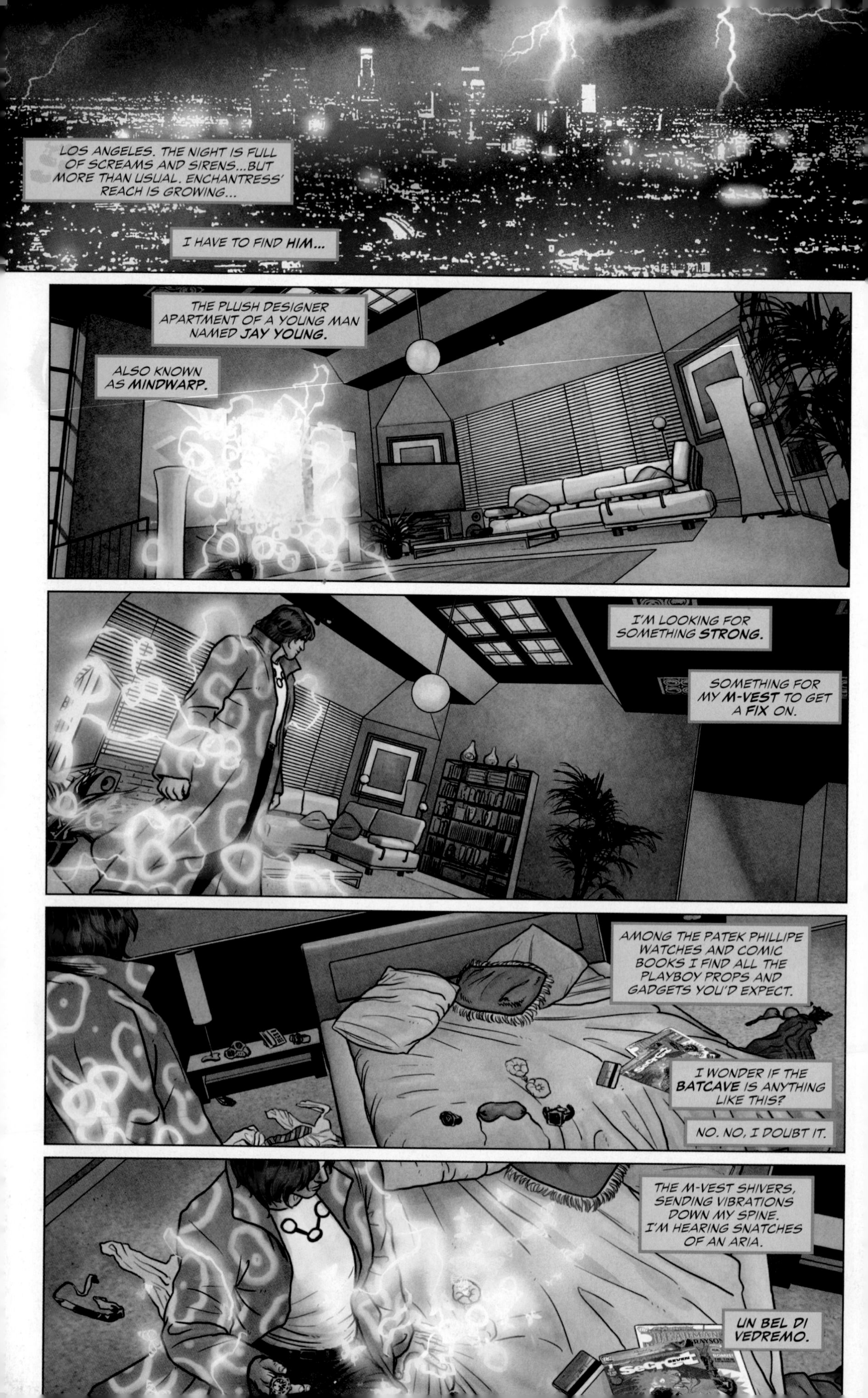
LOS ANGELES. THE NIGHT IS FULL OF SCREAMS AND SIRENS...BUT MORE THAN USUAL. ENCHANTRESS' REACH IS GROWING...
I HAVE TO FIND HIM...
THE PLUSH DESIGNER APARTMENT OF A YOUNG MAN NAMED JAY YOUNG.
ALSO KNOWN AS MINDWARP.
I'M LOOKING FOR SOMETHING STRONG.
SOMETHING FOR MY M-VEST TO GET A FIX ON.
AMONG THE PATEK PHILLIPE WATCHES AND COMIC BOOKS I FIND ALL THE PLAYBOY PROPS AND GADGETS YOU'D EXPECT.
I WONDER IF THE BATCAVE IS ANYTHING LIKE THIS?
NO. NO, I DOUBT IT.
THE M-VEST SHIVERS, SENDING VIBRATIONS DOWN MY SPINE. I'M HEARING SNATCHES OF AN ARIA.
UN BEL DI VEDREMO.

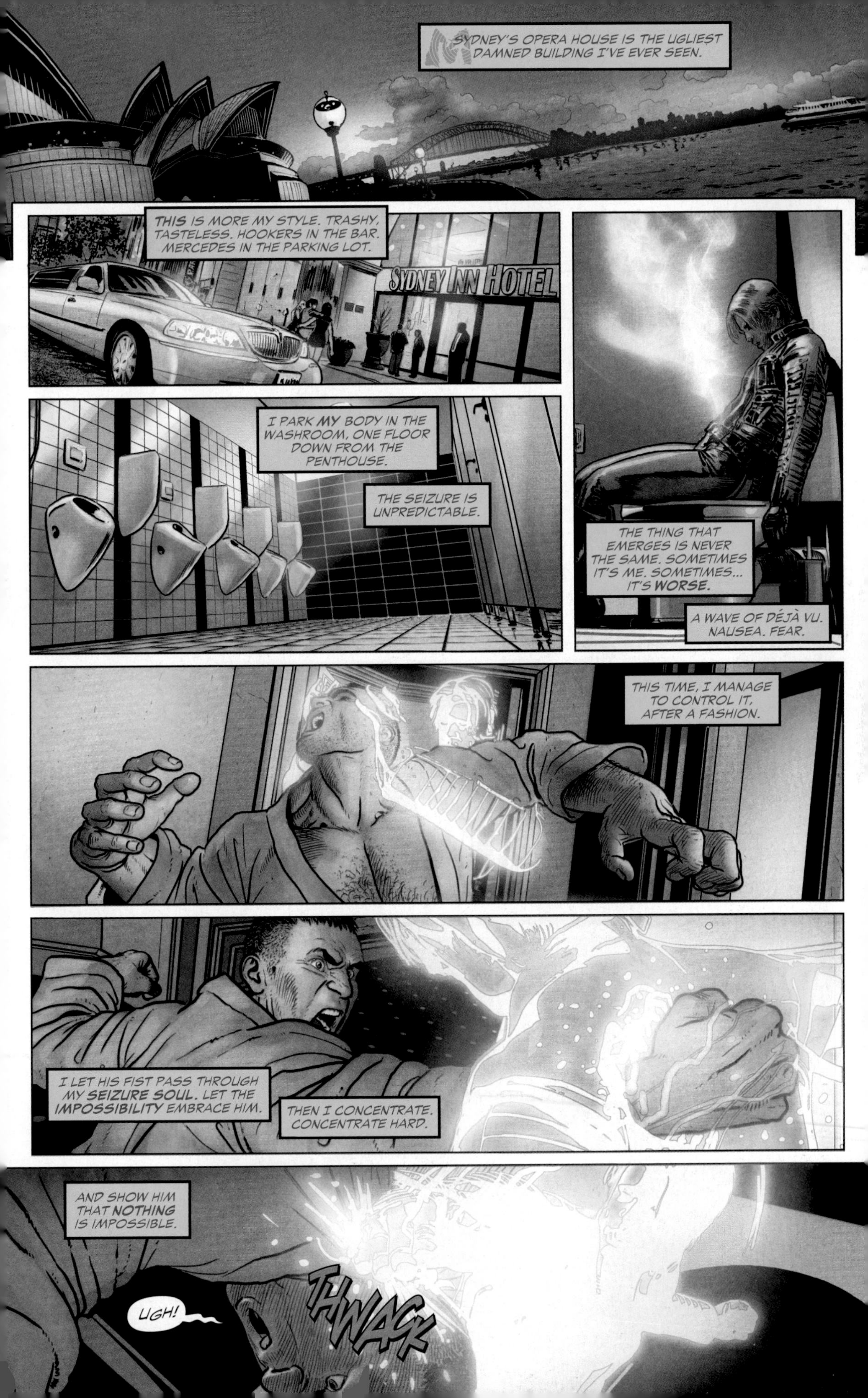
SYDNEY'S OPERA HOUSE IS THE UGLIEST DAMNED BUILDING I'VE EVER SEEN.
THIS IS MORE MY STYLE. TRASHY, TASTELESS. HOOKERS IN THE BAR. MERCEDES IN THE PARKING LOT.
SYDNEY INN HOTEL
I PARK MY BODY IN THE WASHROOM, ONE FLOOR DOWN FROM THE PENTHOUSE.
THE SEIZURE IS UNPREDICTABLE.
THE THING THAT EMERGES IS NEVER THE SAME. SOMETIMES IT'S ME. SOMETIMES... IT'S WORSE.
A WAVE OF DÉJÀ VU. NAUSEA. FEAR.
THIS TIME, I MANAGE TO CONTROL IT, AFTER A FASHION.
I LET HIS FIST PASS THROUGH MY SEIZURE SOUL. LET THE IMPOSSIBILITY EMBRACE HIM.
THEN I CONCENTRATE. CONCENTRATE HARD.
AND SHOW HIM THAT NOTHING IS IMPOSSIBLE.
UGH!
THWACK

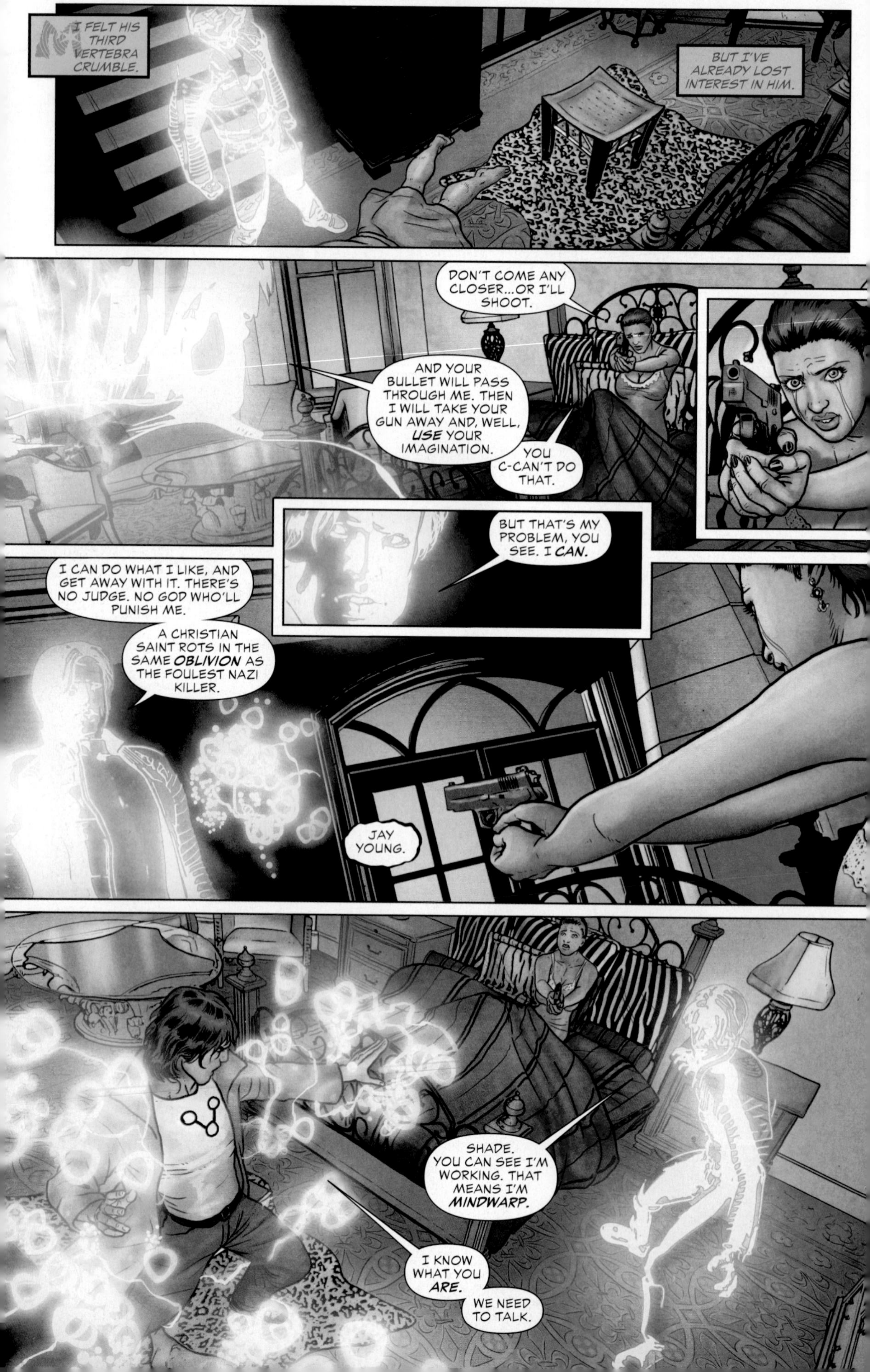

I FELT HIS THIRD VERTEBRA CRUMBLE.
BUT I'VE ALREADY LOST INTEREST IN HIM.
DON'T COME ANY CLOSER...OR I'LL SHOOT.
AND YOUR BULLET WILL PASS THROUGH ME. THEN I WILL TAKE YOUR GUN AWAY AND, WELL, USE YOUR IMAGINATION.
YOU C-CAN'T DO THAT.
BUT THAT'S MY PROBLEM, YOU SEE. I CAN.
I CAN DO WHAT I LIKE, AND GET AWAY WITH IT. THERE'S NO JUDGE. NO GOD WHO'LL PUNISH ME.
A CHRISTIAN SAINT ROTS IN THE SAME OBLIVION AS THE FOULEST NAZI KILLER.
JAY YOUNG.
SHADE. YOU CAN SEE I'M WORKING. THAT MEANS I'M MINDWARP.
I KNOW WHAT YOU ARE.
WE NEED TO TALK.

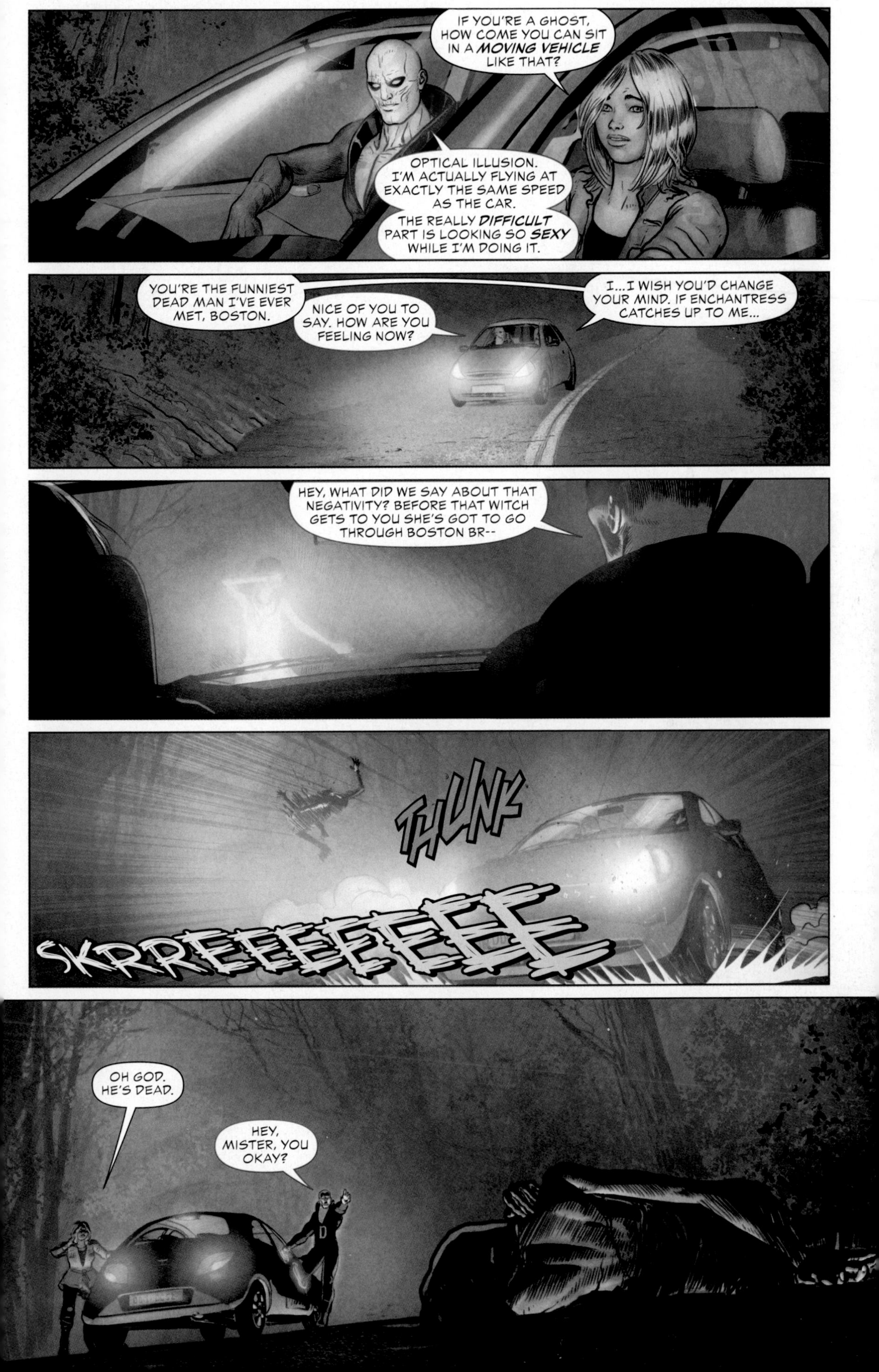
IF YOU'RE A GHOST, HOW COME YOU CAN SIT IN A MOVING VEHICLE LIKE THAT?
OPTICAL ILLUSION. I'M ACTUALLY FLYING AT EXACTLY THE SAME SPEED AS THE CAR.
THE REALLY DIFFICULT PART IS LOOKING SO SEXY WHILE I'M DOING IT.
YOU'RE THE FUNNIEST DEAD MAN I'VE EVER MET, BOSTON.
NICE OF YOU TO SAY. HOW ARE YOU FEELING NOW?
I...I WISH YOU'D CHANGE YOUR MIND. IF ENCHANTRESS CATCHES UP TO ME...
HEY, WHAT DID WE SAY ABOUT THAT NEGATIVITY? BEFORE THAT WITCH GETS TO YOU SHE'S GOT TO GO THROUGH BOSTON BR--
THUNK
SKRREEEEEEEEEE
OH GOD. HE'S DEAD.
HEY, MISTER, YOU OKAY?

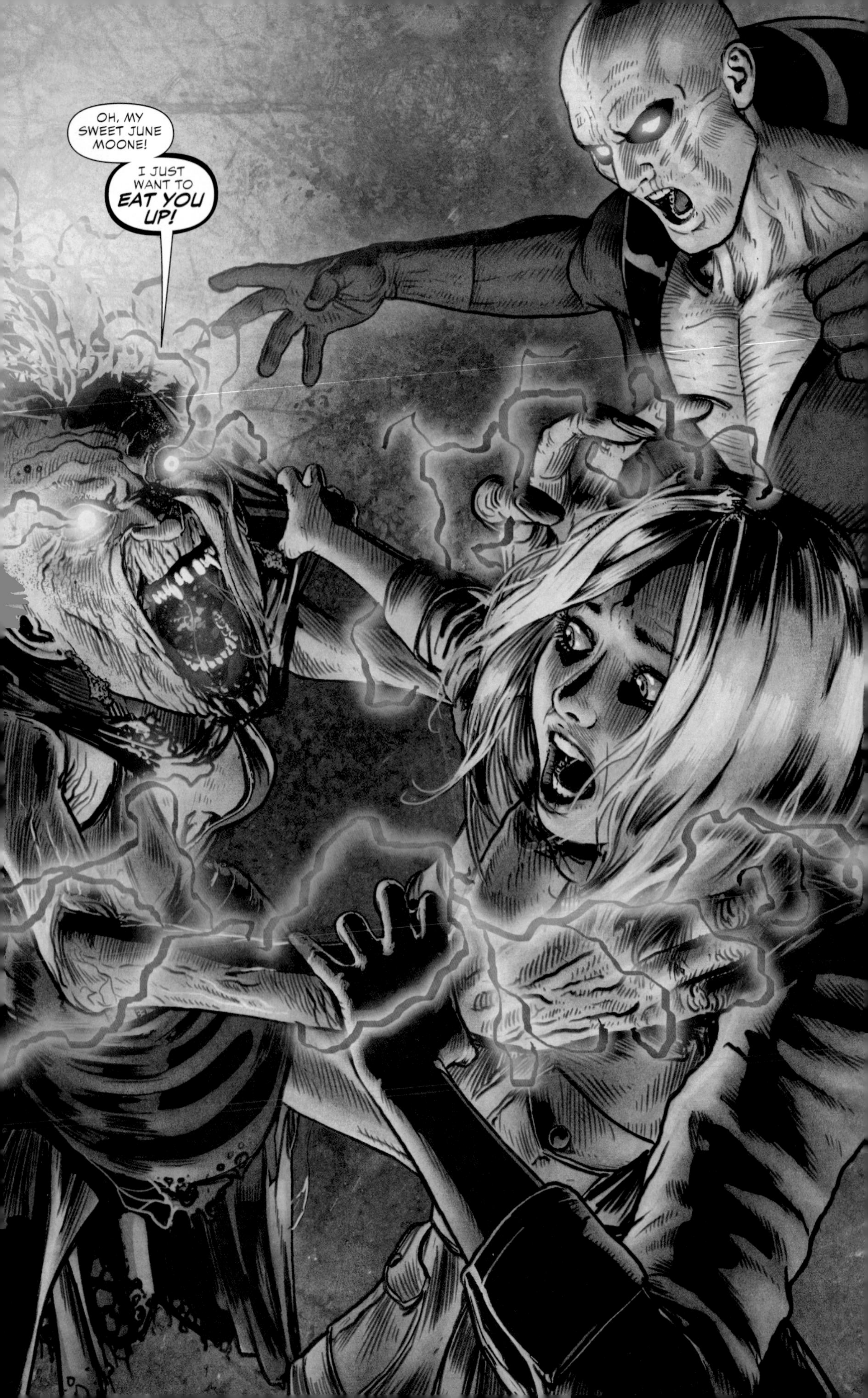
OH, MY SWEET JUNE MOONE!
I JUST WANT TO EAT YOU UP!

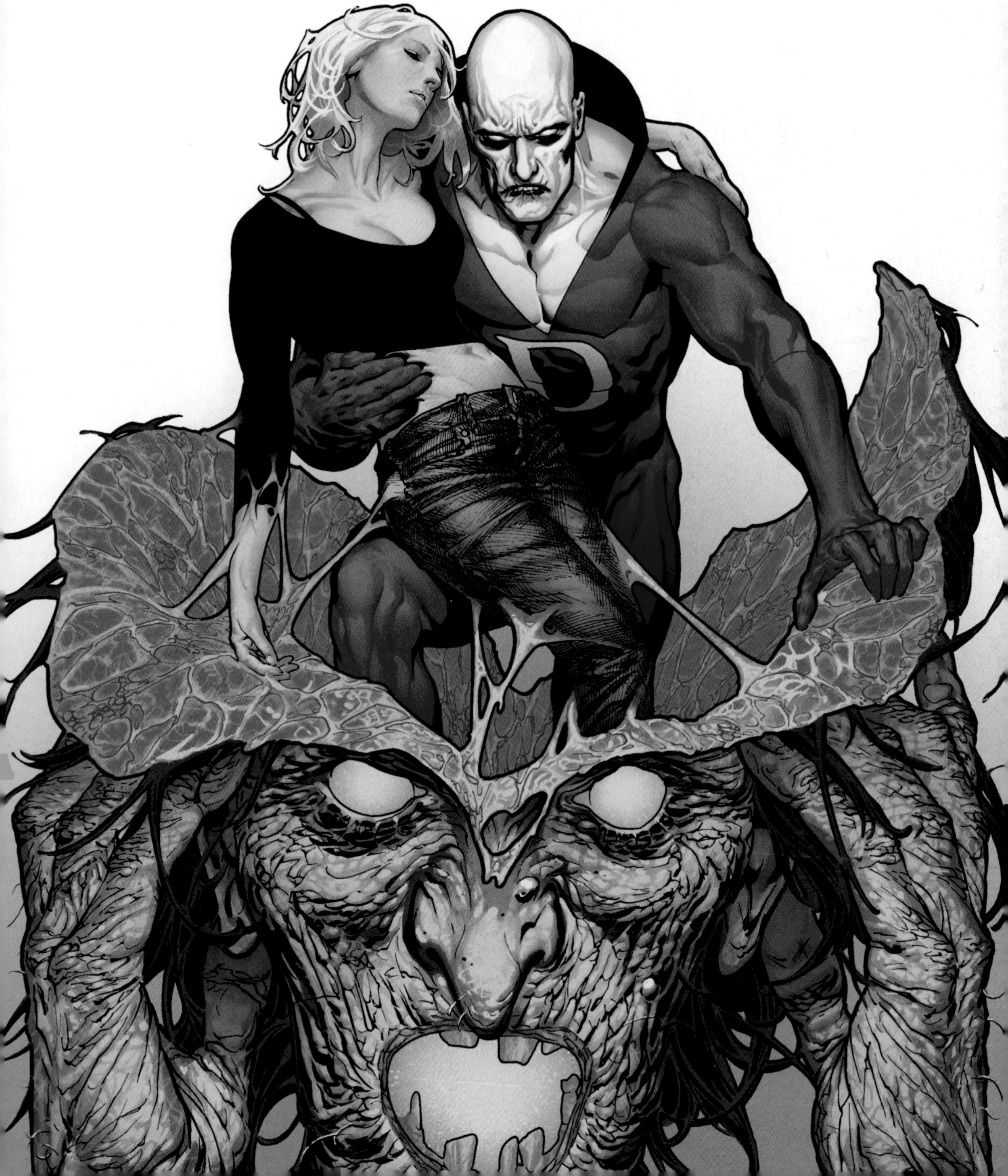

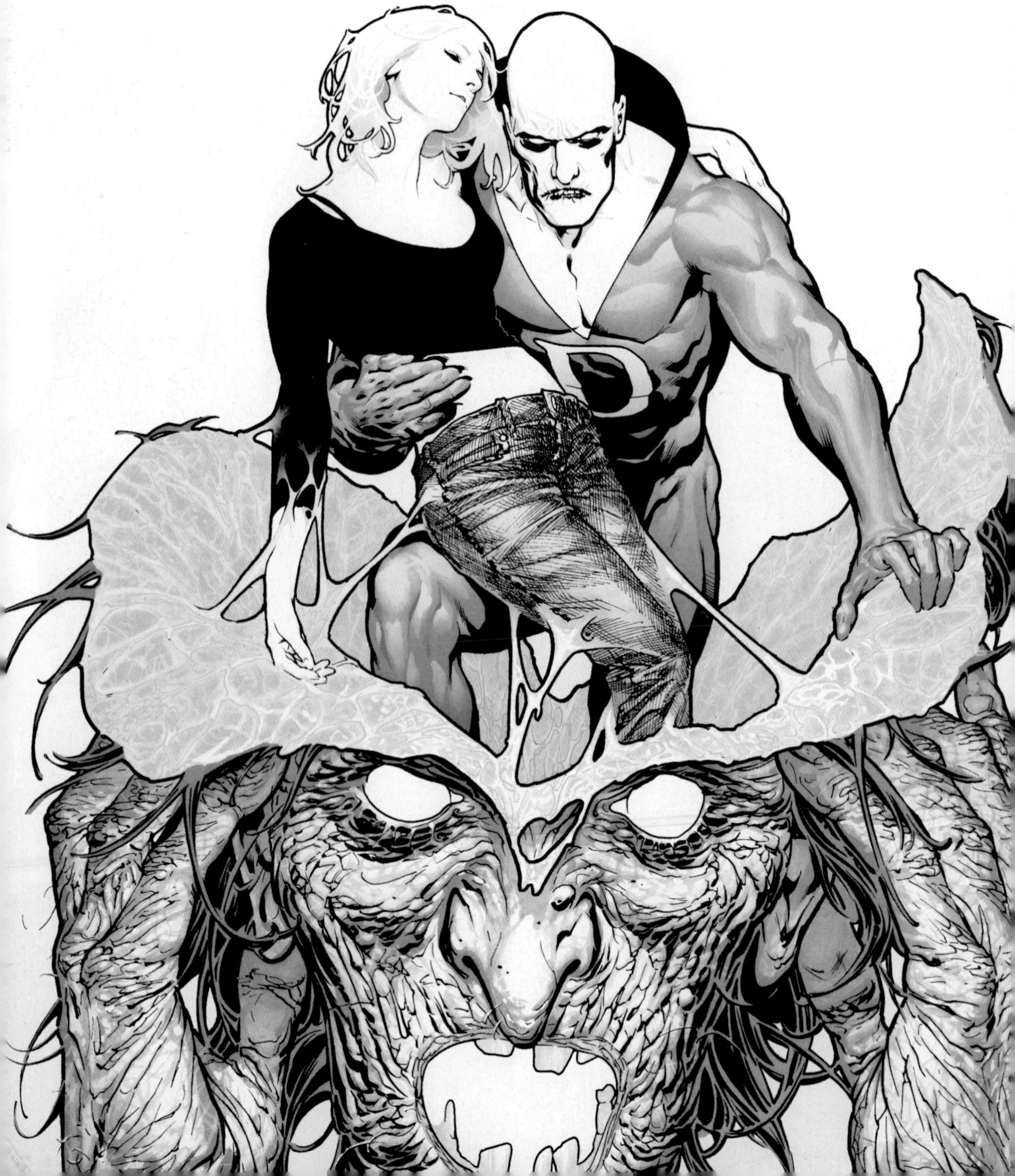

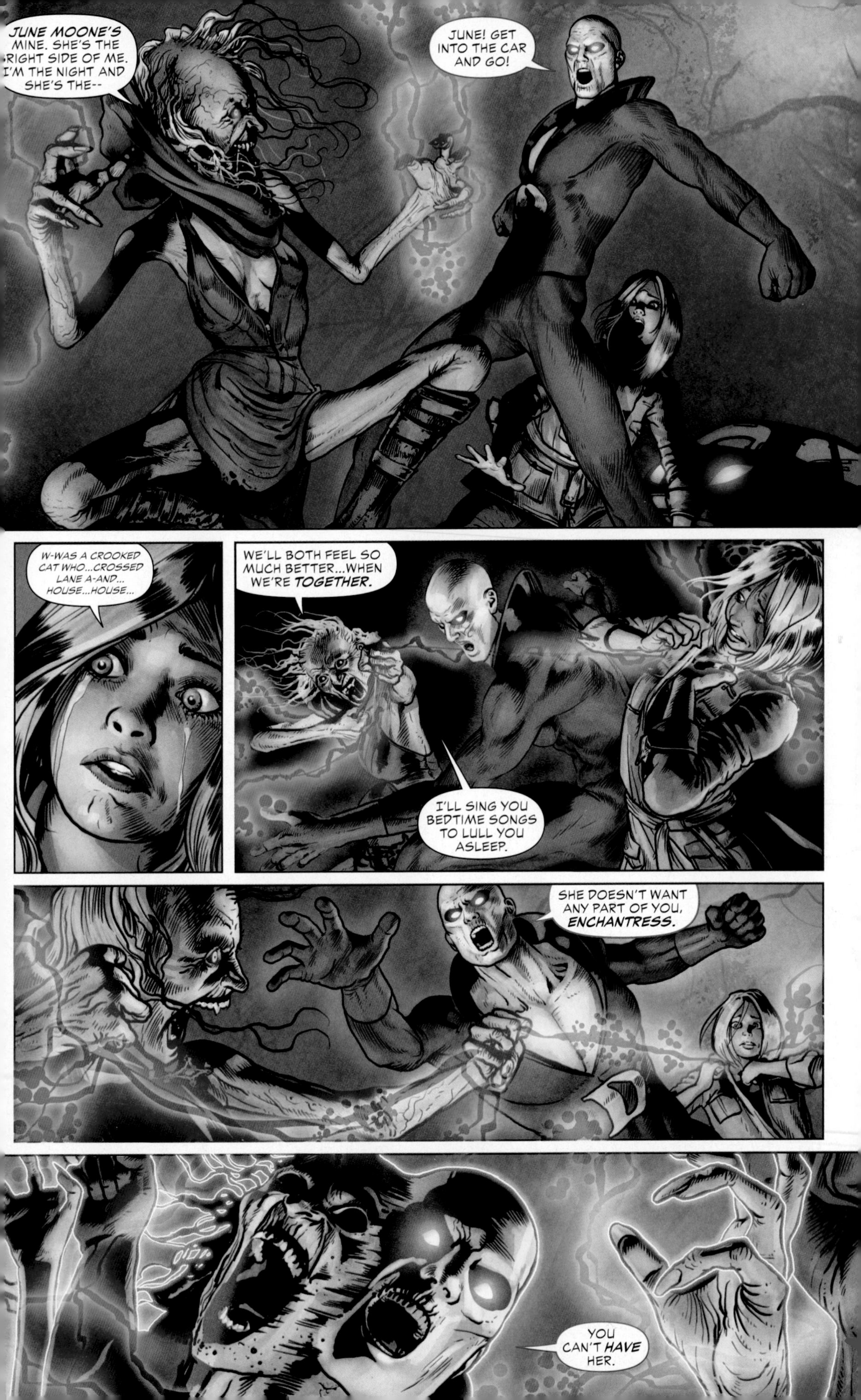
JUNE MOONE'S MINE. SHE'S THE RIGHT SIDE OF ME. I'M THE NIGHT AND SHE'S THE--
JUNE! GET INTO THE CAR AND GO!
W-WAS A CROOKED CAT WHO...CROSSED LANE A-AND... HOUSE...HOUSE...
WE'LL BOTH FEEL SO MUCH BETTER...WHEN WE'RE TOGETHER.
I'LL SING YOU BEDTIME SONGS TO LULL YOU ASLEEP.
SHE DOESN'T WANT ANY PART OF YOU, ENCHANTRESS.
YOU CAN'T HAVE HER.

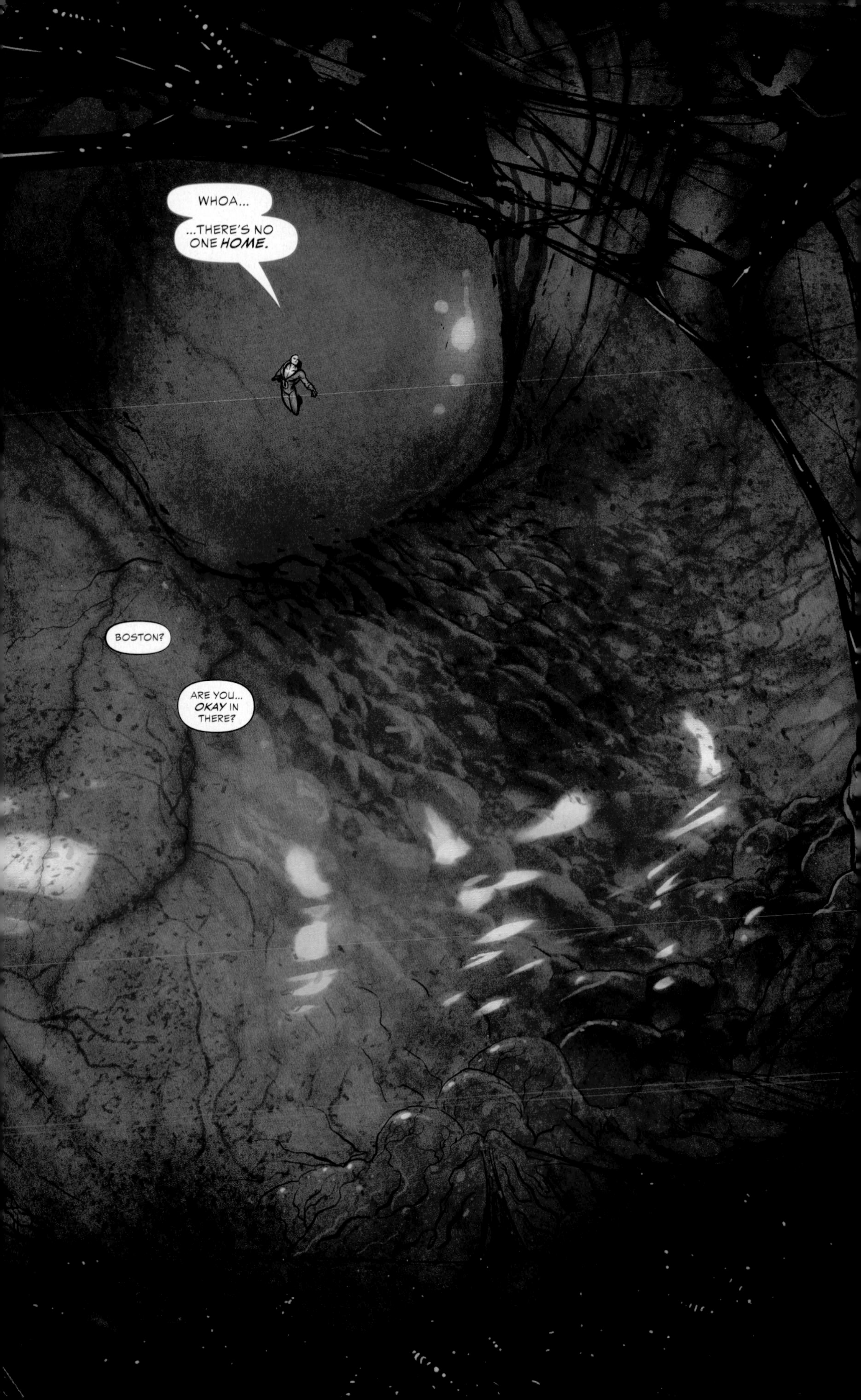
WHOA...
...THERE'S NO ONE HOME.
BOSTON?
ARE YOU... OKAY IN THERE?

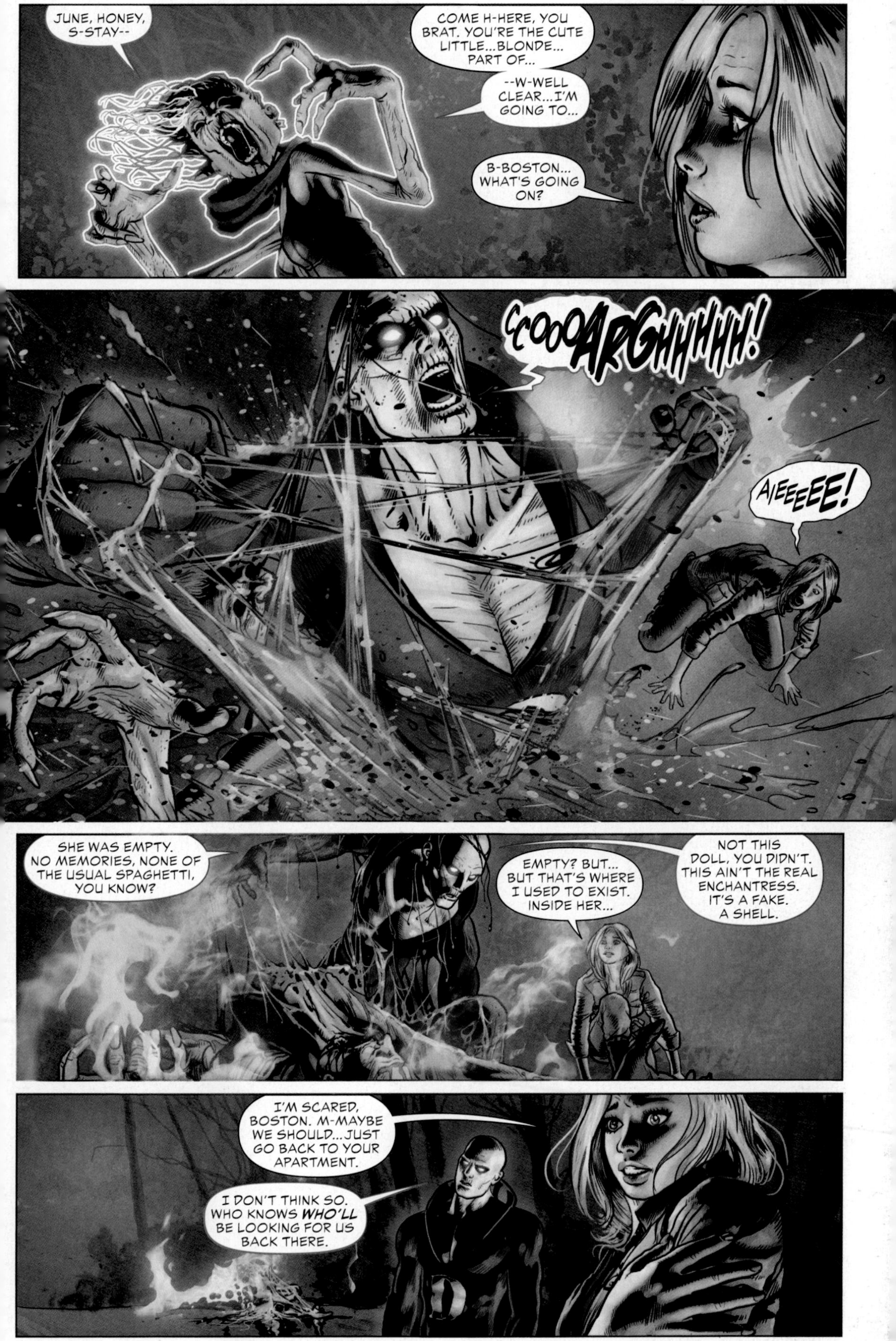
JUNE, HONEY, S-STAY--
COME H-HERE, YOU BRAT. YOU'RE THE CUTE LITTLE...BLONDE... PART OF...
--W-WELL CLEAR...I'M GOING TO...
B-BOSTON... WHAT'S GOING ON?
CCOOOARGHHHHHH!
AIEEEEE!
SHE WAS EMPTY. NO MEMORIES, NONE OF THE USUAL SPAGHETTI, YOU KNOW?
EMPTY? BUT... BUT THAT'S WHERE I USED TO EXIST. INSIDE HER...
NOT THIS DOLL, YOU DIDN'T. THIS AIN'T THE REAL ENCHANTRESS. IT'S A FAKE. A SHELL.
I'M SCARED, BOSTON. M-MAYBE WE SHOULD...JUST GO BACK TO YOUR APARTMENT.
I DON'T THINK SO. WHO KNOWS *WHO'LL* BE LOOKING FOR US BACK THERE.

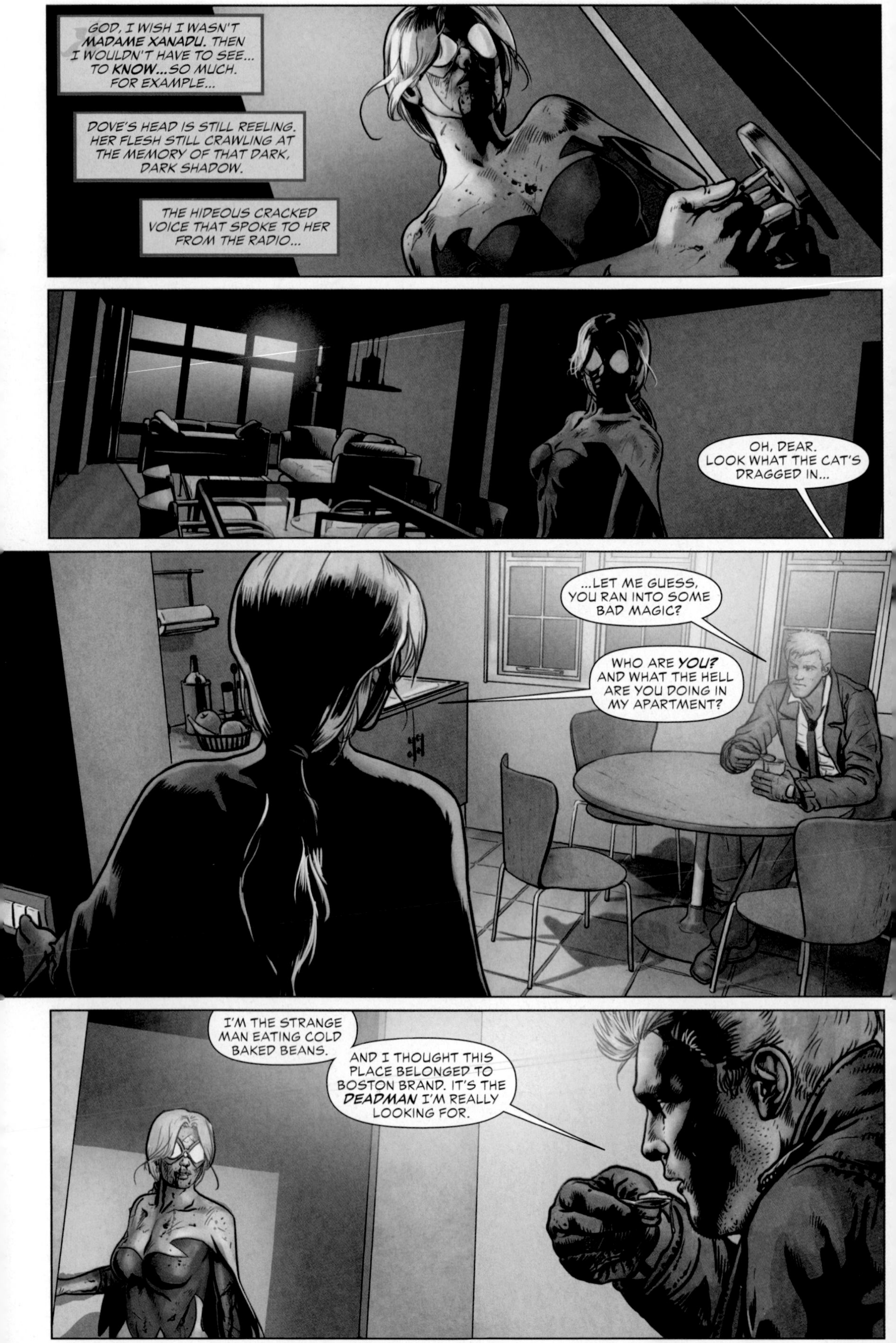
GOD, I WISH I WASN'T MADAME XANADU. THEN I WOULDN'T HAVE TO SEE... TO KNOW...SO MUCH. FOR EXAMPLE...
DOVE'S HEAD IS STILL REELING. HER FLESH STILL CRAWLING AT THE MEMORY OF THAT DARK, DARK SHADOW.
THE HIDEOUS CRACKED VOICE THAT SPOKE TO HER FROM THE RADIO...
OH, DEAR. LOOK WHAT THE CAT'S DRAGGED IN...
...LET ME GUESS, YOU RAN INTO SOME BAD MAGIC?
WHO ARE YOU? AND WHAT THE HELL ARE YOU DOING IN MY APARTMENT?
I'M THE STRANGE MAN EATING COLD BAKED BEANS.
AND I THOUGHT THIS PLACE BELONGED TO BOSTON BRAND. IT'S THE DEADMAN I'M REALLY LOOKING FOR.

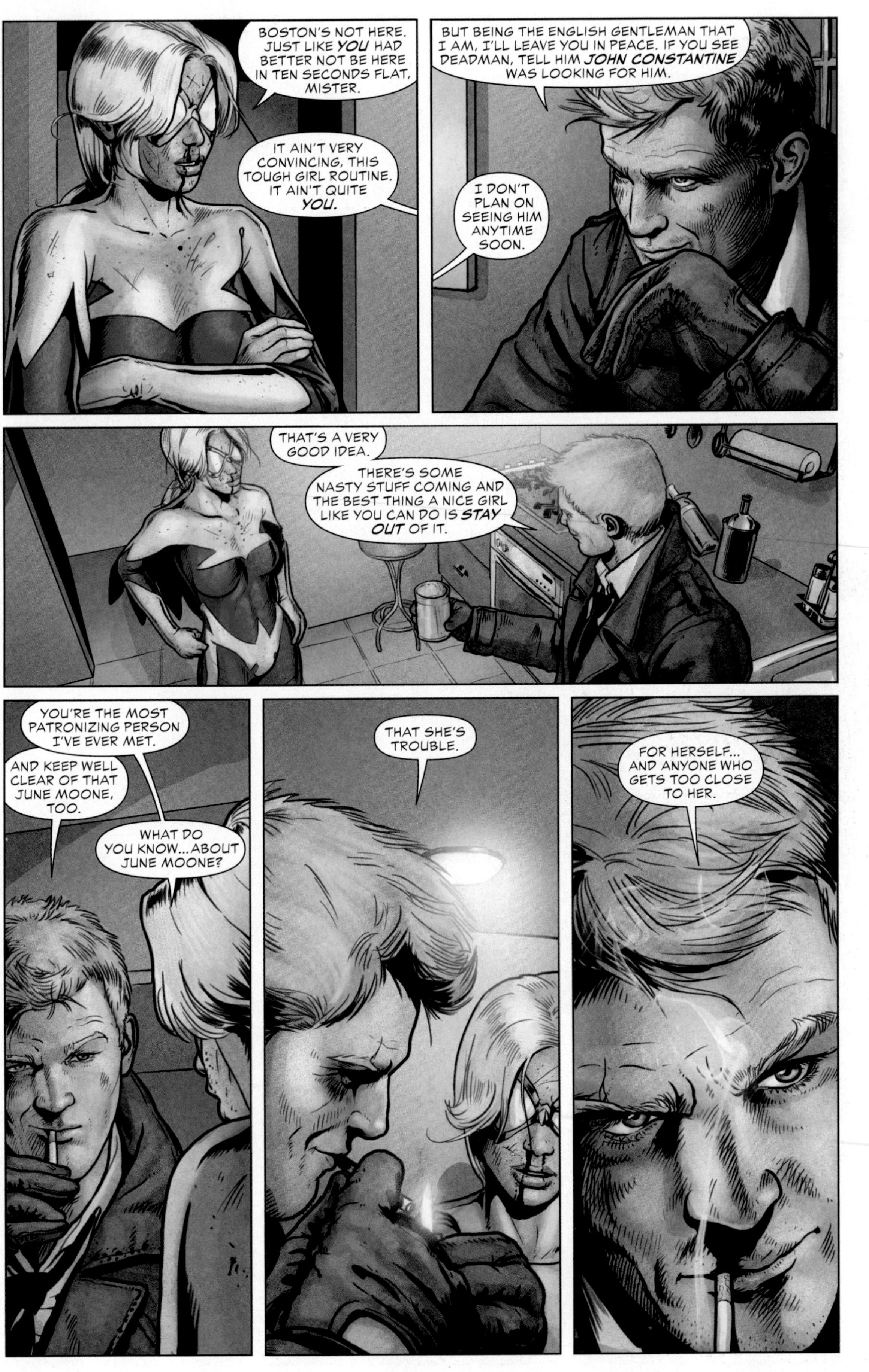
BOSTON'S NOT HERE. JUST LIKE YOU HAD BETTER NOT BE HERE IN TEN SECONDS FLAT, MISTER.
IT AIN'T VERY CONVINCING, THIS TOUGH GIRL ROUTINE. IT AIN'T QUITE YOU.
BUT BEING THE ENGLISH GENTLEMAN THAT I AM, I'LL LEAVE YOU IN PEACE. IF YOU SEE DEADMAN, TELL HIM JOHN CONSTANTINE WAS LOOKING FOR HIM.
I DON'T PLAN ON SEEING HIM ANYTIME SOON.
THAT'S A VERY GOOD IDEA.
THERE'S SOME NASTY STUFF COMING AND THE BEST THING A NICE GIRL LIKE YOU CAN DO IS STAY OUT OF IT.
YOU'RE THE MOST PATRONIZING PERSON I'VE EVER MET.
AND KEEP WELL CLEAR OF THAT JUNE MOONE, TOO.
WHAT DO YOU KNOW...ABOUT JUNE MOONE?
THAT SHE'S TROUBLE.
FOR HERSELF... AND ANYONE WHO GETS TOO CLOSE TO HER.

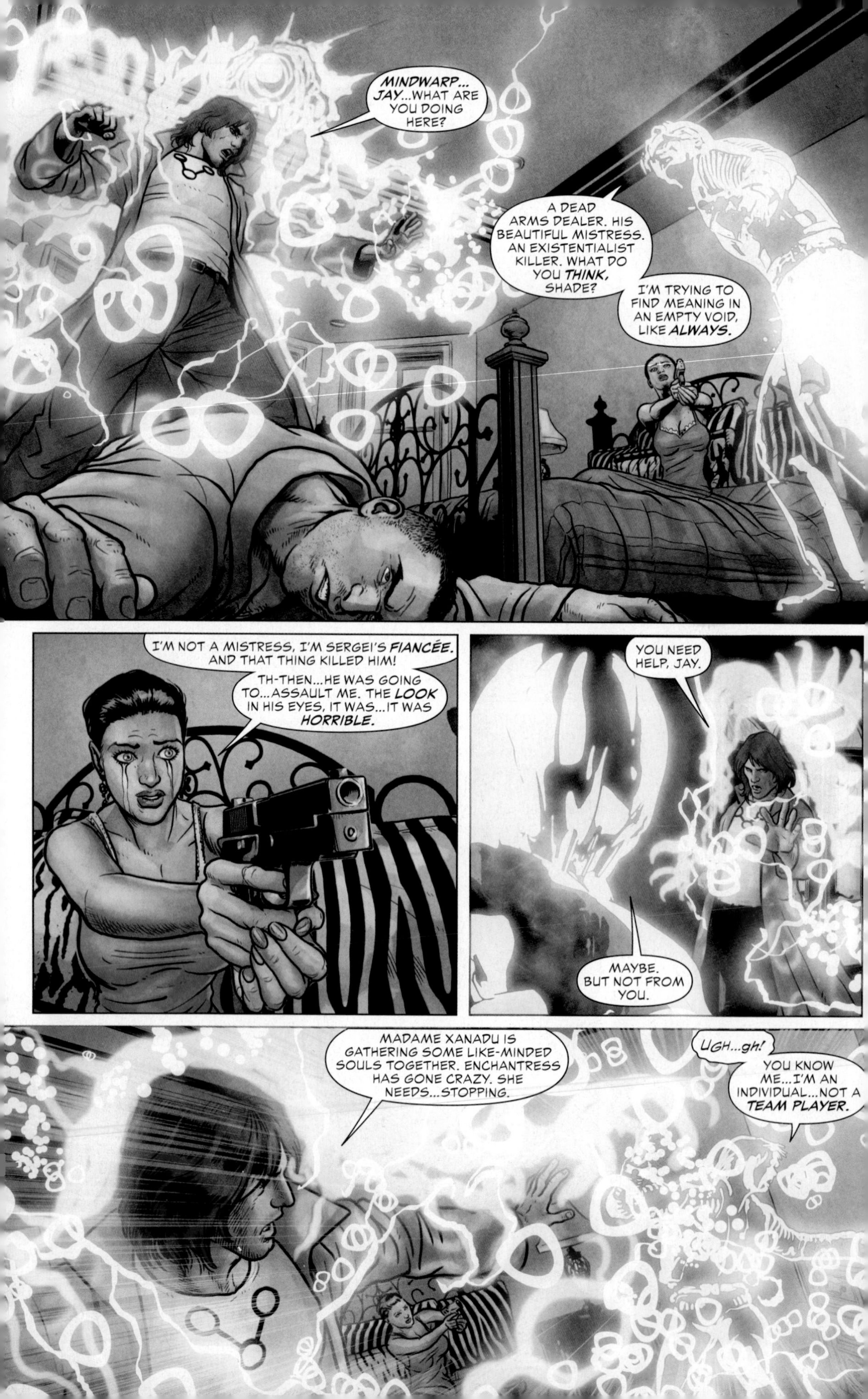
MINDWARP... JAY...WHAT ARE YOU DOING HERE?
A DEAD ARMS DEALER. HIS BEAUTIFUL MISTRESS. AN EXISTENTIALIST KILLER. WHAT DO YOU THINK, SHADE?
I'M TRYING TO FIND MEANING IN AN EMPTY VOID, LIKE ALWAYS.
I'M NOT A MISTRESS, I'M SERGEI'S FIANCÉE. AND THAT THING KILLED HIM!
TH-THEN...HE WAS GOING TO...ASSAULT ME. THE LOOK IN HIS EYES, IT WAS...IT WAS HORRIBLE.
YOU NEED HELP, JAY.
MAYBE. BUT NOT FROM YOU.
MADAME XANADU IS GATHERING SOME LIKE-MINDED SOULS TOGETHER. ENCHANTRESS HAS GONE CRAZY. SHE NEEDS...STOPPING.
UGH...gh!
YOU KNOW ME...I'M AN INDIVIDUAL...NOT A TEAM PLAYER.

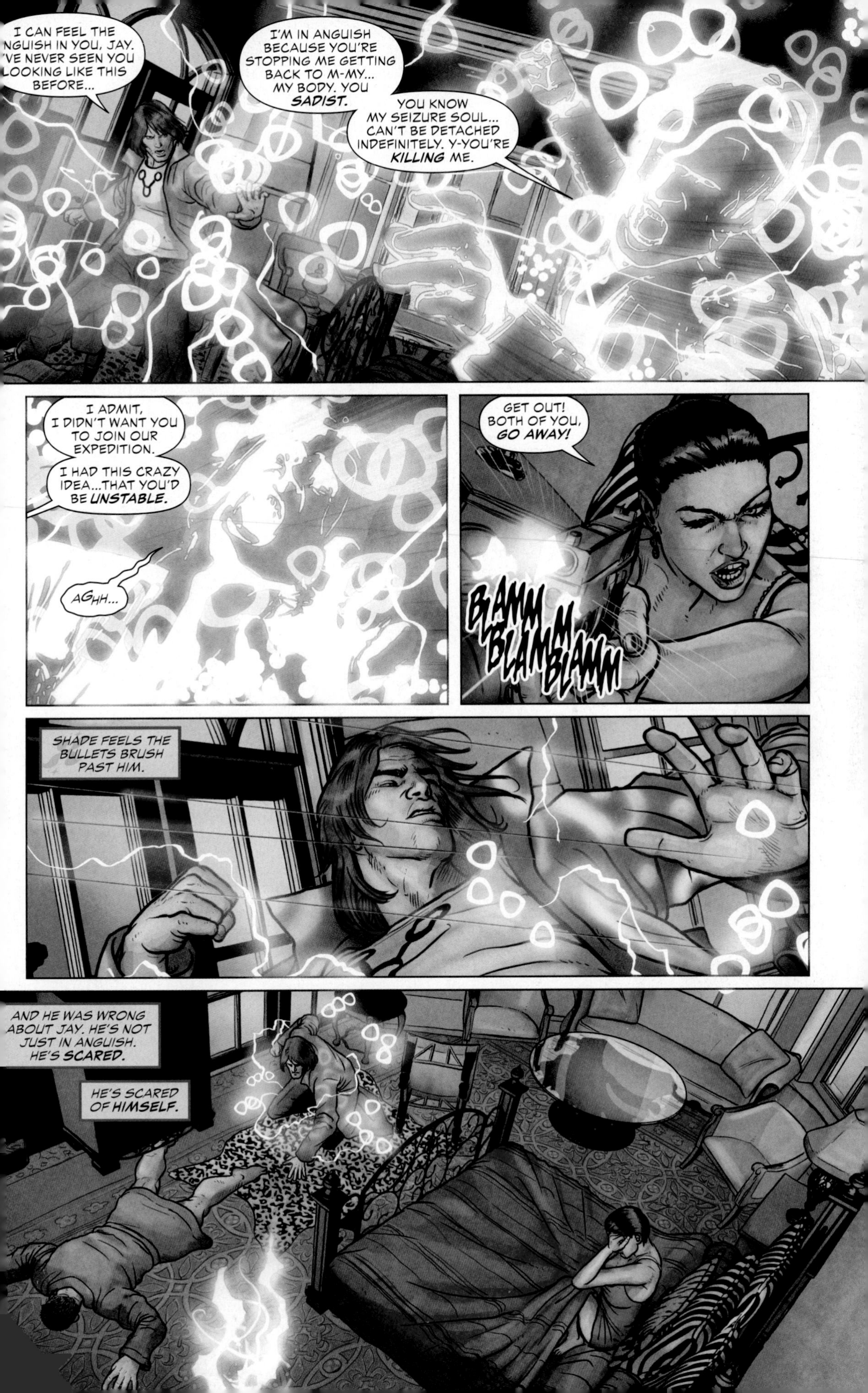
I CAN FEEL THE ANGUISH IN YOU, JAY. I'VE NEVER SEEN YOU LOOKING LIKE THIS BEFORE...
I'M IN ANGUISH BECAUSE YOU'RE STOPPING ME GETTING BACK TO M-MY... MY BODY. YOU SADIST.
YOU KNOW MY SEIZURE SOUL... CAN'T BE DETACHED INDEFINITELY. Y-YOU'RE KILLING ME.
I ADMIT, I DIDN'T WANT YOU TO JOIN OUR EXPEDITION.
I HAD THIS CRAZY IDEA...THAT YOU'D BE UNSTABLE.
AGHH...
GET OUT! BOTH OF YOU, GO AWAY!
BLAMM BLAMM BLAMM BLAMM
SHADE FEELS THE BULLETS BRUSH PAST HIM.
AND HE WAS WRONG ABOUT JAY. HE'S NOT JUST IN ANGUISH. HE'S SCARED.
HE'S SCARED OF HIMSELF.

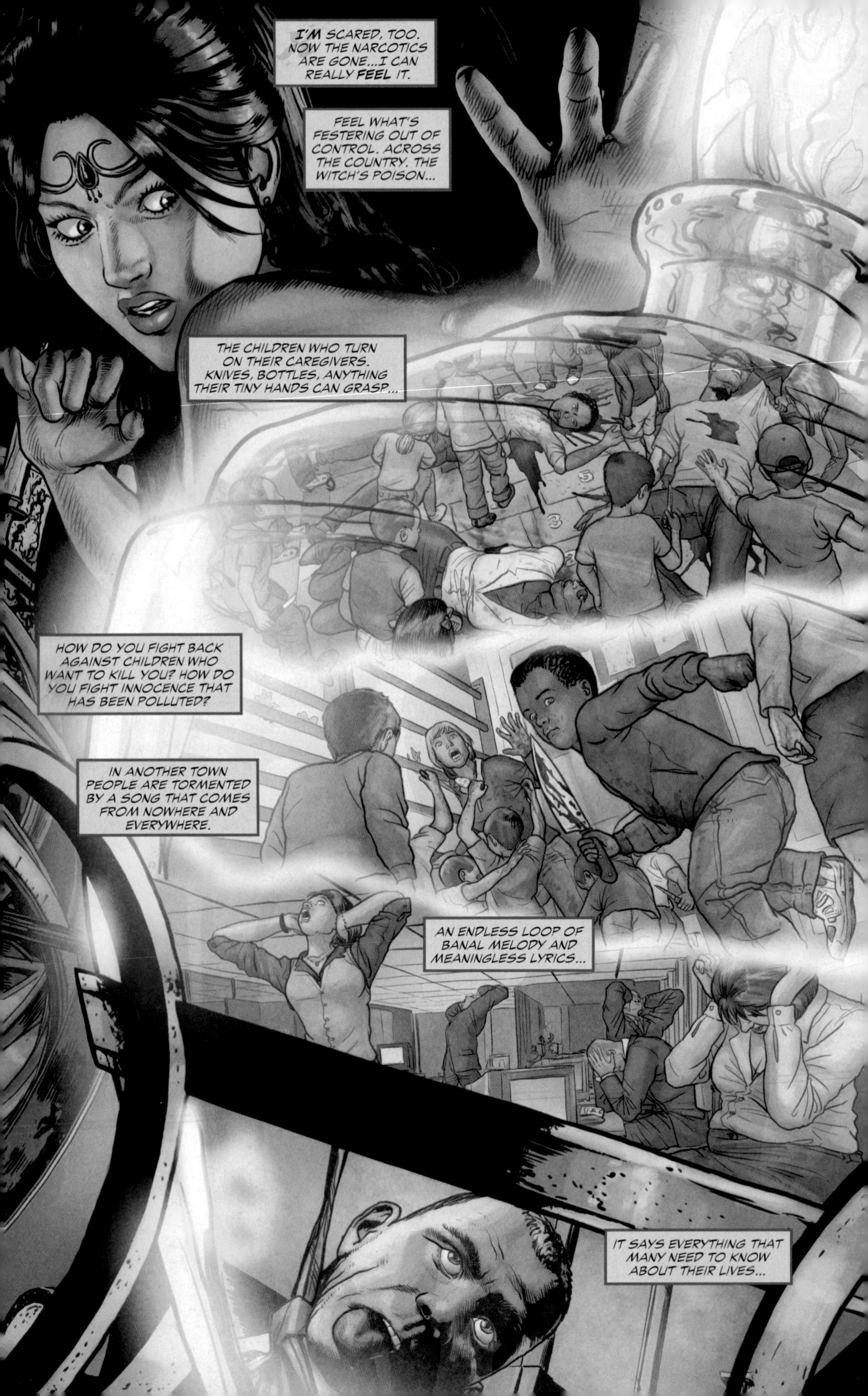
I'M SCARED, TOO. NOW THE NARCOTICS ARE GONE...I CAN REALLY FEEL IT.
FEEL WHAT'S FESTERING OUT OF CONTROL. ACROSS THE COUNTRY. THE WITCH'S POISON...
THE CHILDREN WHO TURN ON THEIR CAREGIVERS. KNIVES, BOTTLES, ANYTHING THEIR TINY HANDS CAN GRASP...
HOW DO YOU FIGHT BACK AGAINST CHILDREN WHO WANT TO KILL YOU? HOW DO YOU FIGHT INNOCENCE THAT HAS BEEN POLLUTED?
IN ANOTHER TOWN PEOPLE ARE TORMENTED BY A SONG THAT COMES FROM NOWHERE AND EVERYWHERE.
AN ENDLESS LOOP OF BANAL MELODY AND MEANINGLESS LYRICS...
IT SAYS EVERYTHING THAT MANY NEED TO KNOW ABOUT THEIR LIVES...

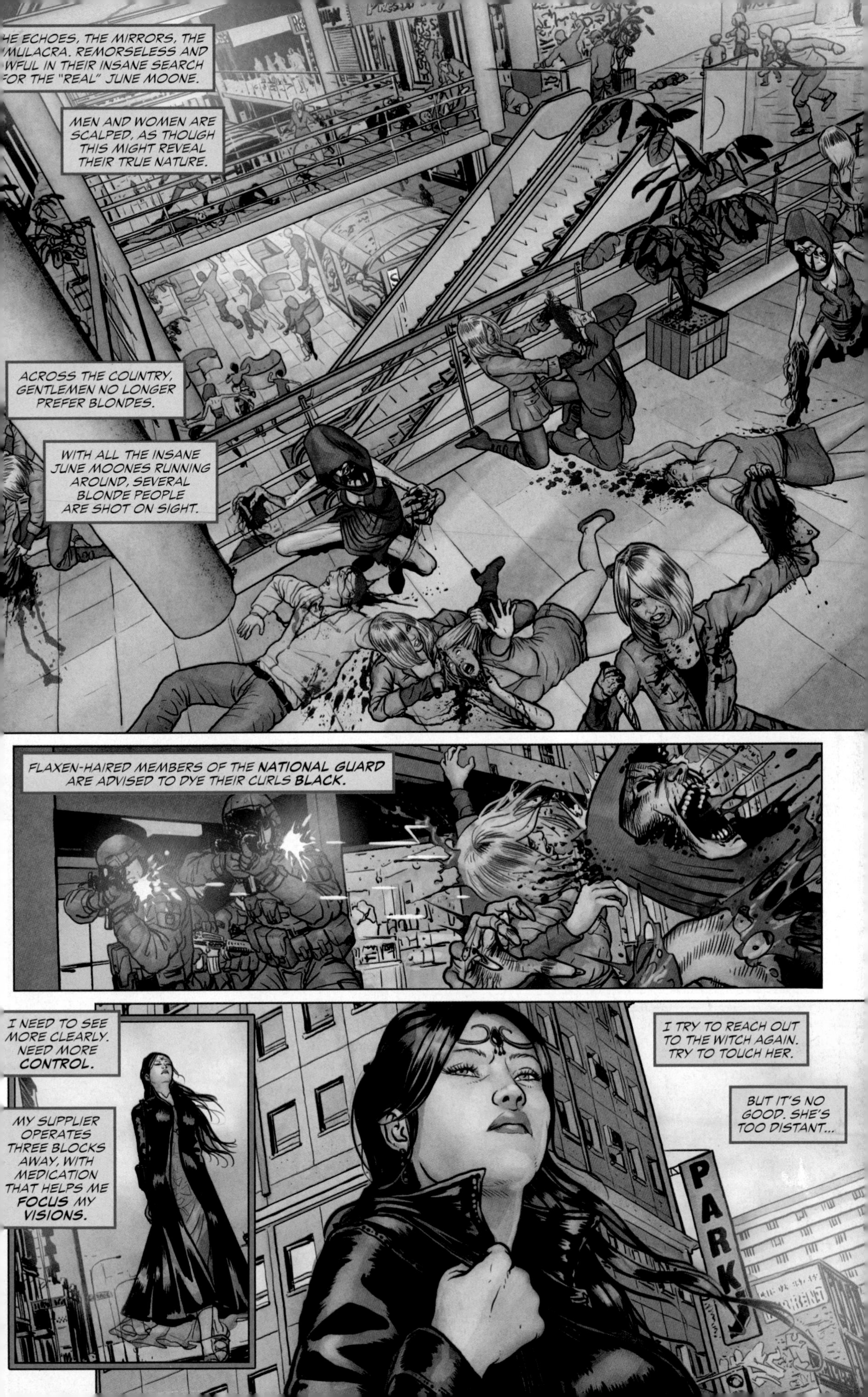

HE ECHOES, THE MIRRORS, THE MULACRA. REMORSELESS AND WFUL IN THEIR INSANE SEARCH FOR THE "REAL" JUNE MOONE.
MEN AND WOMEN ARE SCALPED, AS THOUGH THIS MIGHT REVEAL THEIR TRUE NATURE.
ACROSS THE COUNTRY, GENTLEMEN NO LONGER PREFER BLONDES.
WITH ALL THE INSANE JUNE MOONES RUNNING AROUND, SEVERAL BLONDE PEOPLE ARE SHOT ON SIGHT.
FLAXEN-HAIRED MEMBERS OF THE NATIONAL GUARD ARE ADVISED TO DYE THEIR CURLS BLACK.
I NEED TO SEE MORE CLEARLY. NEED MORE CONTROL.
MY SUPPLIER OPERATES THREE BLOCKS AWAY, WITH MEDICATION THAT HELPS ME FOCUS MY VISIONS.
I TRY TO REACH OUT TO THE WITCH AGAIN. TRY TO TOUCH HER.
BUT IT'S NO GOOD. SHE'S TOO DISTANT...
PARK

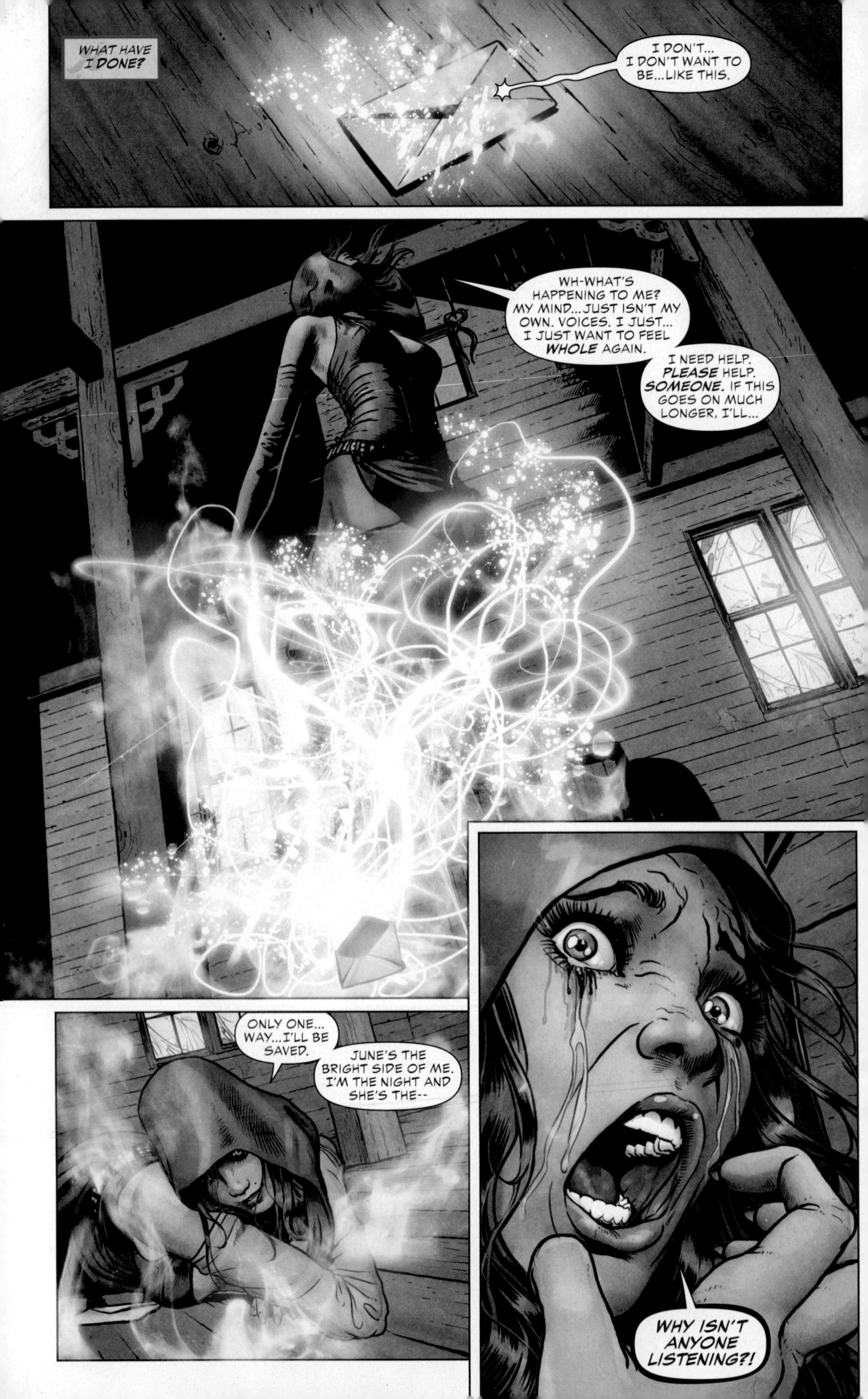
WHAT HAVE I DONE?
I DON'T... I DON'T WANT TO BE...LIKE THIS.
WH-WHAT'S HAPPENING TO ME? MY MIND...JUST ISN'T MY OWN. VOICES. I JUST... I JUST WANT TO FEEL WHOLE AGAIN.
I NEED HELP. PLEASE HELP. SOMEONE. IF THIS GOES ON MUCH LONGER, I'LL...
ONLY ONE... WAY...I'LL BE SAVED.
JUNE'S THE BRIGHT SIDE OF ME. I'M THE NIGHT AND SHE'S THE--
WHY ISN'T ANYONE LISTENING?!

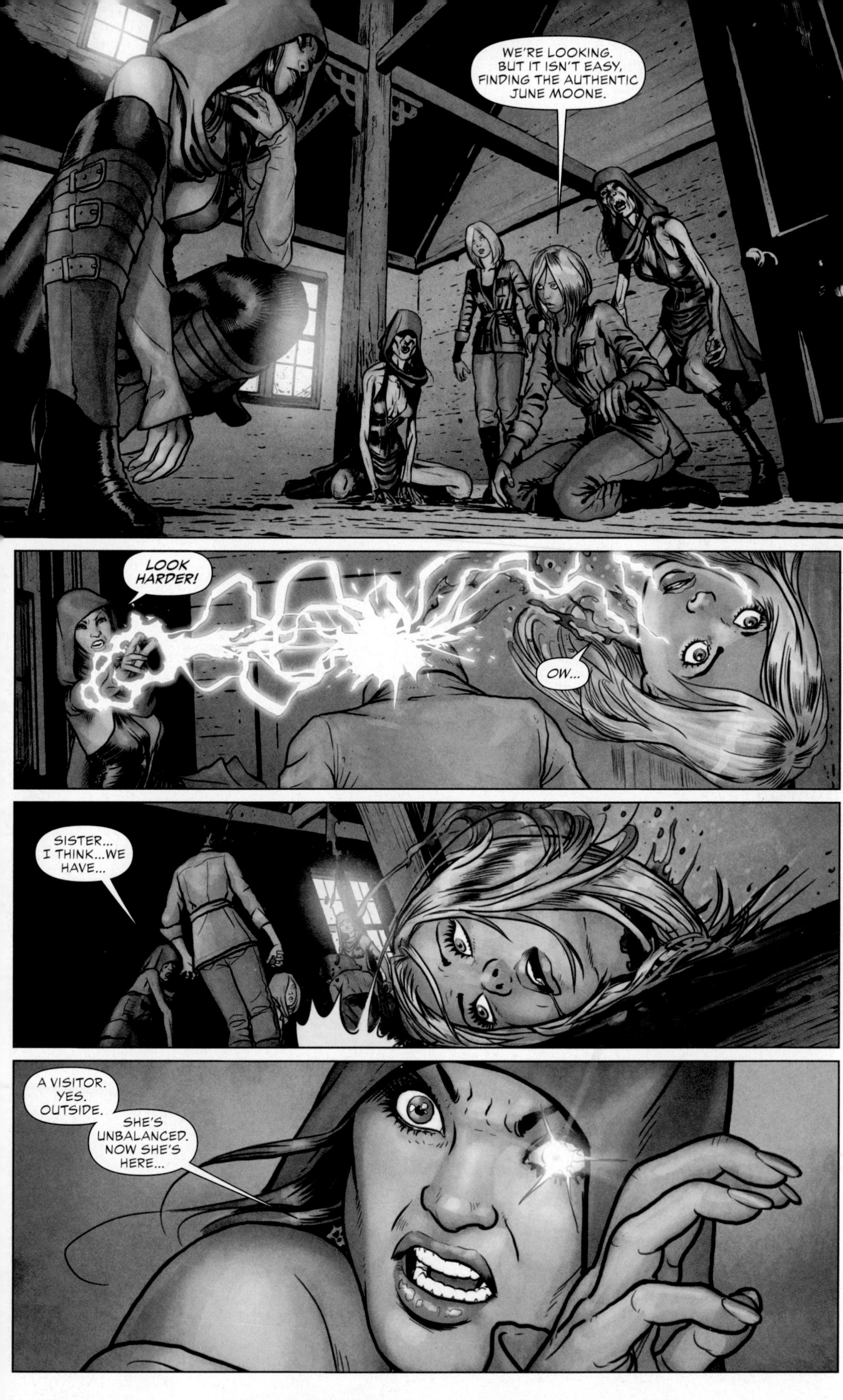
WE'RE LOOKING. BUT IT ISN'T EASY, FINDING THE AUTHENTIC JUNE MOONE.
LOOK HARDER!
OW...
SISTER... I THINK...WE HAVE...
A VISITOR. YES. OUTSIDE.
SHE'S UNBALANCED. NOW SHE'S HERE...

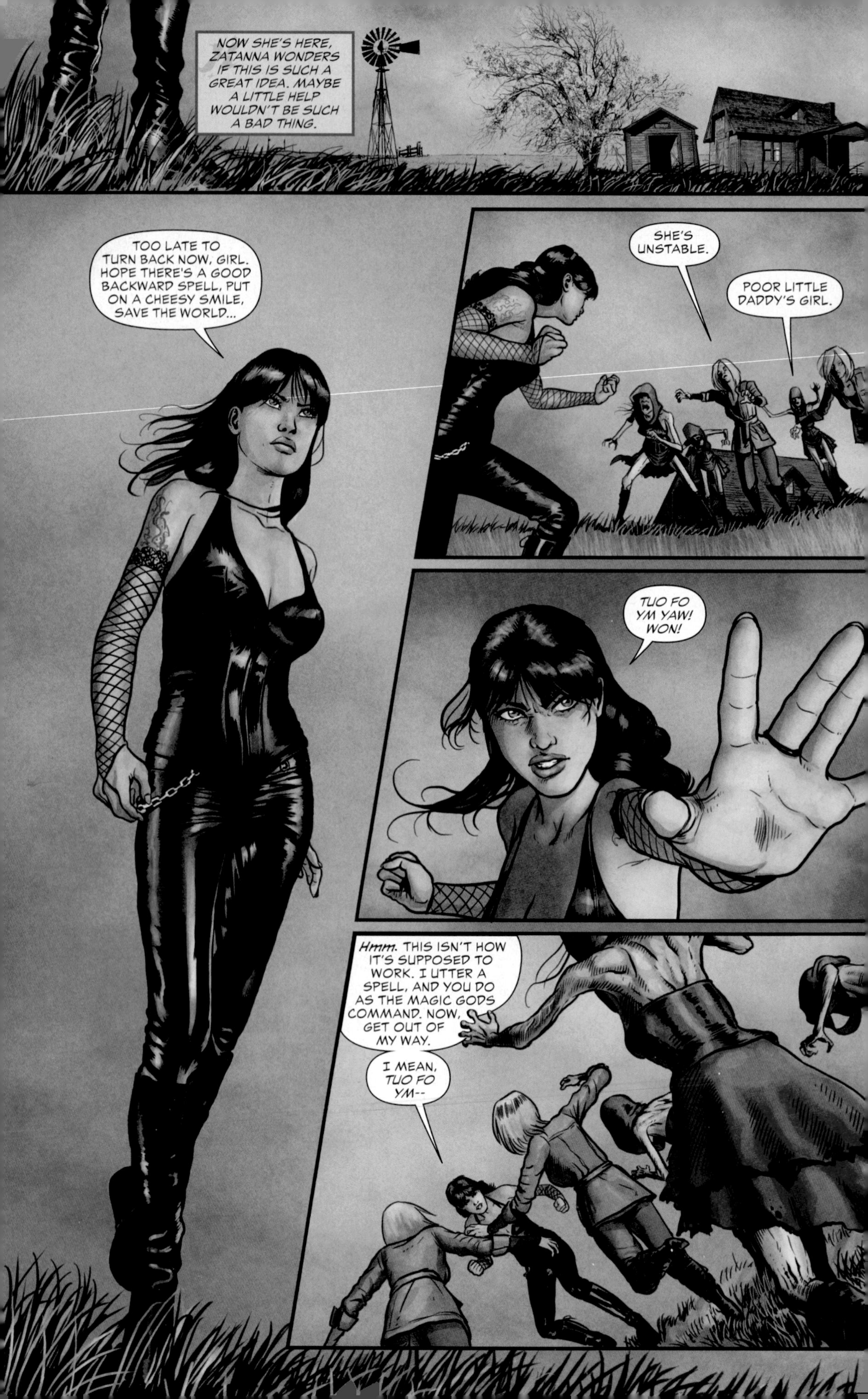
NOW SHE'S HERE, ZATANNA WONDERS IF THIS IS SUCH A GREAT IDEA. MAYBE A LITTLE HELP WOULDN'T BE SUCH A BAD THING.
TOO LATE TO TURN BACK NOW, GIRL. HOPE THERE'S A GOOD BACKWARD SPELL, PUT ON A CHEESY SMILE, SAVE THE WORLD...
SHE'S UNSTABLE.
POOR LITTLE DADDY'S GIRL.
TUO FO YM YAW! WON!
Hmm. THIS ISN'T HOW IT'S SUPPOSED TO WORK. I UTTER A SPELL, AND YOU DO AS THE MAGIC GODS COMMAND. NOW, GET OUT OF MY WAY.
I MEAN, TUO FO YM--

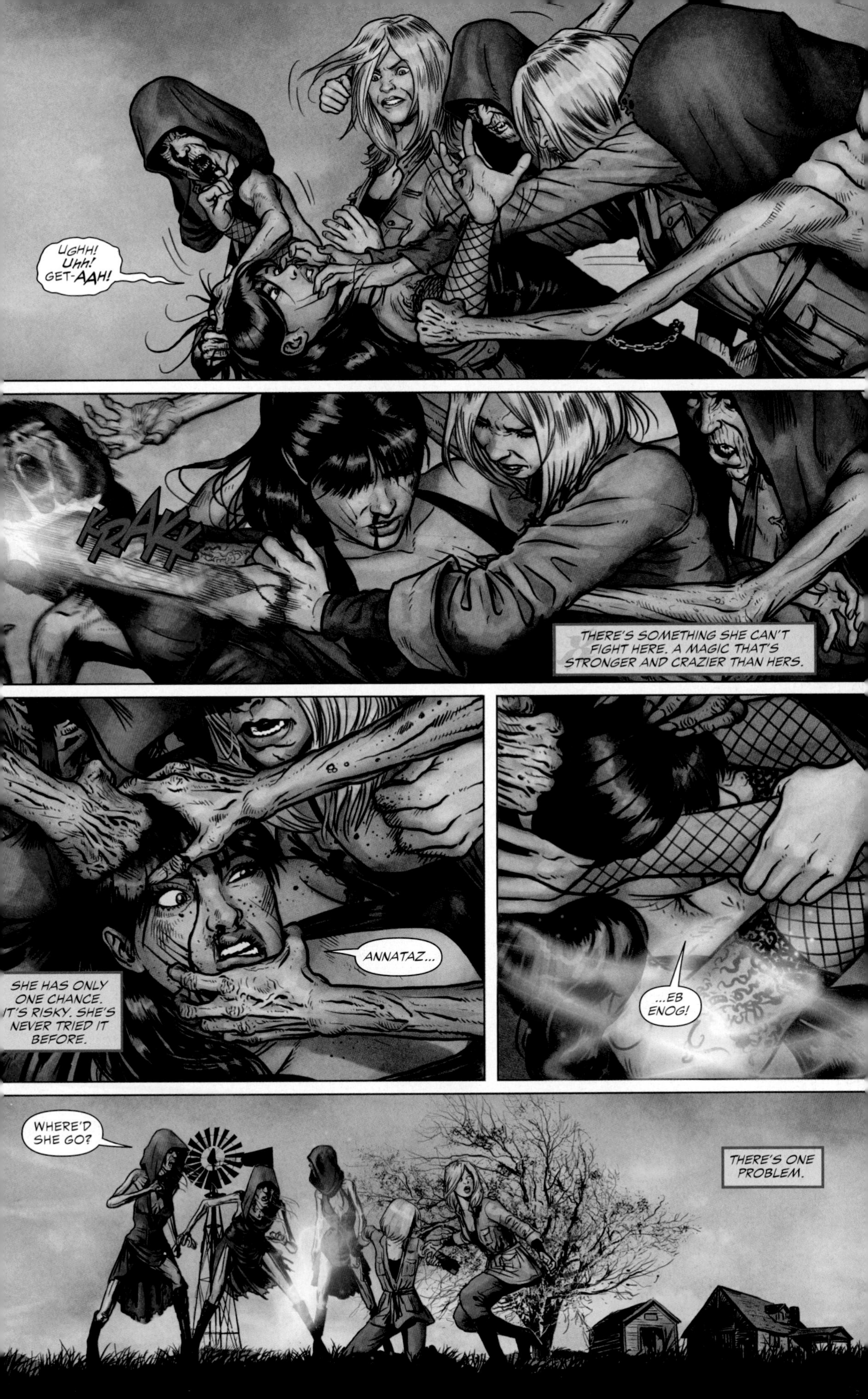
UGHH! Uhh! GET-AAH!
KRAKK
THERE'S SOMETHING SHE CAN'T FIGHT HERE. A MAGIC THAT'S STRONGER AND CRAZIER THAN HERS.
ANNATAZ...
SHE HAS ONLY ONE CHANCE. IT'S RISKY. SHE'S NEVER TRIED IT BEFORE.
...EB ENOG!
WHERE'D SHE GO?
THERE'S ONE PROBLEM.

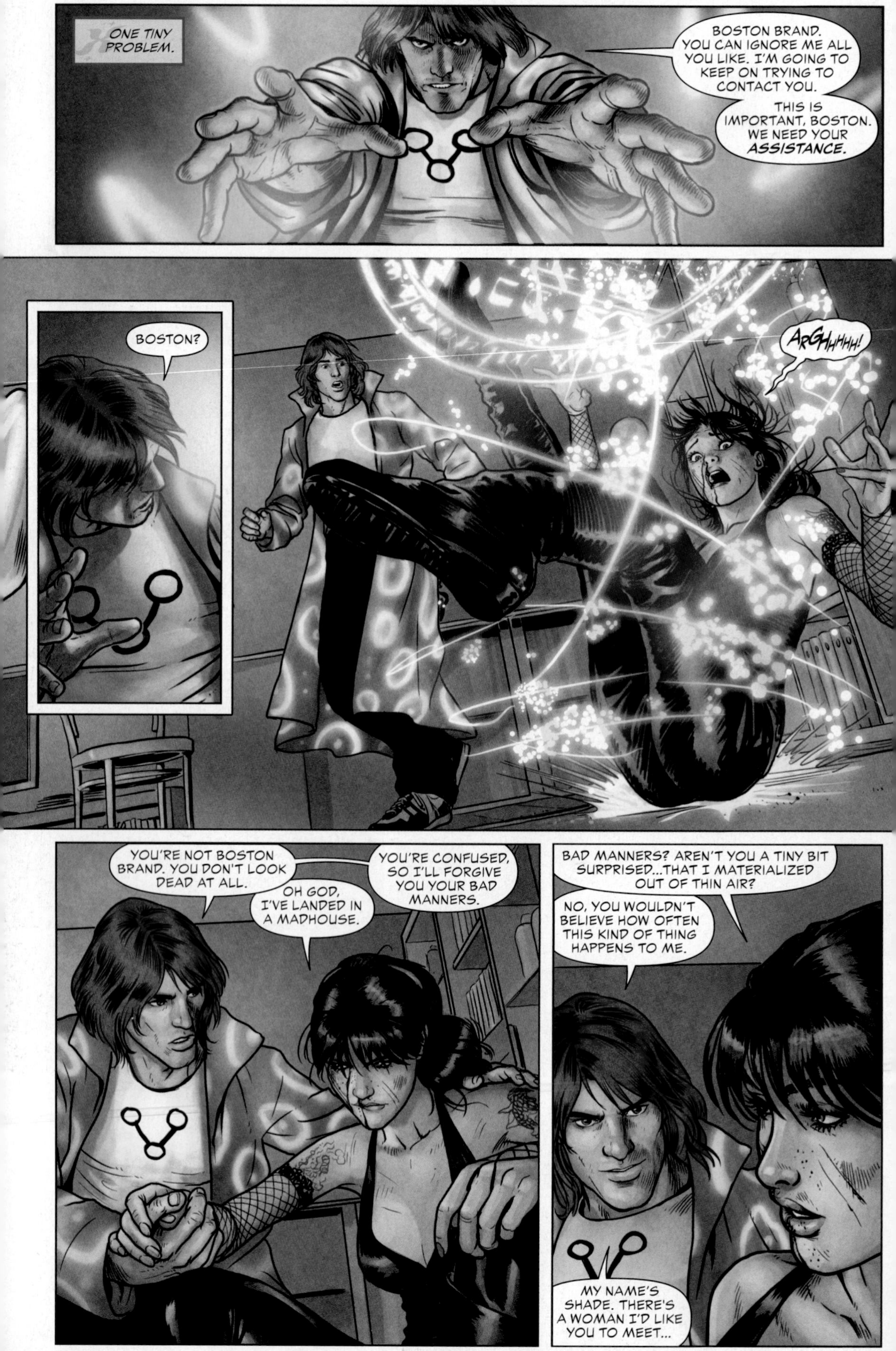
ONE TINY PROBLEM.
BOSTON BRAND. YOU CAN IGNORE ME ALL YOU LIKE. I'M GOING TO KEEP ON TRYING TO CONTACT YOU.
THIS IS IMPORTANT, BOSTON. WE NEED YOUR ASSISTANCE.
BOSTON?
ARGHHHHH!
YOU'RE NOT BOSTON BRAND. YOU DON'T LOOK DEAD AT ALL.
OH GOD, I'VE LANDED IN A MADHOUSE.
YOU'RE CONFUSED, SO I'LL FORGIVE YOU YOUR BAD MANNERS.
BAD MANNERS? AREN'T YOU A TINY BIT SURPRISED...THAT I MATERIALIZED OUT OF THIN AIR?
NO, YOU WOULDN'T BELIEVE HOW OFTEN THIS KIND OF THING HAPPENS TO ME.
MY NAME'S SHADE. THERE'S A WOMAN I'D LIKE YOU TO MEET...

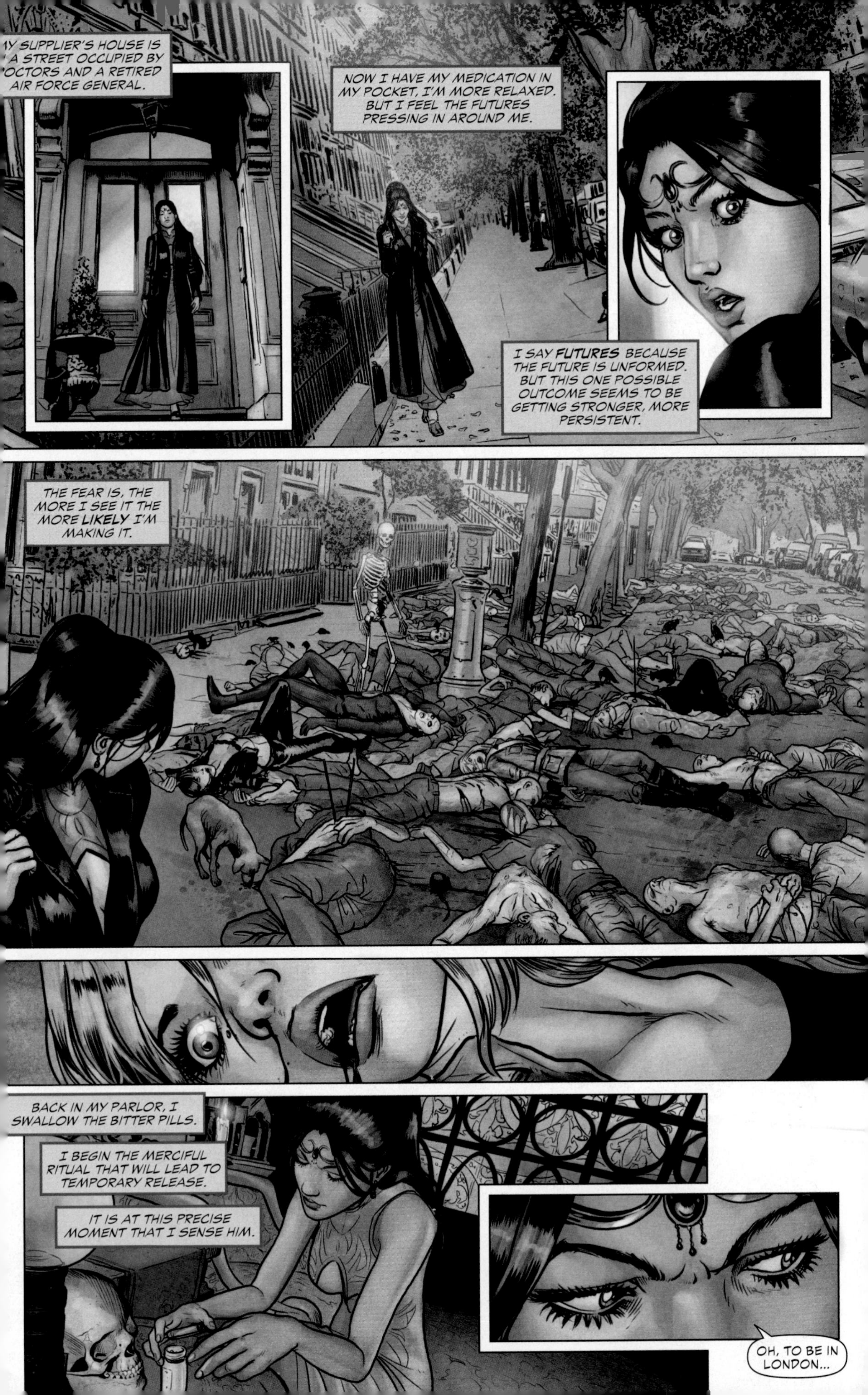
MY SUPPLIER'S HOUSE IS
A STREET OCCUPIED BY
OCTORS AND A RETIRED
AIR FORCE GENERAL.
NOW I HAVE MY MEDICATION IN MY POCKET, I'M MORE RELAXED. BUT I FEEL THE FUTURES PRESSING IN AROUND ME.
I SAY FUTURES BECAUSE THE FUTURE IS UNFORMED. BUT THIS ONE POSSIBLE OUTCOME SEEMS TO BE GETTING STRONGER, MORE PERSISTENT.
THE FEAR IS, THE MORE I SEE IT THE MORE LIKELY I'M MAKING IT.
BACK IN MY PARLOR, I SWALLOW THE BITTER PILLS.
I BEGIN THE MERCIFUL RITUAL THAT WILL LEAD TO TEMPORARY RELEASE.
IT IS AT THIS PRECISE MOMENT THAT I SENSE HIM.
OH, TO BE IN LONDON...

...NOW THAT LONDON IS HERE.

I WANT A WORD WITH YOU.

I'M BUSY. GET OUT. AND IN THE FUTURE--

SLPPP

DON'T TALK TO ME ABOUT THE *FUTURE.*

Ugh!

I'LL KILL YOU!

SLPPP

KILL ME? YOU MEAN LIKE YOU KILLED ALL THE OTHERS?

I NEVER WANTED... TO HURT ANYONE...

MAYBE NOT DELIBERATELY. BUT YOU WERE RESPONSIBLE FOR THIS CARNAGE.

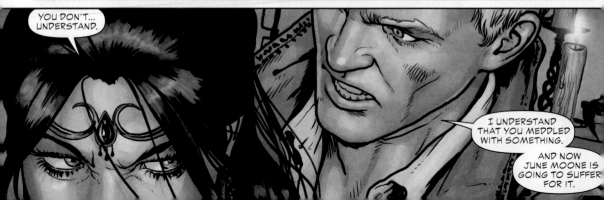

YOU DON'T... UNDERSTAND.

I UNDERSTAND THAT YOU MEDDLED WITH SOMETHING.

AND NOW JUNE MOONE IS GOING TO SUFFER FOR IT.

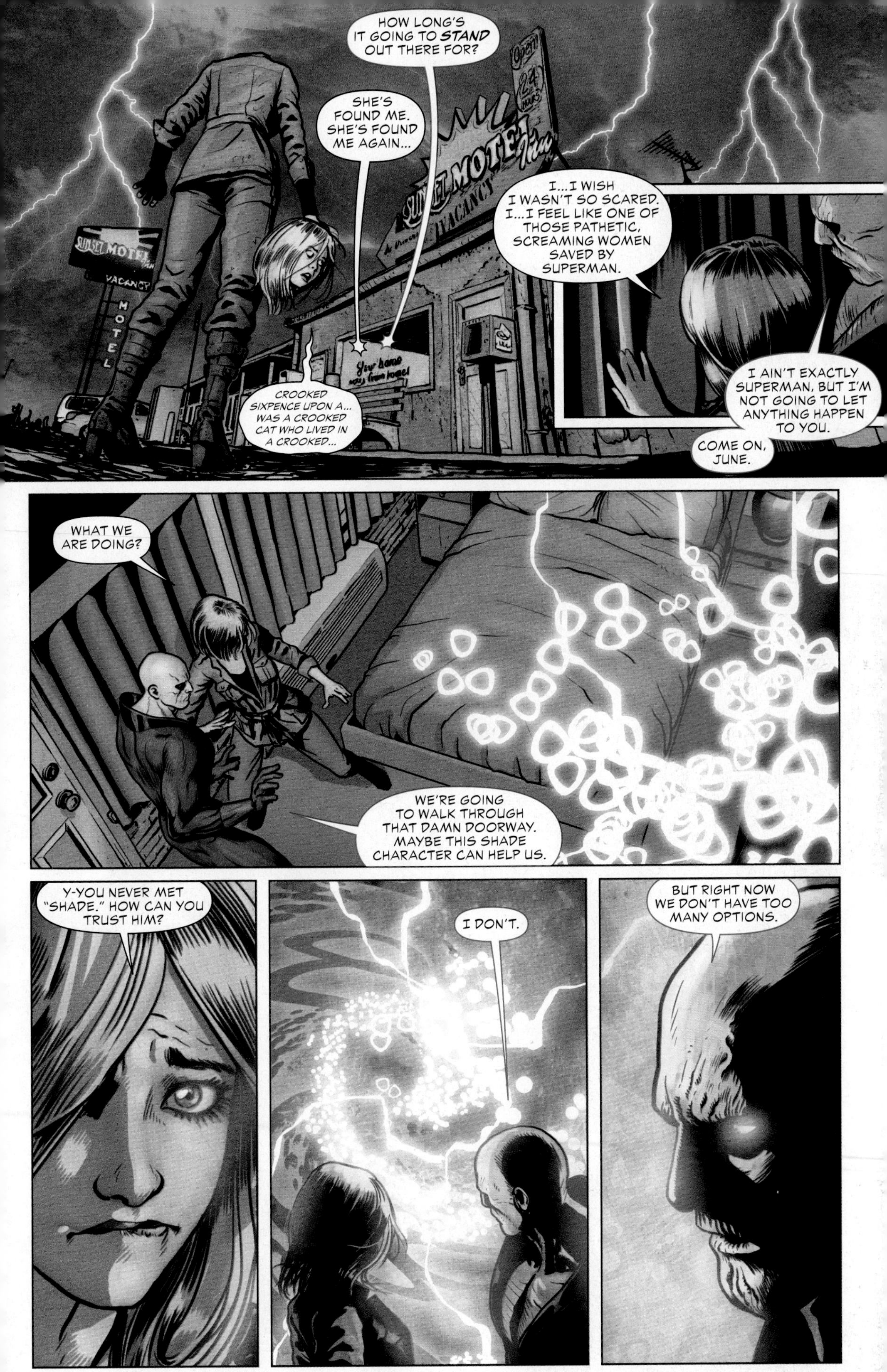
HOW LONG'S IT GOING TO STAND OUT THERE FOR?
SHE'S FOUND ME. SHE'S FOUND ME AGAIN...
CROOKED SIXPENCE UPON A... WAS A CROOKED CAT WHO LIVED IN A CROOKED...
SUNSET MOTEL Inn
VACANCY
Open 24 HOURS
I...I WISH I WASN'T SO SCARED. I...I FEEL LIKE ONE OF THOSE PATHETIC, SCREAMING WOMEN SAVED BY SUPERMAN.
I AIN'T EXACTLY SUPERMAN, BUT I'M NOT GOING TO LET ANYTHING HAPPEN TO YOU.
COME ON, JUNE.
WHAT WE ARE DOING?
WE'RE GOING TO WALK THROUGH THAT DAMN DOORWAY. MAYBE THIS SHADE CHARACTER CAN HELP US.
Y-YOU NEVER MET "SHADE." HOW CAN YOU TRUST HIM?
I DON'T.
BUT RIGHT NOW WE DON'T HAVE TOO MANY OPTIONS.

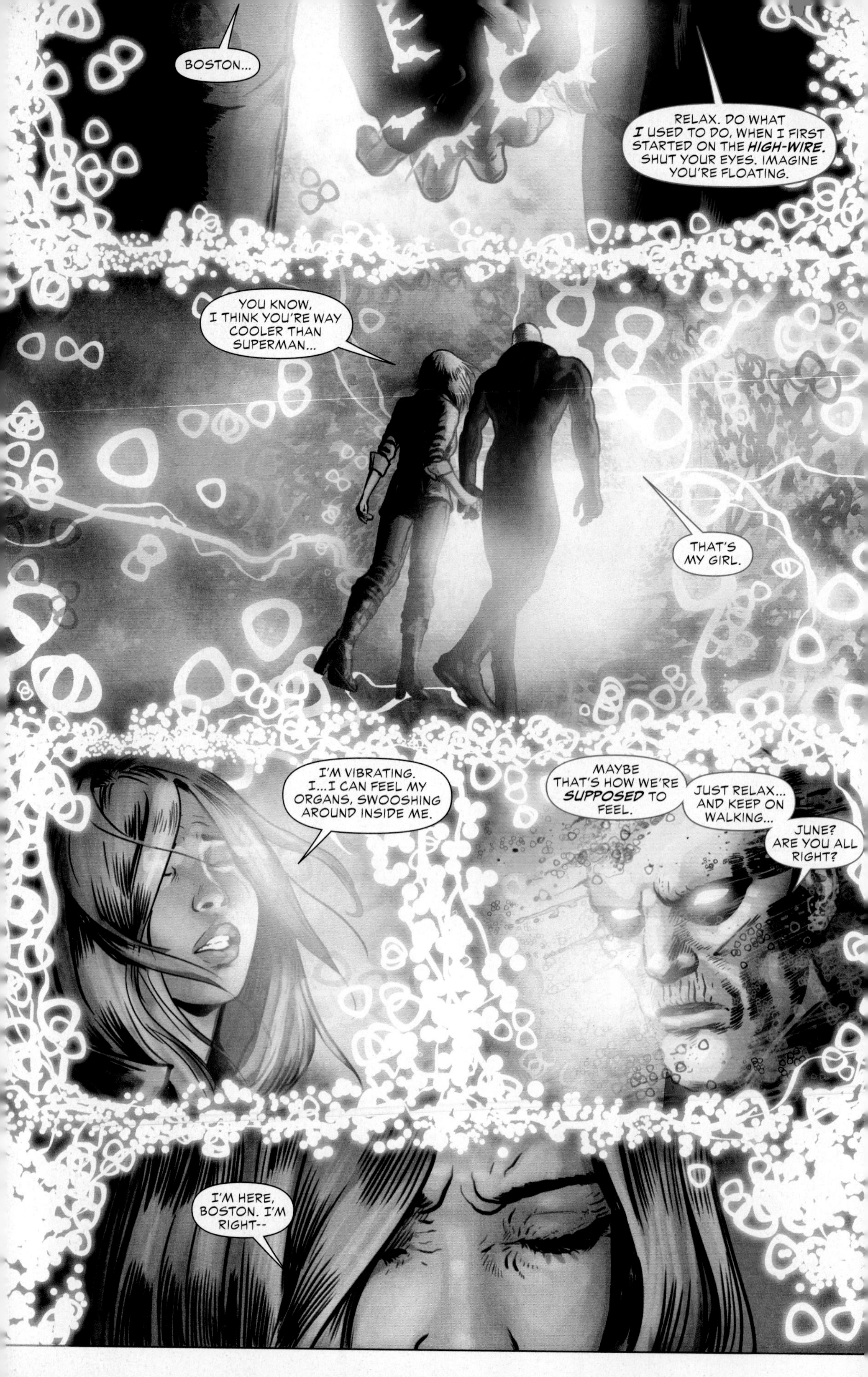
BOSTON...
RELAX. DO WHAT I USED TO DO, WHEN I FIRST STARTED ON THE HIGH-WIRE. SHUT YOUR EYES. IMAGINE YOU'RE FLOATING.
YOU KNOW, I THINK YOU'RE WAY COOLER THAN SUPERMAN...
THAT'S MY GIRL.
I'M VIBRATING. I...I CAN FEEL MY ORGANS, SWOOSHING AROUND INSIDE ME.
MAYBE THAT'S HOW WE'RE SUPPOSED TO FEEL.
JUST RELAX... AND KEEP ON WALKING...
JUNE? ARE YOU ALL RIGHT?
I'M HERE, BOSTON. I'M RIGHT--

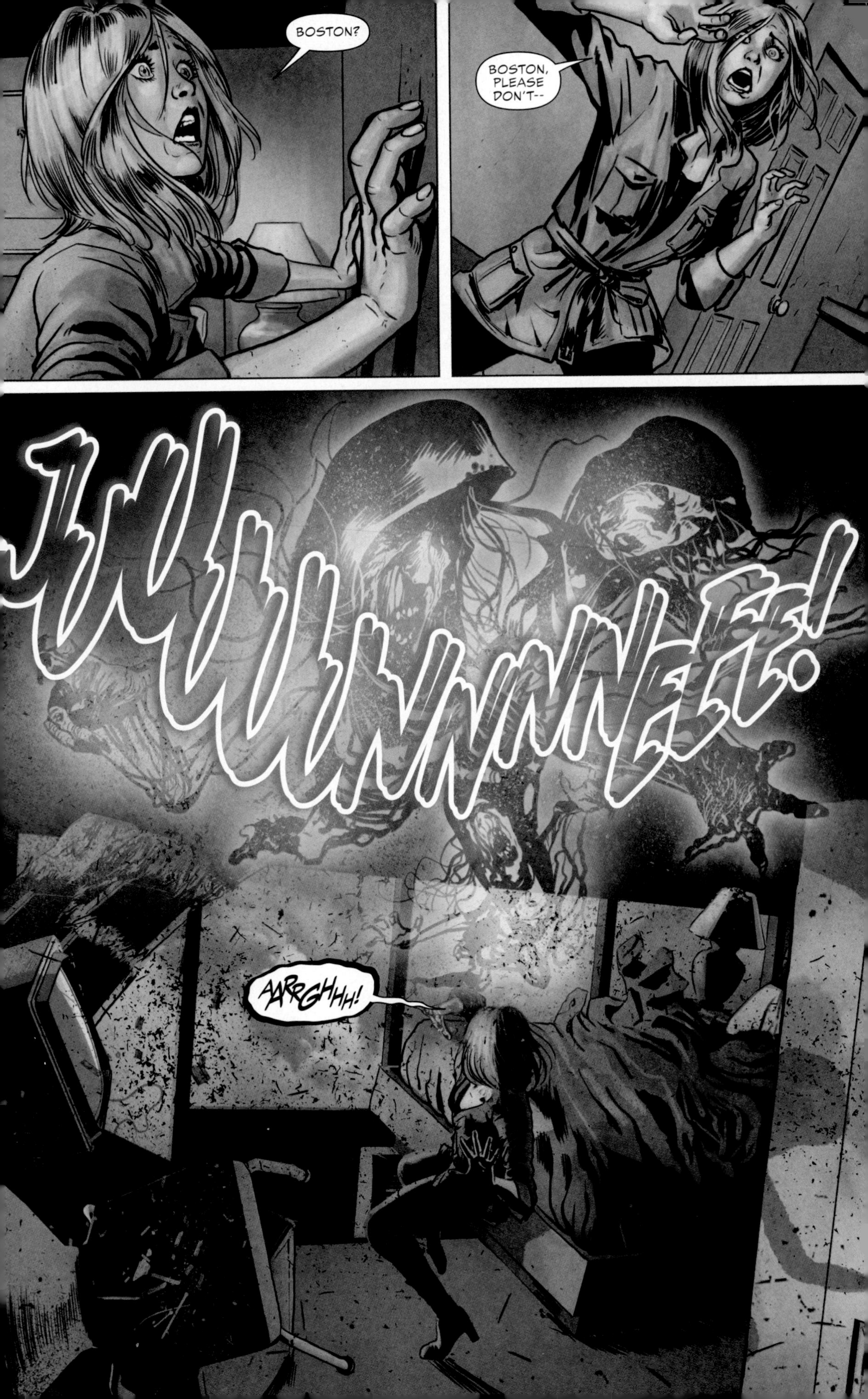
BOSTON?
BOSTON, PLEASE DON'T--
JUUUNNNNEEE!
AARRGHHH!

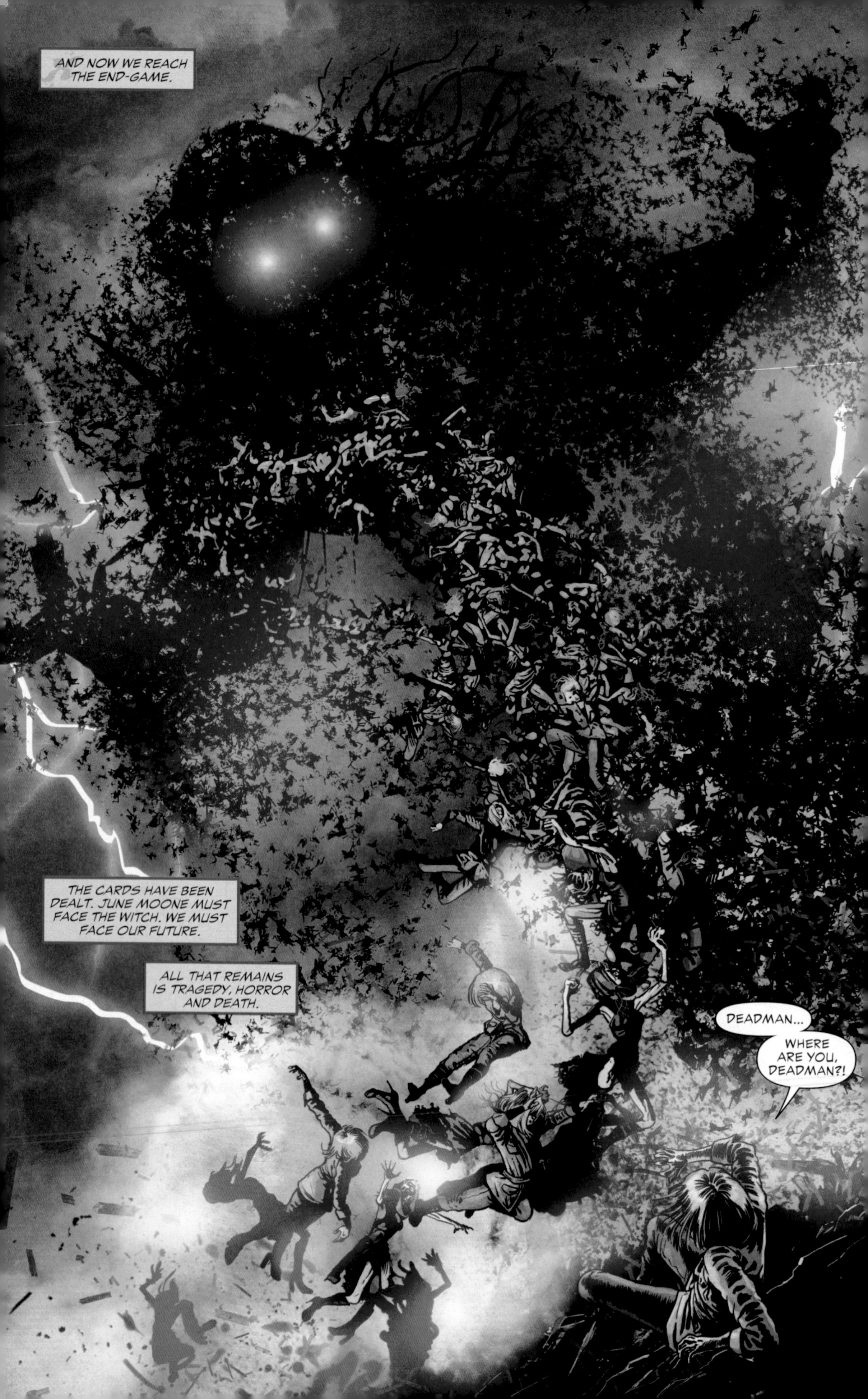
AND NOW WE REACH THE END-GAME.
THE CARDS HAVE BEEN DEALT. JUNE MOONE MUST FACE THE WITCH. WE MUST FACE OUR FUTURE.
ALL THAT REMAINS IS TRAGEDY, HORROR AND DEATH.
DEADMAN...
WHERE ARE YOU, DEADMAN?!

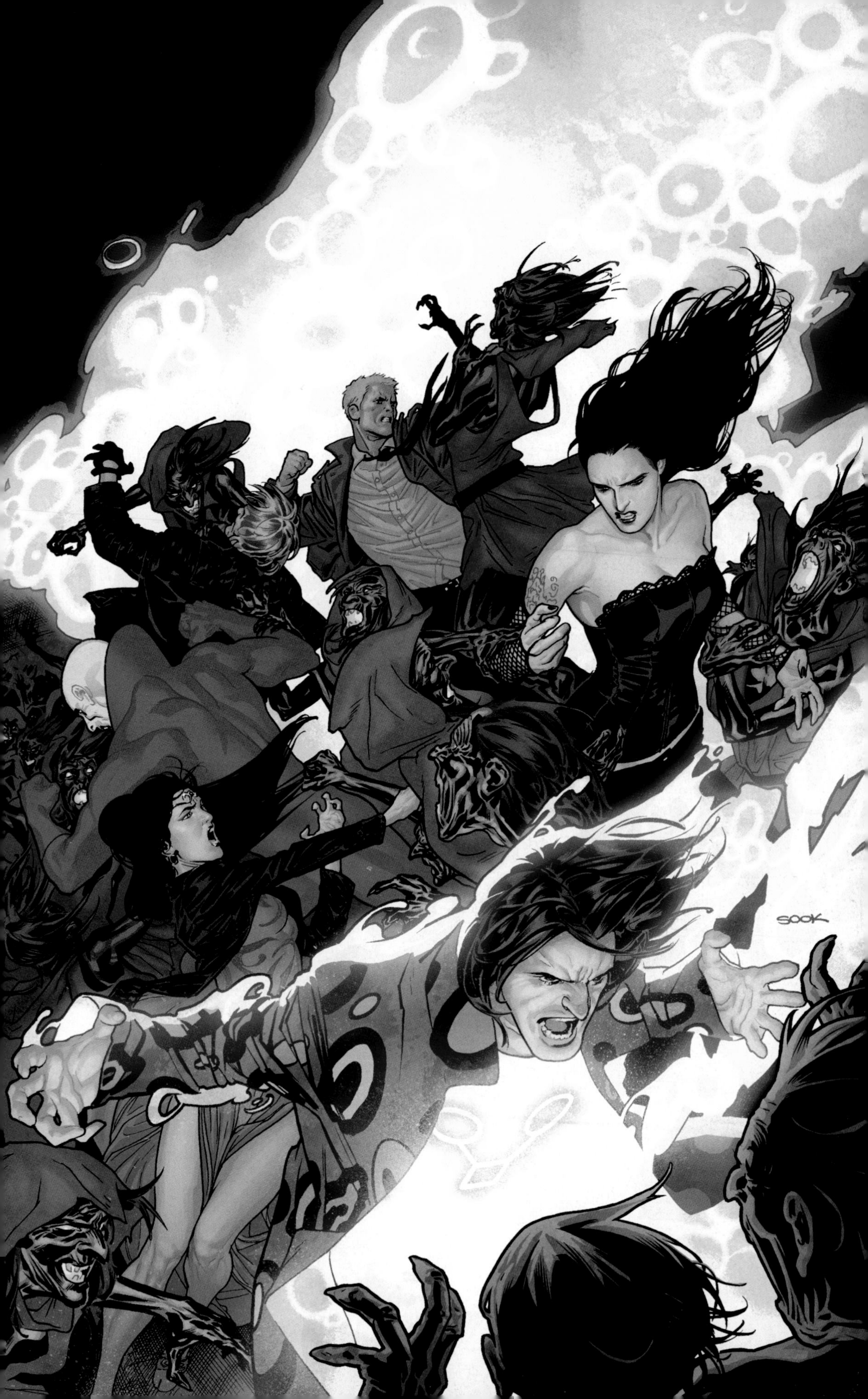
SOOK

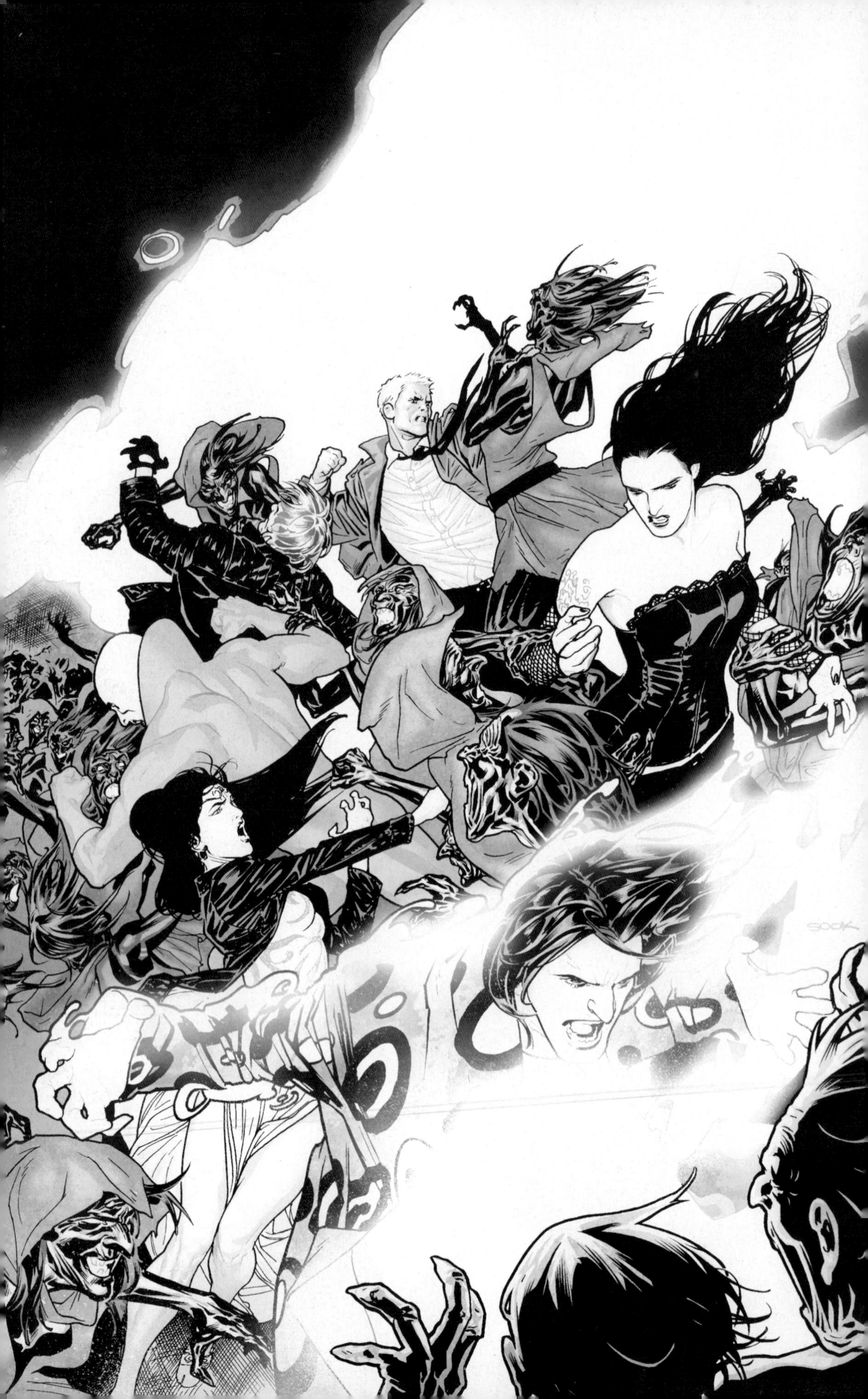
SOOK

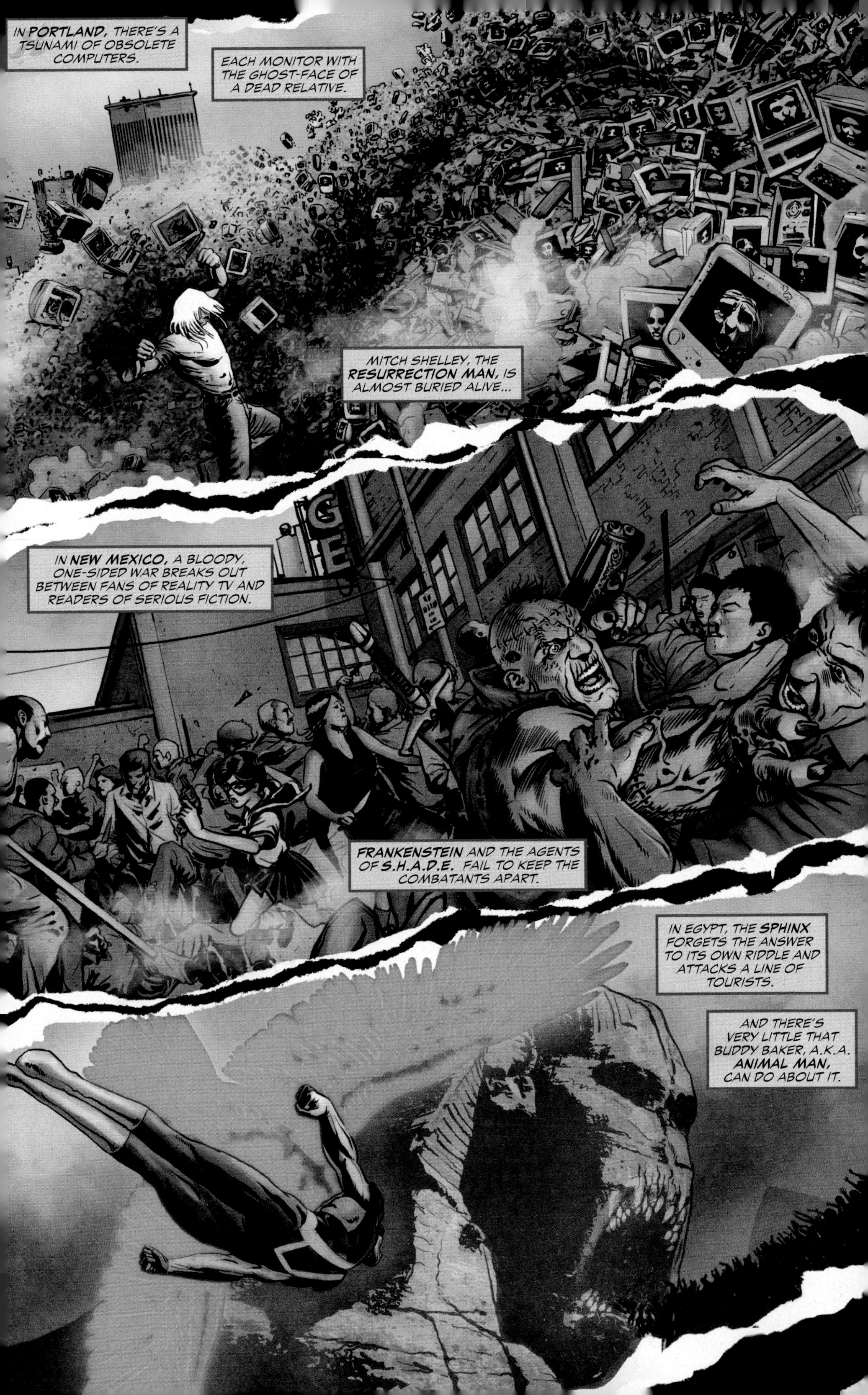
IN **PORTLAND**, THERE'S A TSUNAMI OF OBSOLETE COMPUTERS.
EACH MONITOR WITH THE GHOST-FACE OF A DEAD RELATIVE.
MITCH SHELLEY, THE **RESURRECTION MAN**, IS ALMOST BURIED ALIVE...
IN **NEW MEXICO**, A BLOODY, ONE-SIDED WAR BREAKS OUT BETWEEN FANS OF REALITY TV AND READERS OF SERIOUS FICTION.
FRANKENSTEIN AND THE AGENTS OF **S.H.A.D.E.** FAIL TO KEEP THE COMBATANTS APART.
IN EGYPT, THE **SPHINX** FORGETS THE ANSWER TO ITS OWN RIDDLE AND ATTACKS A LINE OF TOURISTS.
AND THERE'S VERY LITTLE THAT BUDDY BAKER, A.K.A. **ANIMAL MAN**, CAN DO ABOUT IT.

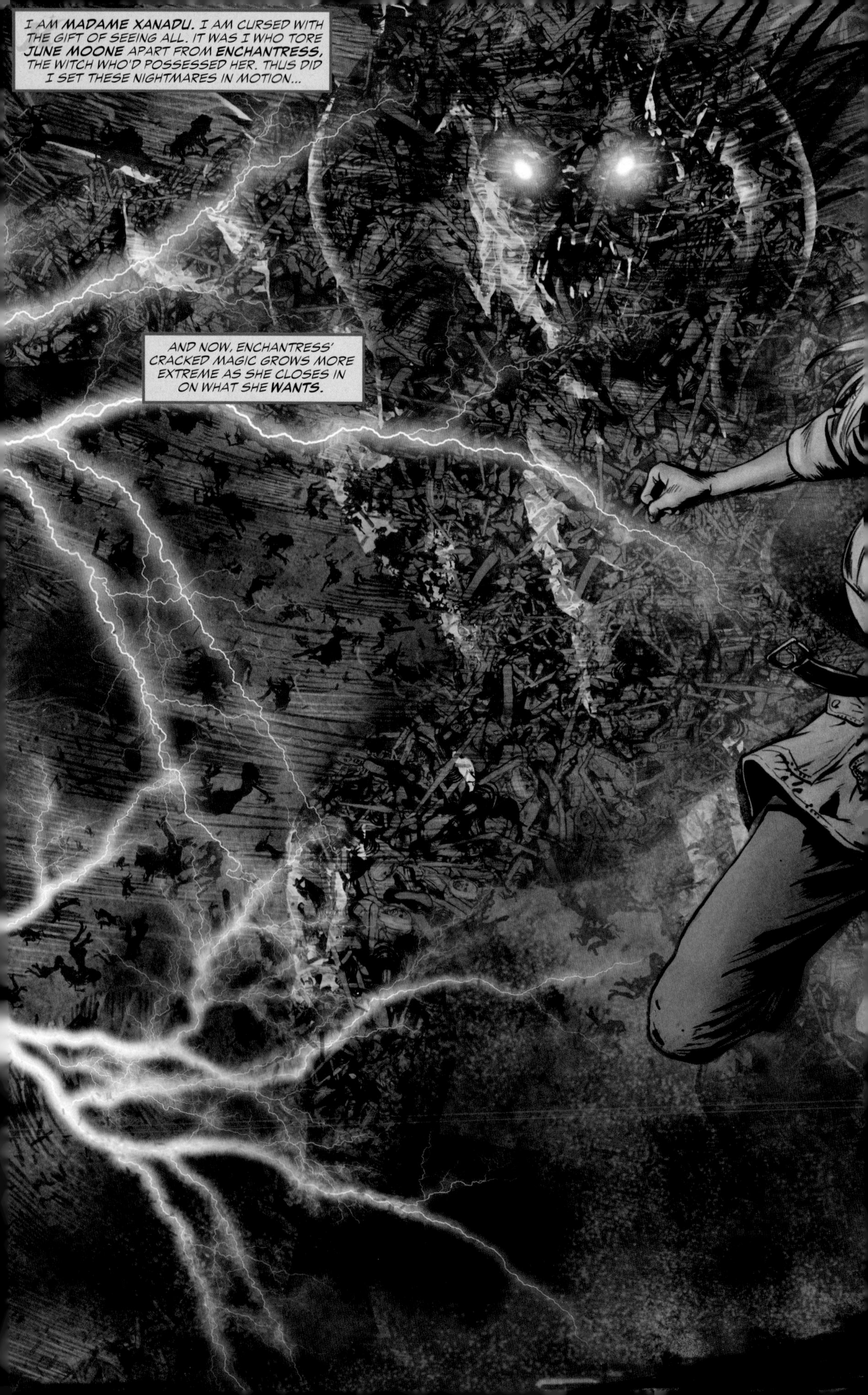

I AM MADAME XANADU. I AM CURSED WITH THE GIFT OF SEEING ALL. IT WAS I WHO TORE JUNE MOONE APART FROM ENCHANTRESS, THE WITCH WHO'D POSSESSED HER. THUS DID I SET THESE NIGHTMARES IN MOTION...
AND NOW, ENCHANTRESS' CRACKED MAGIC GROWS MORE EXTREME AS SHE CLOSES IN ON WHAT SHE WANTS.

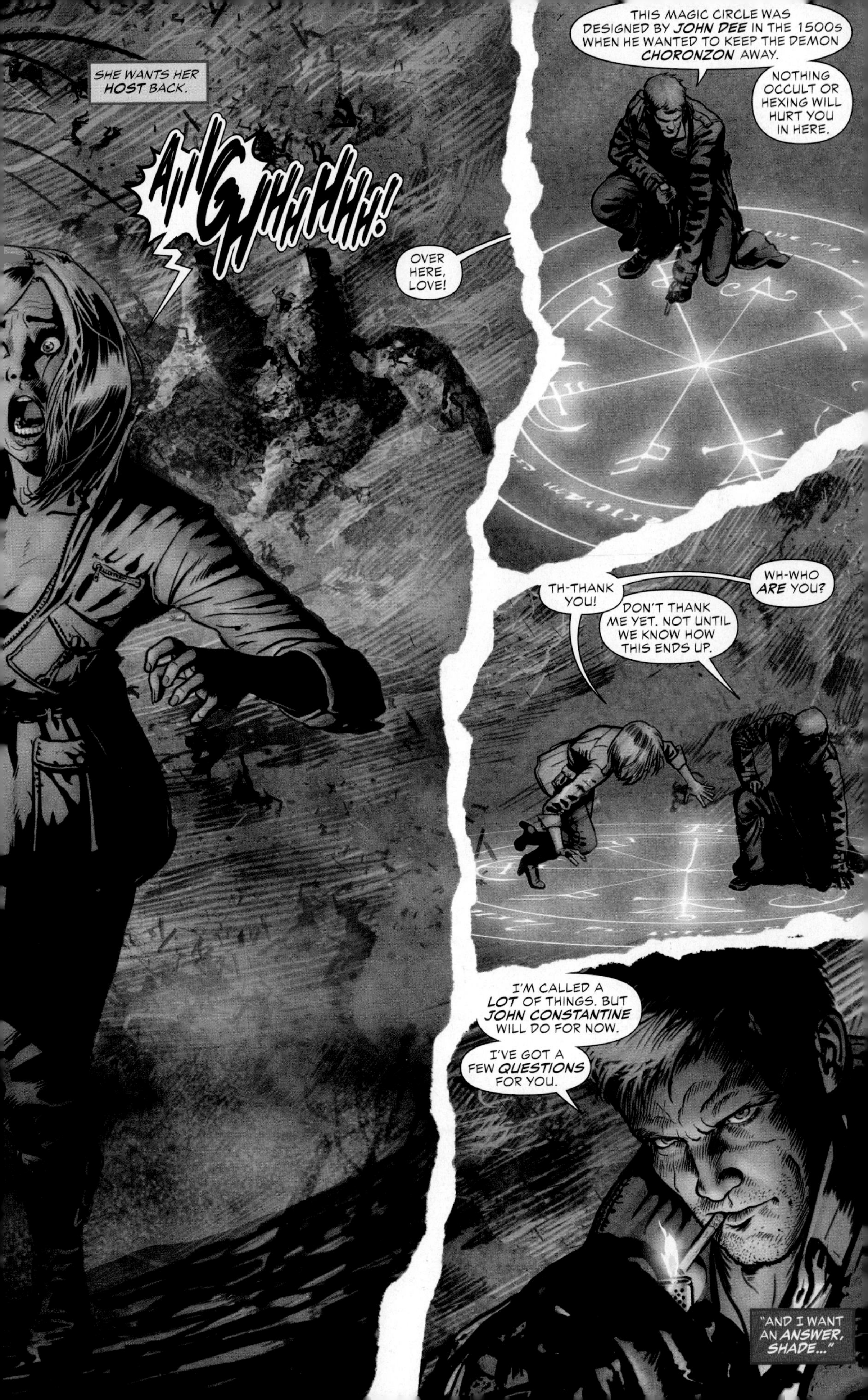
SHE WANTS HER HOST BACK.
AAGGHHHHHHHH!
OVER HERE, LOVE!
THIS MAGIC CIRCLE WAS DESIGNED BY JOHN DEE IN THE 1500s WHEN HE WANTED TO KEEP THE DEMON CHORONZON AWAY.
NOTHING OCCULT OR HEXING WILL HURT YOU IN HERE.
TH-THANK YOU!
DON'T THANK ME YET. NOT UNTIL WE KNOW HOW THIS ENDS UP.
WH-WHO ARE YOU?
I'M CALLED A LOT OF THINGS. BUT JOHN CONSTANTINE WILL DO FOR NOW.
I'VE GOT A FEW QUESTIONS FOR YOU.
"AND I WANT AN ANSWER, SHADE..."

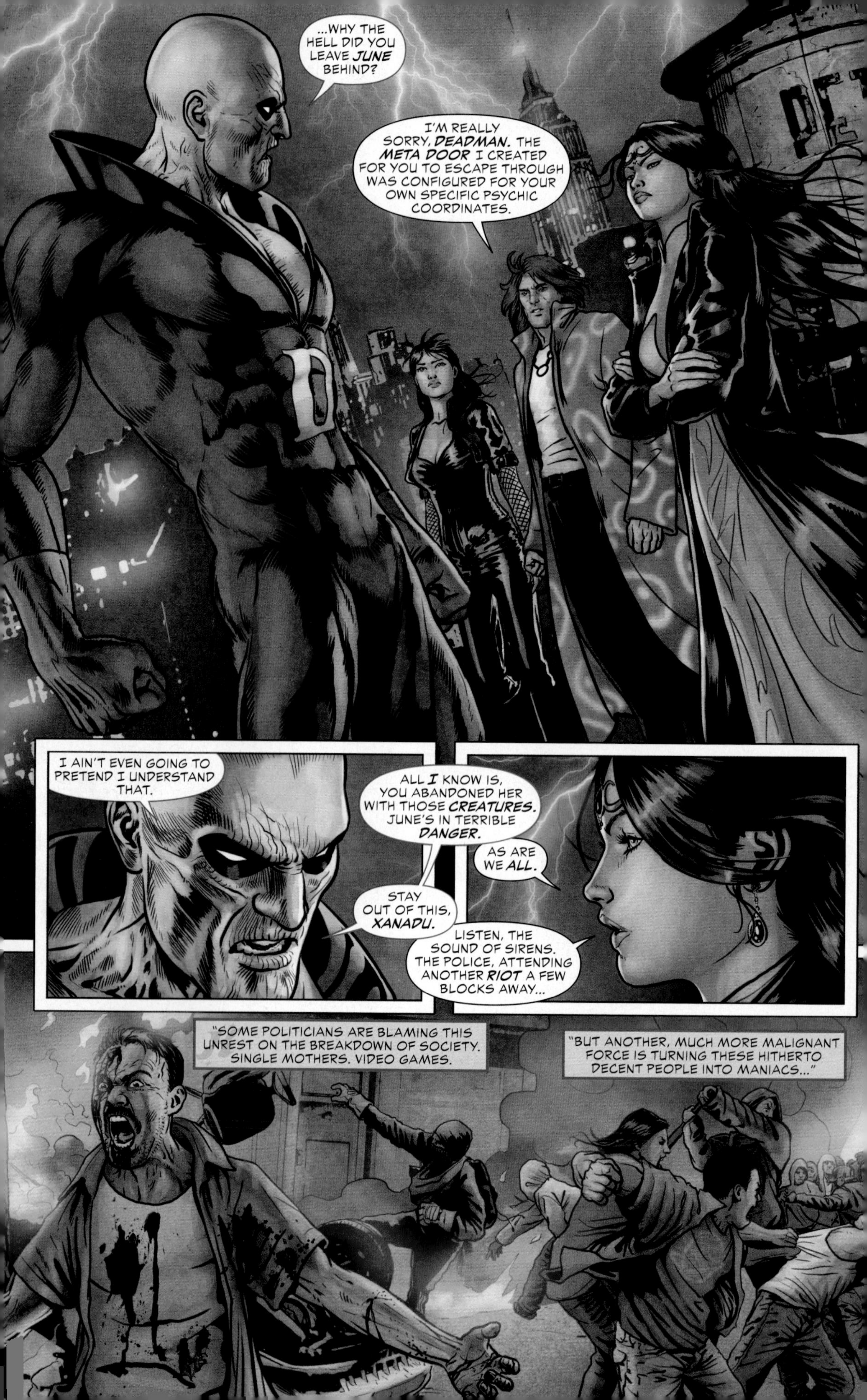
...WHY THE HELL DID YOU LEAVE JUNE BEHIND?
I'M REALLY SORRY, DEADMAN. THE META DOOR I CREATED FOR YOU TO ESCAPE THROUGH WAS CONFIGURED FOR YOUR OWN SPECIFIC PSYCHIC COORDINATES.
I AIN'T EVEN GOING TO PRETEND I UNDERSTAND THAT.
ALL I KNOW IS, YOU ABANDONED HER WITH THOSE CREATURES. JUNE'S IN TERRIBLE DANGER.
AS ARE WE ALL.
STAY OUT OF THIS, XANADU.
LISTEN, THE SOUND OF SIRENS. THE POLICE, ATTENDING ANOTHER RIOT A FEW BLOCKS AWAY...
"SOME POLITICIANS ARE BLAMING THIS UNREST ON THE BREAKDOWN OF SOCIETY. SINGLE MOTHERS. VIDEO GAMES.
"BUT ANOTHER, MUCH MORE MALIGNANT FORCE IS TURNING THESE HITHERTO DECENT PEOPLE INTO MANIACS..."

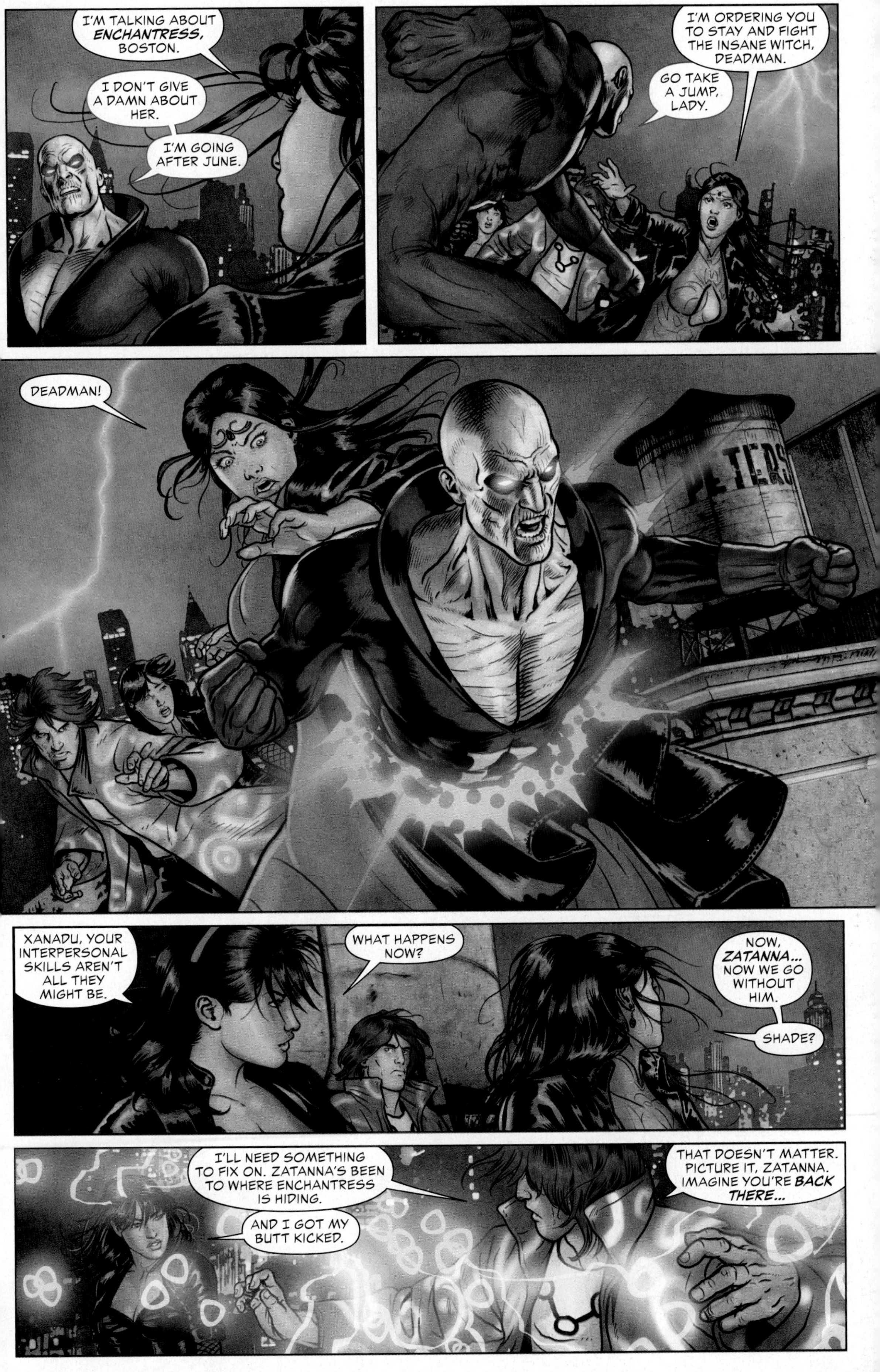

I'M TALKING ABOUT ENCHANTRESS, BOSTON.
I DON'T GIVE A DAMN ABOUT HER.
I'M GOING AFTER JUNE.
I'M ORDERING YOU TO STAY AND FIGHT THE INSANE WITCH, DEADMAN.
GO TAKE A JUMP, LADY.
DEADMAN!
XANADU, YOUR INTERPERSONAL SKILLS AREN'T ALL THEY MIGHT BE.
WHAT HAPPENS NOW?
NOW, ZATANNA... NOW WE GO WITHOUT HIM.
SHADE?
I'LL NEED SOMETHING TO FIX ON. ZATANNA'S BEEN TO WHERE ENCHANTRESS IS HIDING.
AND I GOT MY BUTT KICKED.
THAT DOESN'T MATTER. PICTURE IT, ZATANNA. IMAGINE YOU'RE BACK THERE...

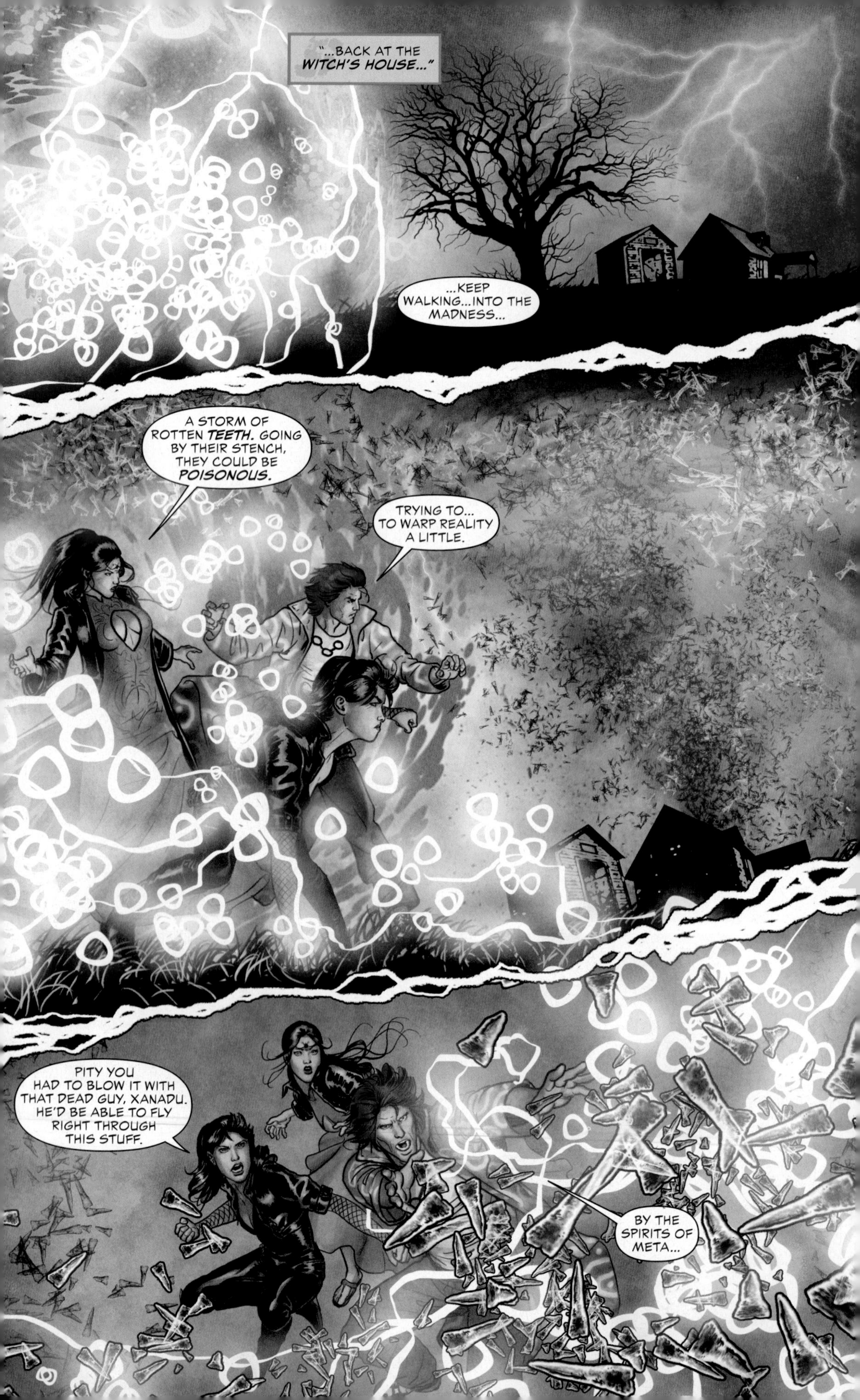
"...BACK AT THE WITCH'S HOUSE..."
...KEEP WALKING...INTO THE MADNESS...
A STORM OF ROTTEN TEETH. GOING BY THEIR STENCH, THEY COULD BE POISONOUS.
TRYING TO... TO WARP REALITY A LITTLE.
PITY YOU HAD TO BLOW IT WITH THAT DEAD GUY, XANADU. HE'D BE ABLE TO FLY RIGHT THROUGH THIS STUFF.
BY THE SPIRITS OF META...

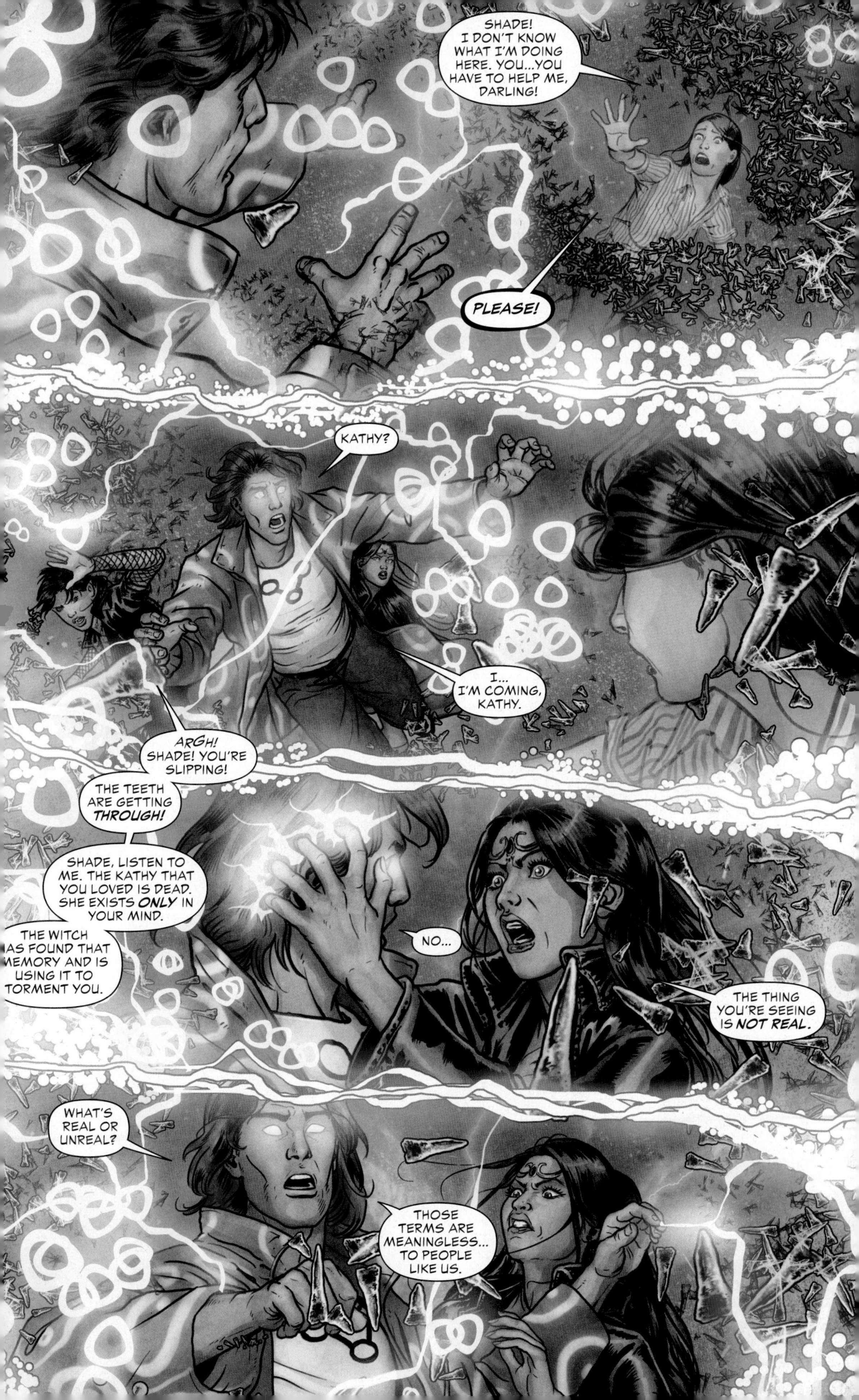
SHADE! I DON'T KNOW WHAT I'M DOING HERE. YOU...YOU HAVE TO HELP ME, DARLING!
PLEASE!
KATHY?
I... I'M COMING, KATHY.
ARGH! SHADE! YOU'RE SLIPPING!
THE TEETH ARE GETTING THROUGH!
SHADE, LISTEN TO ME. THE KATHY THAT YOU LOVED IS DEAD. SHE EXISTS ONLY IN YOUR MIND.
THE WITCH HAS FOUND THAT MEMORY AND IS USING IT TO TORMENT YOU.
NO...
THE THING YOU'RE SEEING IS NOT REAL.
WHAT'S REAL OR UNREAL?
THOSE TERMS ARE MEANINGLESS... TO PEOPLE LIKE US.

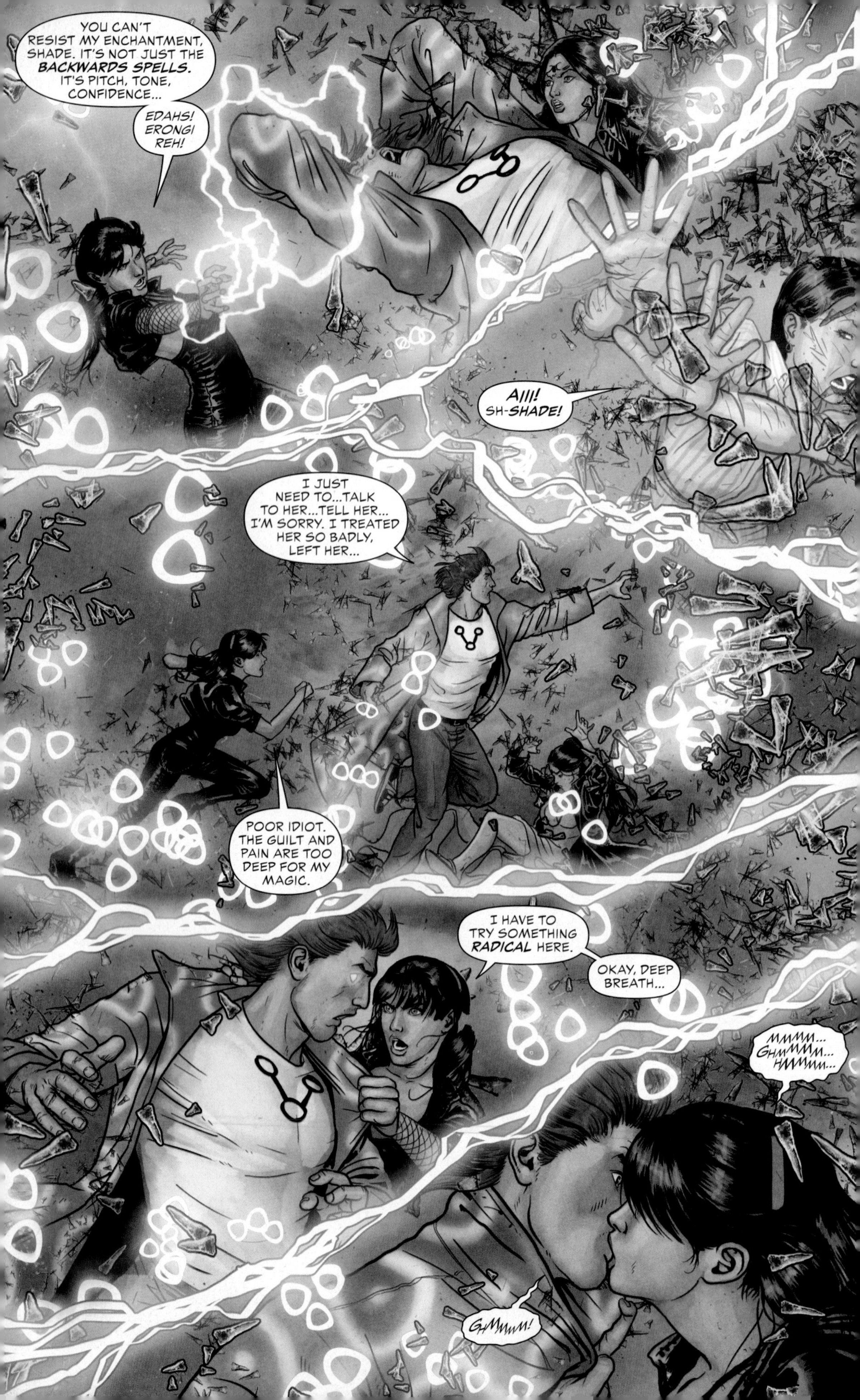
YOU CAN'T RESIST MY ENCHANTMENT, SHADE. IT'S NOT JUST THE BACKWARDS SPELLS. IT'S PITCH, TONE, CONFIDENCE...
EDAHS! ERONGI REH!
AIII! SH-SHADE!
I JUST NEED TO...TALK TO HER...TELL HER... I'M SORRY. I TREATED HER SO BADLY, LEFT HER...
POOR IDIOT. THE GUILT AND PAIN ARE TOO DEEP FOR MY MAGIC.
I HAVE TO TRY SOMETHING RADICAL HERE.
OKAY, DEEP BREATH...
MMMM... GHMMMM... HMMMM...
GHMMMM!

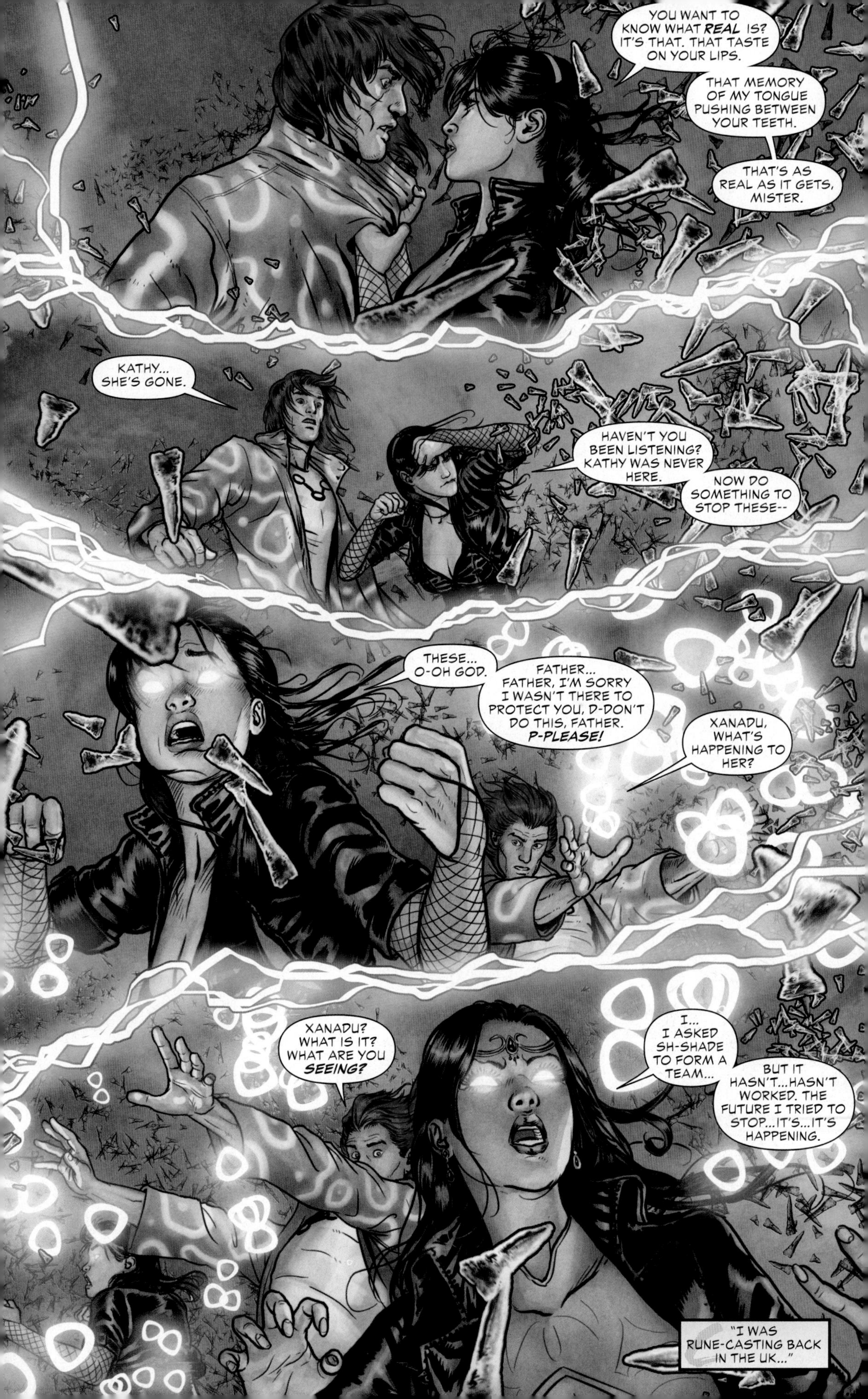
YOU WANT TO KNOW WHAT REAL IS? IT'S THAT. THAT TASTE ON YOUR LIPS.
THAT MEMORY OF MY TONGUE PUSHING BETWEEN YOUR TEETH.
THAT'S AS REAL AS IT GETS, MISTER.
KATHY... SHE'S GONE.
HAVEN'T YOU BEEN LISTENING? KATHY WAS NEVER HERE.
NOW DO SOMETHING TO STOP THESE--
THESE... O-OH GOD.
FATHER... FATHER, I'M SORRY I WASN'T THERE TO PROTECT YOU, D-DON'T DO THIS, FATHER. P-PLEASE!
XANADU, WHAT'S HAPPENING TO HER?
XANADU? WHAT IS IT? WHAT ARE YOU SEEING?
I... I ASKED SH-SHADE TO FORM A TEAM...
BUT IT HASN'T...HASN'T WORKED. THE FUTURE I TRIED TO STOP...IT'S...IT'S HAPPENING.
"I WAS RUNE-CASTING BACK IN THE UK..."

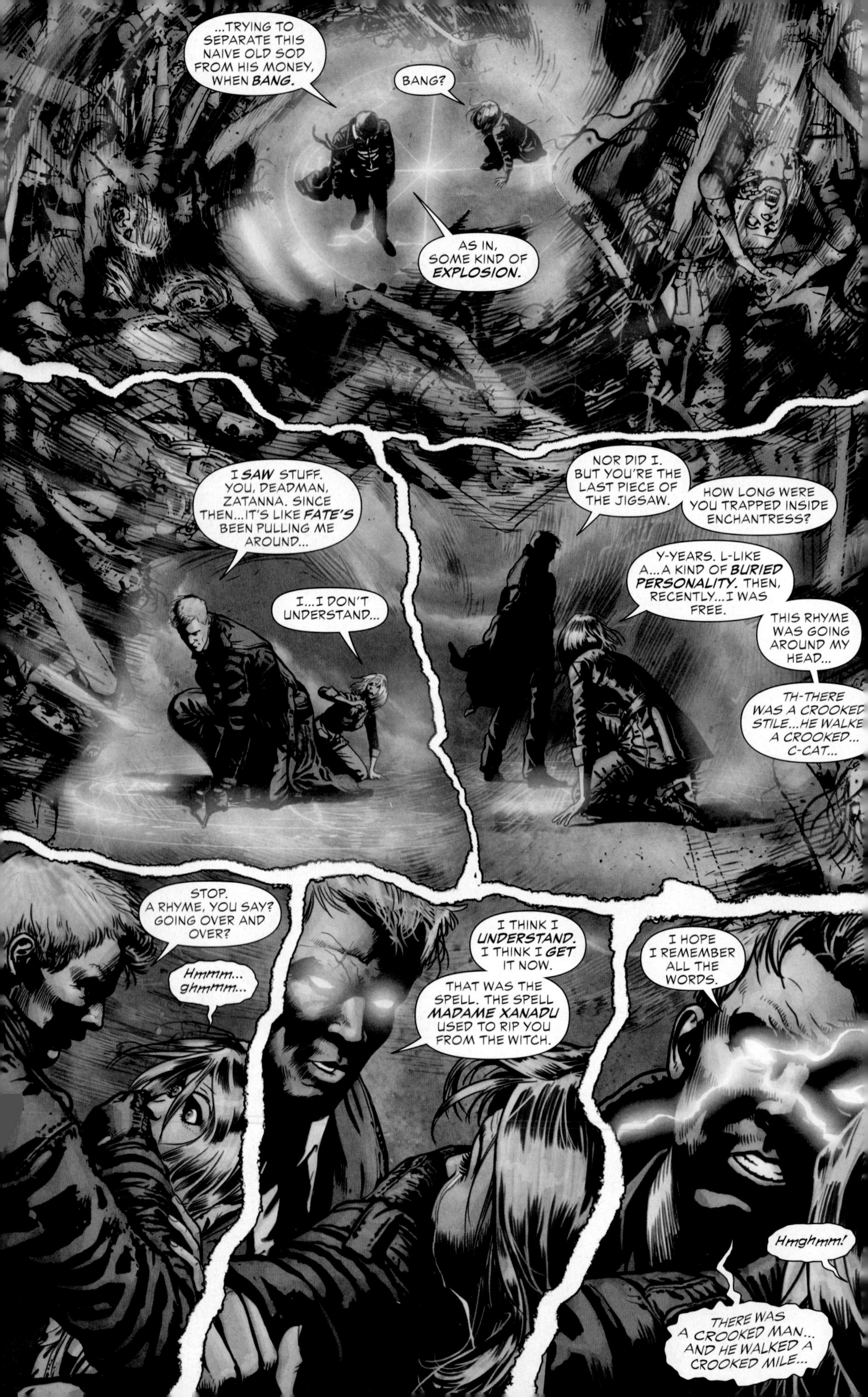
...TRYING TO SEPARATE THIS NAIVE OLD SOD FROM HIS MONEY, WHEN **BANG.**
BANG?
AS IN, SOME KIND OF ***EXPLOSION.***
I ***SAW*** STUFF. YOU, DEADMAN, ZATANNA. SINCE THEN...IT'S LIKE ***FATE'S*** BEEN PULLING ME AROUND...
I...I DON'T UNDERSTAND...
NOR DID I. BUT YOU'RE THE LAST PIECE OF THE JIGSAW.
HOW LONG WERE YOU TRAPPED INSIDE ENCHANTRESS?
Y-YEARS. L-LIKE A...A KIND OF ***BURIED PERSONALITY.*** THEN, RECENTLY...I WAS FREE.
THIS RHYME WAS GOING AROUND MY HEAD...
TH-THERE WAS A CROOKED STILE...HE WALKE A CROOKED... C-CAT...
STOP. A RHYME, YOU SAY? GOING OVER AND OVER?
Hmmm... ghmmm...
I THINK I ***UNDERSTAND.*** I THINK I ***GET*** IT NOW.
THAT WAS THE SPELL. THE SPELL ***MADAME XANADU*** USED TO RIP YOU FROM THE WITCH.
I HOPE I REMEMBER ALL THE WORDS.
Hmghmm!
THERE WAS A CROOKED MAN... AND HE WALKED A CROOKED MILE...

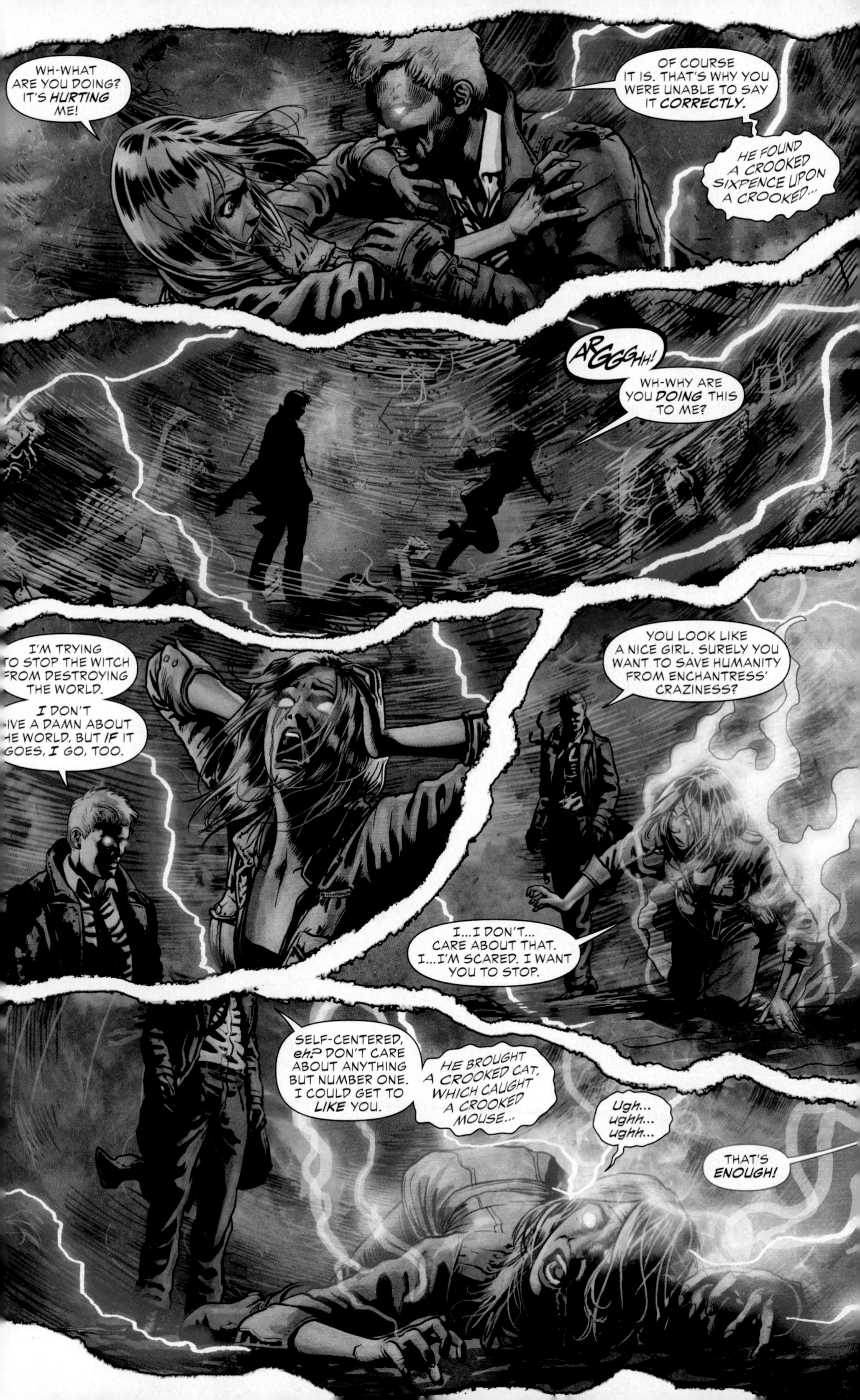
WH-WHAT ARE YOU DOING? IT'S **HURTING** ME!
OF COURSE IT IS. THAT'S WHY YOU WERE UNABLE TO SAY IT **CORRECTLY.**
HE FOUND A CROOKED SIXPENCE UPON A CROOKED...
ARGGGHH!
WH-WHY ARE YOU **DOING** THIS TO ME?
I'M TRYING TO STOP THE WITCH FROM DESTROYING THE WORLD.
I DON'T GIVE A DAMN ABOUT THE WORLD, BUT **IF** IT GOES, **I** GO, TOO.
YOU LOOK LIKE A NICE GIRL. SURELY YOU WANT TO SAVE HUMANITY FROM ENCHANTRESS' CRAZINESS?
I...I DON'T... CARE ABOUT THAT. I...I'M SCARED. I WANT YOU TO STOP.
SELF-CENTERED, *eh?* DON'T CARE ABOUT ANYTHING BUT NUMBER ONE. I COULD GET TO **LIKE** YOU.
HE BROUGHT A CROOKED CAT, WHICH CAUGHT A CROOKED MOUSE...
Ugh... ughh... ughh...
THAT'S **ENOUGH!**

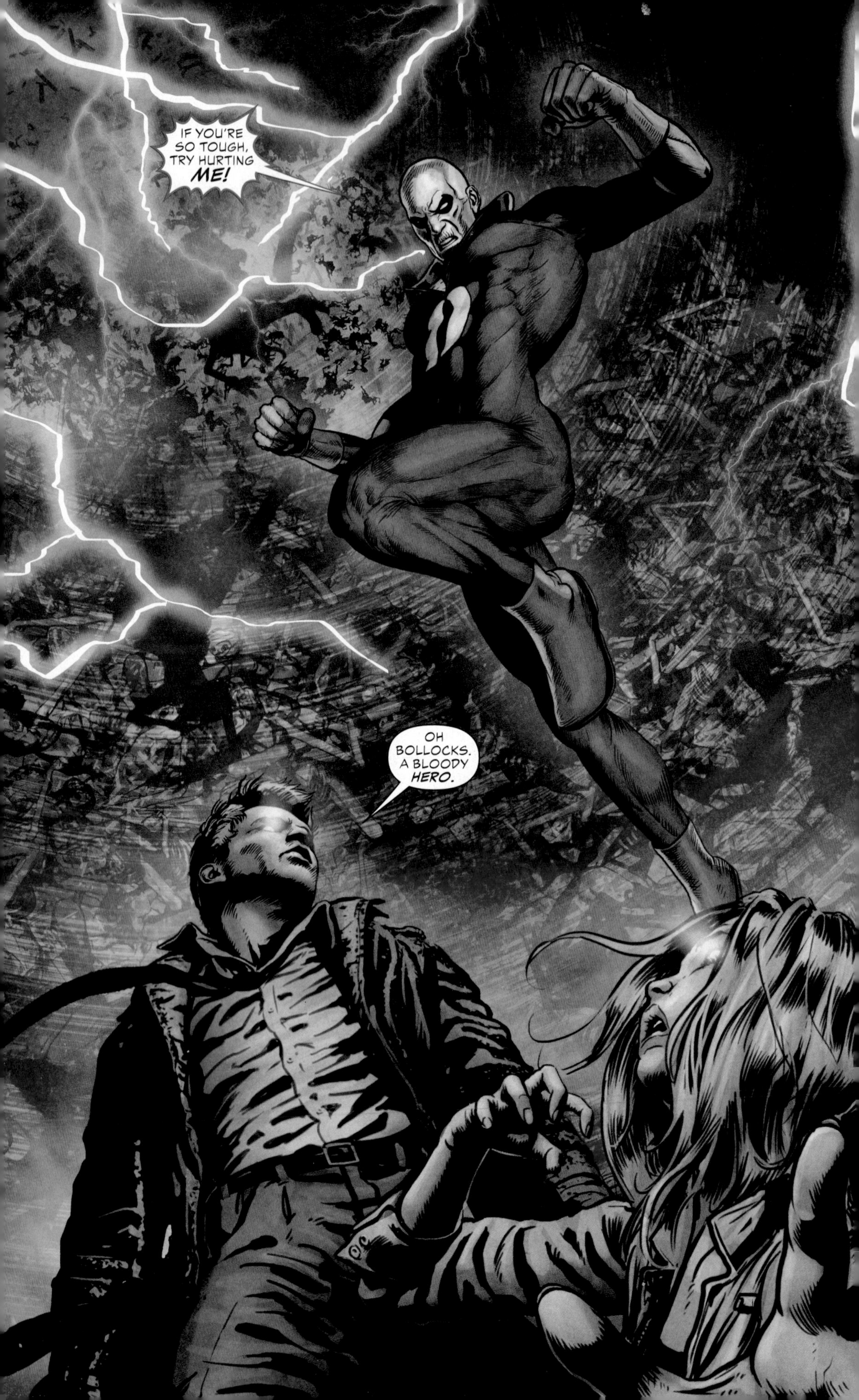
IF YOU'RE SO TOUGH, TRY HURTING ME!
OH BOLLOCKS. A BLOODY HERO.

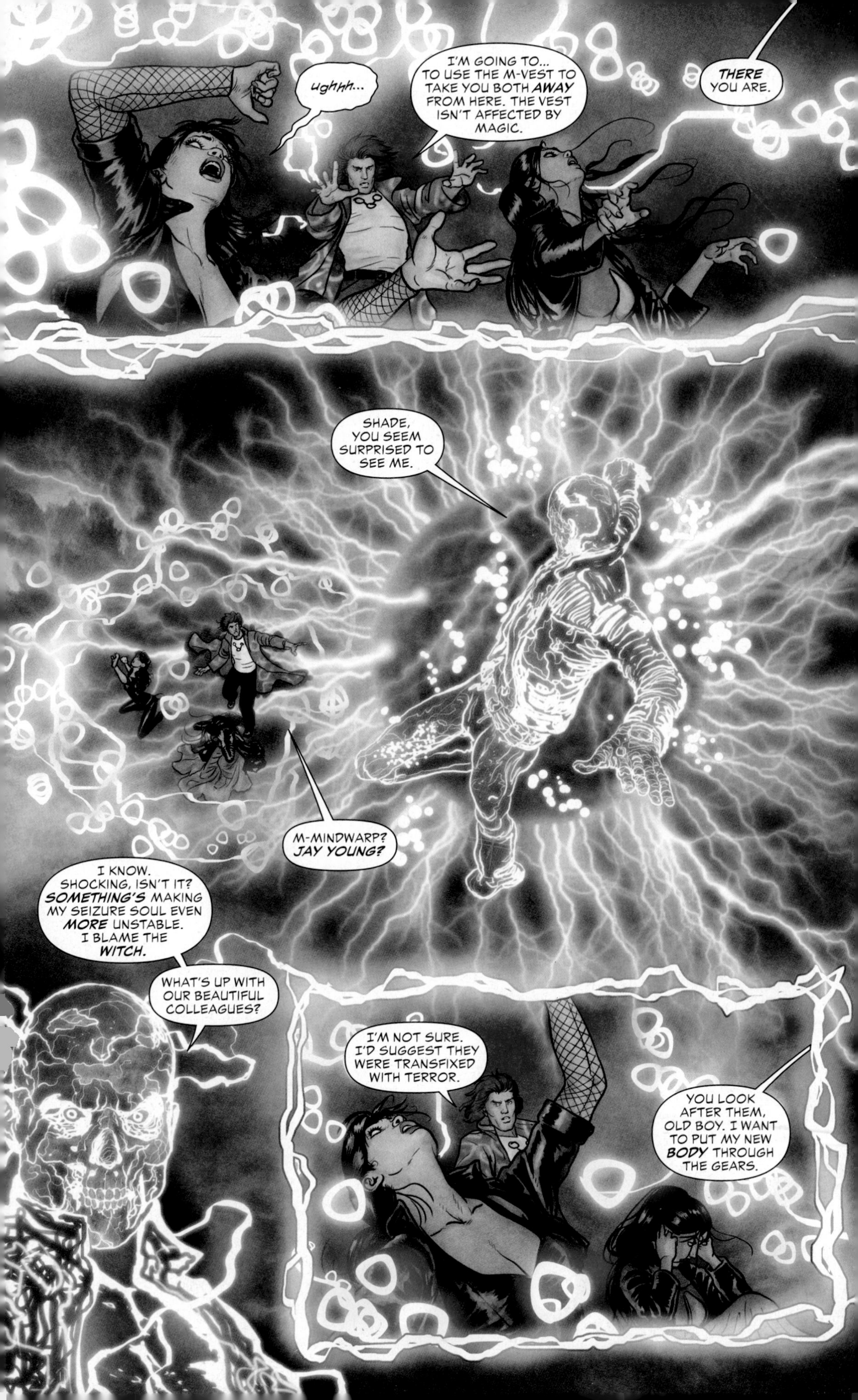
ughhh...
I'M GOING TO... TO USE THE M-VEST TO TAKE YOU BOTH AWAY FROM HERE. THE VEST ISN'T AFFECTED BY MAGIC.
THERE YOU ARE.
SHADE, YOU SEEM SURPRISED TO SEE ME.
M-MINDWARP? JAY YOUNG?
I KNOW. SHOCKING, ISN'T IT? SOMETHING'S MAKING MY SEIZURE SOUL EVEN MORE UNSTABLE. I BLAME THE WITCH.
WHAT'S UP WITH OUR BEAUTIFUL COLLEAGUES?
I'M NOT SURE. I'D SUGGEST THEY WERE TRANSFIXED WITH TERROR.
YOU LOOK AFTER THEM, OLD BOY. I WANT TO PUT MY NEW BODY THROUGH THE GEARS.

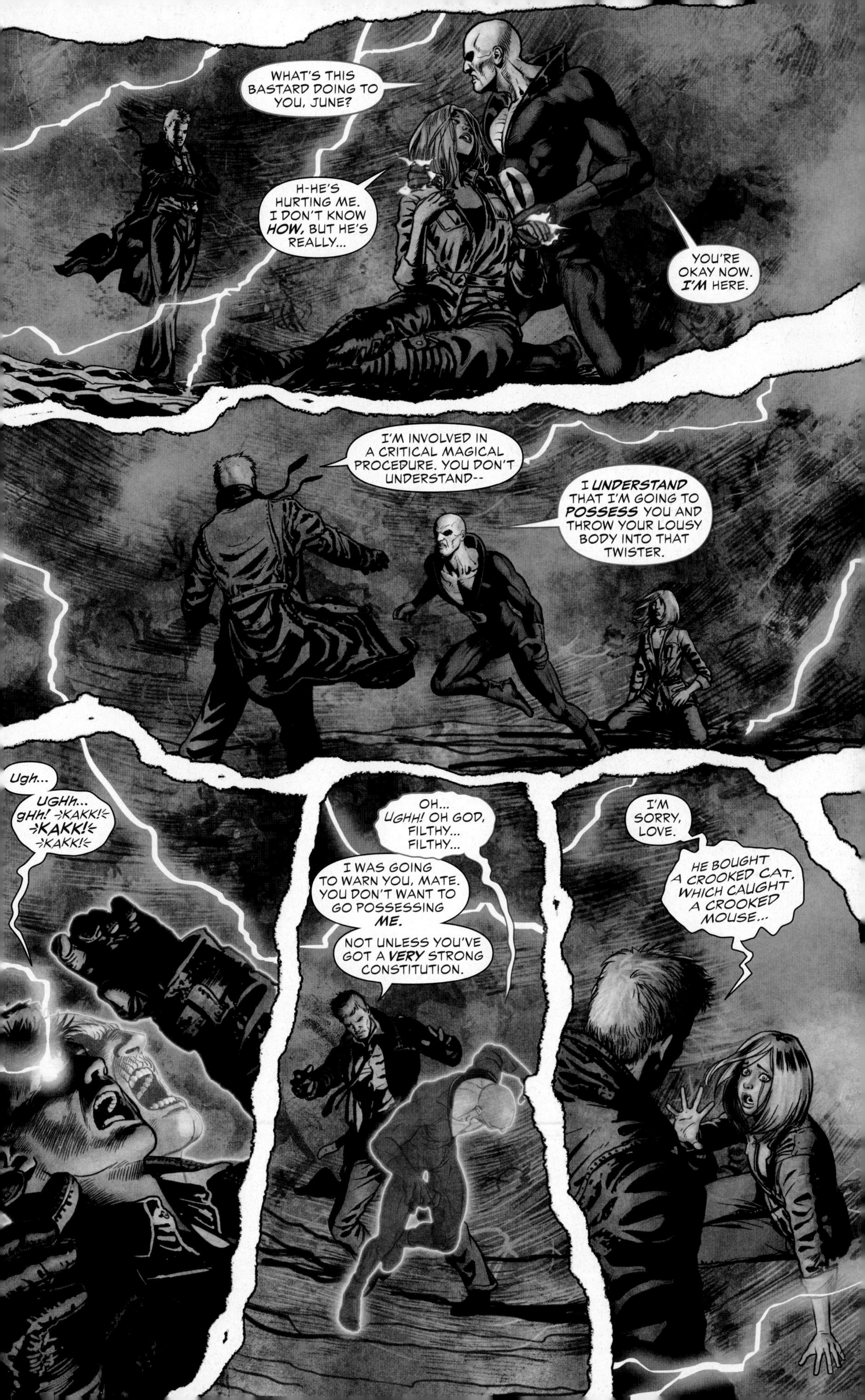
WHAT'S THIS BASTARD DOING TO YOU, JUNE?
H-HE'S HURTING ME. I DON'T KNOW HOW, BUT HE'S REALLY...
YOU'RE OKAY NOW. I'M HERE.
I'M INVOLVED IN A CRITICAL MAGICAL PROCEDURE. YOU DON'T UNDERSTAND--
I UNDERSTAND THAT I'M GOING TO POSSESS YOU AND THROW YOUR LOUSY BODY INTO THAT TWISTER.
Ugh... UGHh... gHh! KAKK! KAKK! KAKK!
OH... UGHH! OH GOD, FILTHY... FILTHY...
I WAS GOING TO WARN YOU, MATE. YOU DON'T WANT TO GO POSSESSING ME.
NOT UNLESS YOU'VE GOT A VERY STRONG CONSTITUTION.
I'M SORRY, LOVE.
HE BOUGHT A CROOKED CAT, WHICH CAUGHT A CROOKED MOUSE...

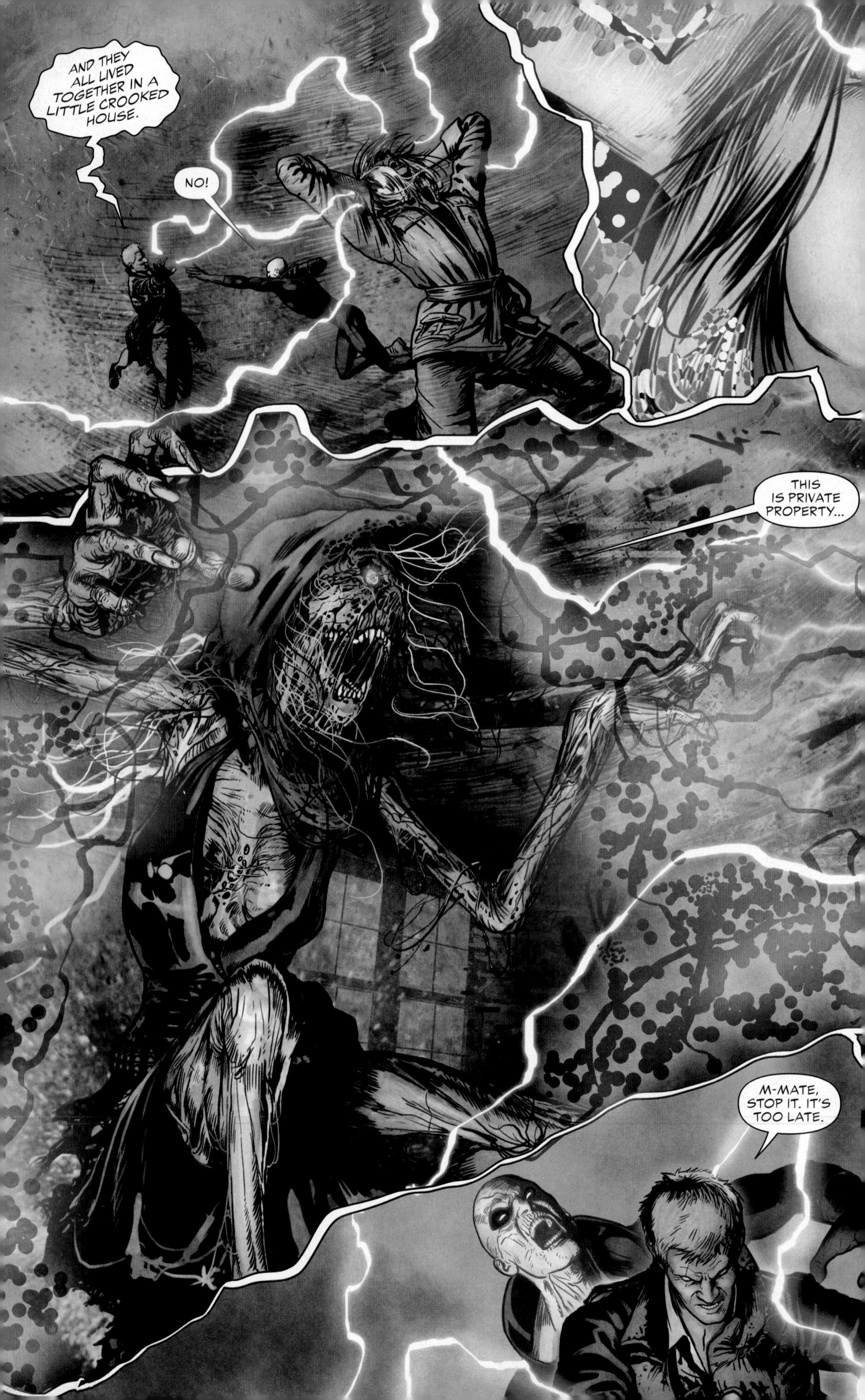
AND THEY ALL LIVED TOGETHER IN A LITTLE CROOKED HOUSE.
NO!
THIS IS PRIVATE PROPERTY...
M-MATE, STOP IT. IT'S TOO LATE.

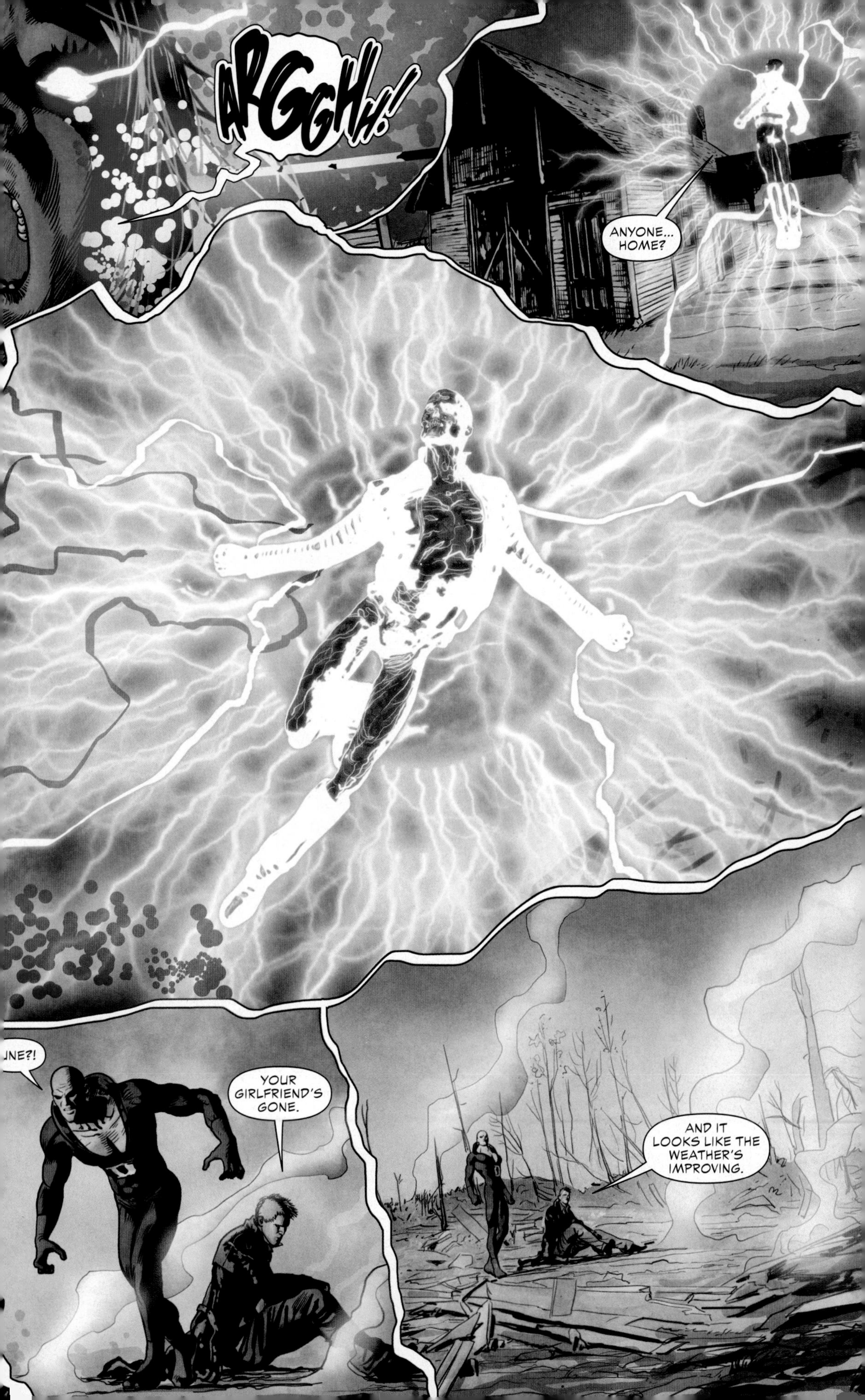
ARGGH!!
ANYONE... HOME?
UNE?!
YOUR GIRLFRIEND'S GONE.
AND IT LOOKS LIKE THE WEATHER'S IMPROVING.

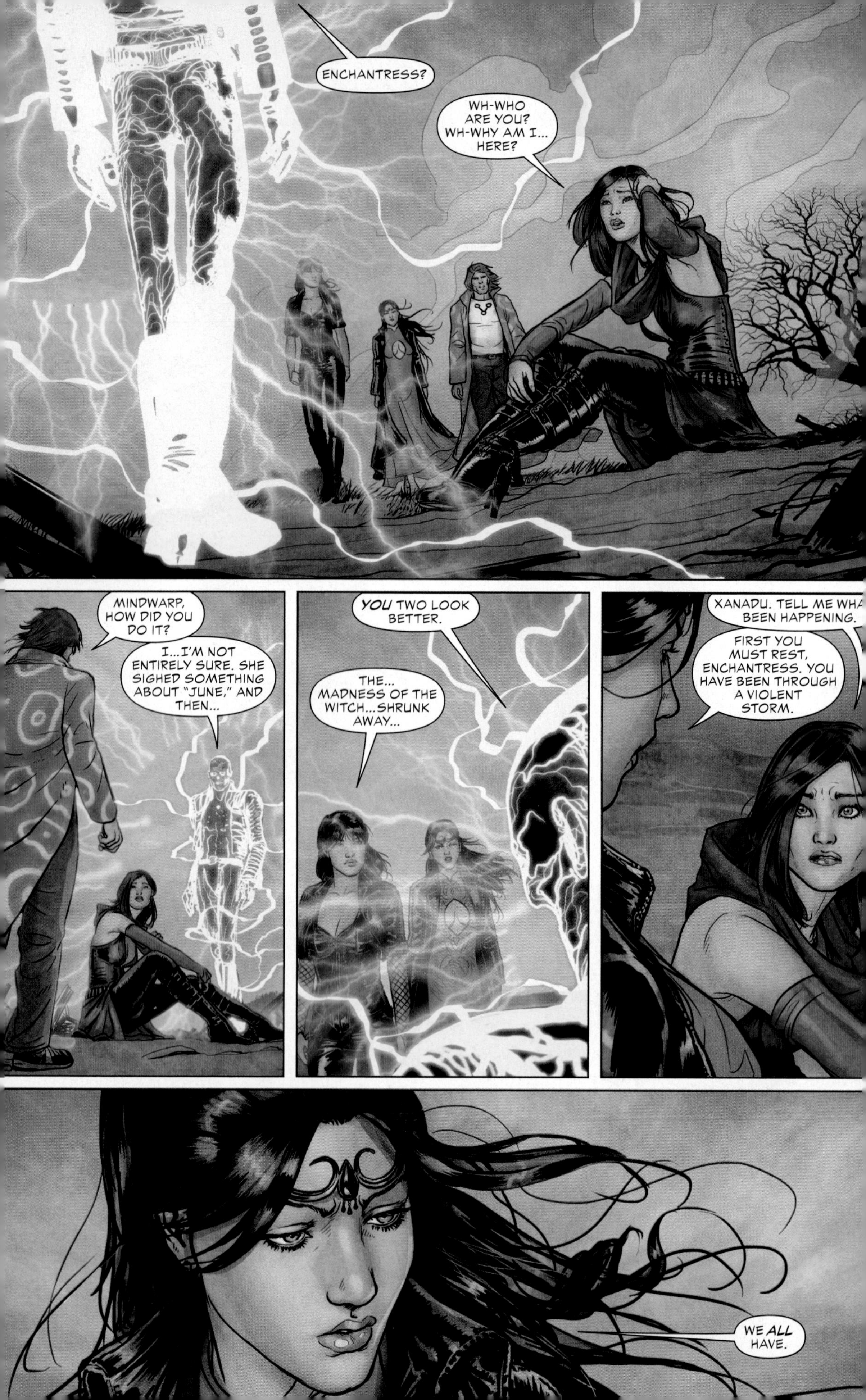
ENCHANTRESS?
WH-WHO ARE YOU? WH-WHY AM I... HERE?
MINDWARP, HOW DID YOU DO IT?
I...I'M NOT ENTIRELY SURE. SHE SIGHED SOMETHING ABOUT "JUNE," AND THEN...
YOU TWO LOOK BETTER.
THE... MADNESS OF THE WITCH...SHRUNK AWAY...
FIRST YOU MUST REST, ENCHANTRESS. YOU HAVE BEEN THROUGH A VIOLENT STORM.
WE *ALL* HAVE.

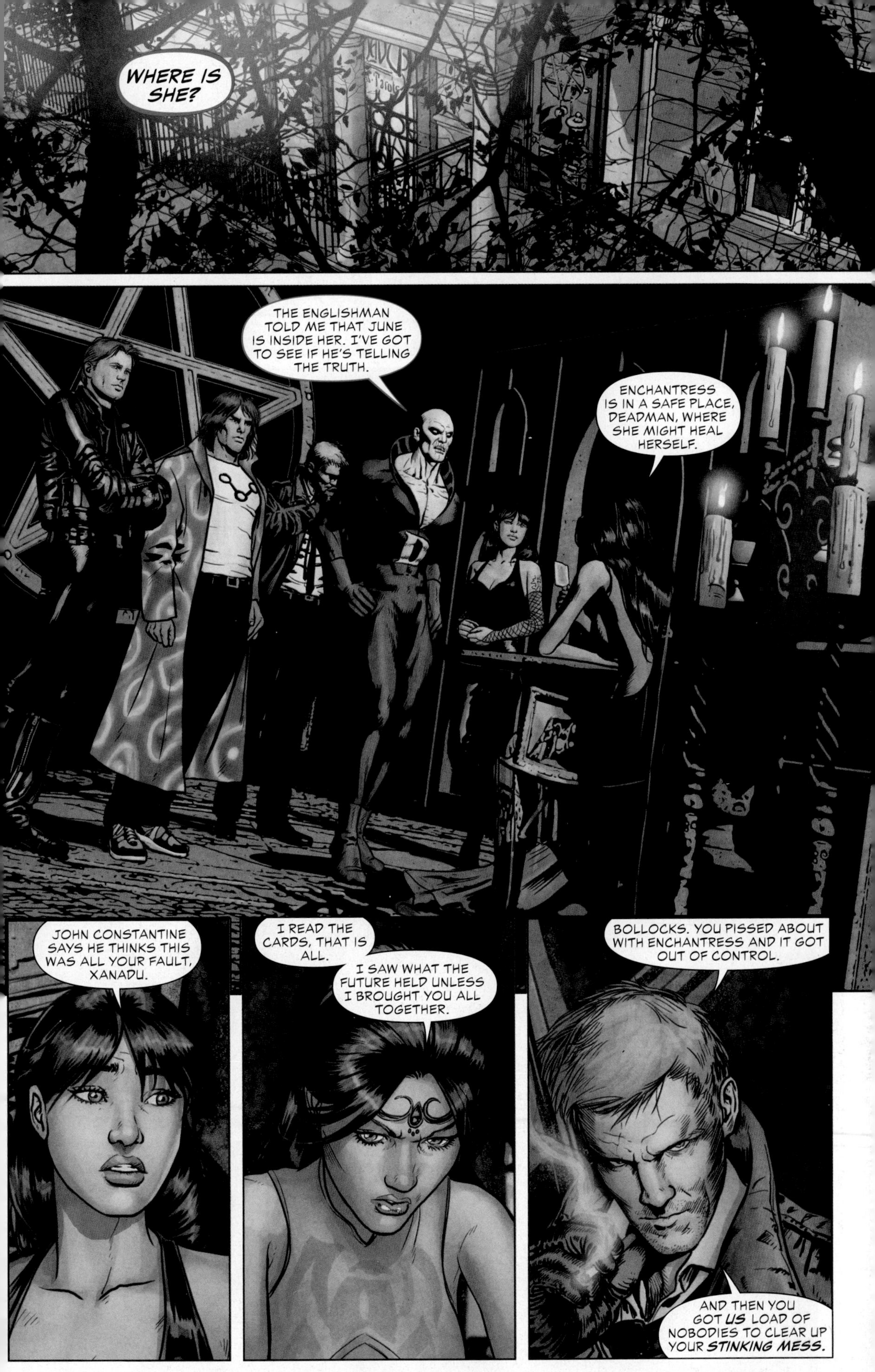
WHERE IS SHE?
THE ENGLISHMAN TOLD ME THAT JUNE IS INSIDE HER. I'VE GOT TO SEE IF HE'S TELLING THE TRUTH.
ENCHANTRESS IS IN A SAFE PLACE, DEADMAN, WHERE SHE MIGHT HEAL HERSELF.
JOHN CONSTANTINE SAYS HE THINKS THIS WAS ALL YOUR FAULT, XANADU.
I READ THE CARDS, THAT IS ALL.
I SAW WHAT THE FUTURE HELD UNLESS I BROUGHT YOU ALL TOGETHER.
BOLLOCKS. YOU PISSED ABOUT WITH ENCHANTRESS AND IT GOT OUT OF CONTROL.
AND THEN YOU GOT *US* LOAD OF NOBODIES TO CLEAR UP YOUR *STINKING MESS.*

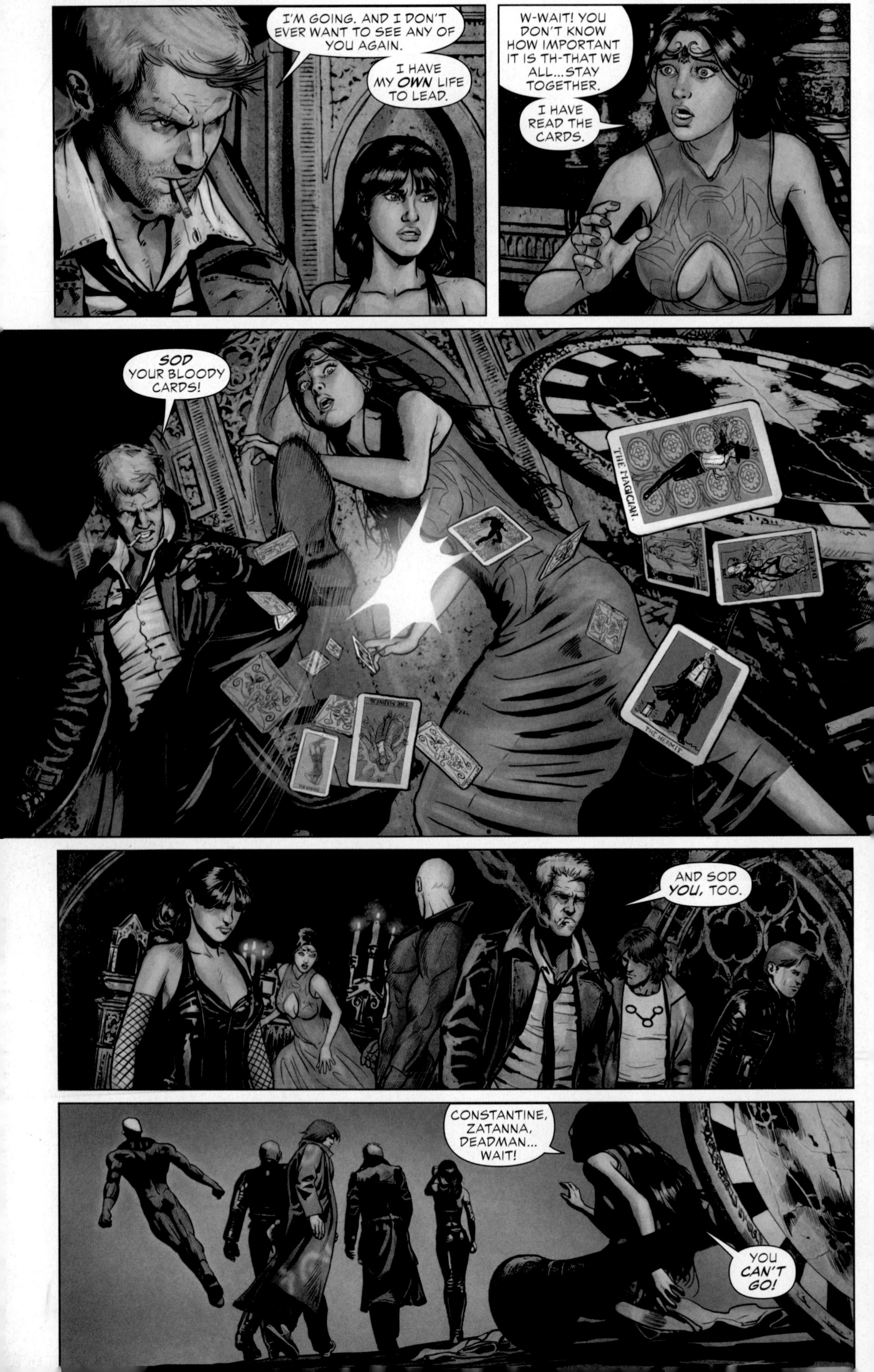
I'M GOING. AND I DON'T EVER WANT TO SEE ANY OF YOU AGAIN.
I HAVE MY OWN LIFE TO LEAD.
W-WAIT! YOU DON'T KNOW HOW IMPORTANT IT IS TH-THAT WE ALL...STAY TOGETHER.
I HAVE READ THE CARDS.
SOD YOUR BLOODY CARDS!
THE MAGICIAN
DEATH
THE HERMIT
AND SOD YOU, TOO.
CONSTANTINE, ZATANNA, DEADMAN... WAIT!
YOU CAN'T GO!

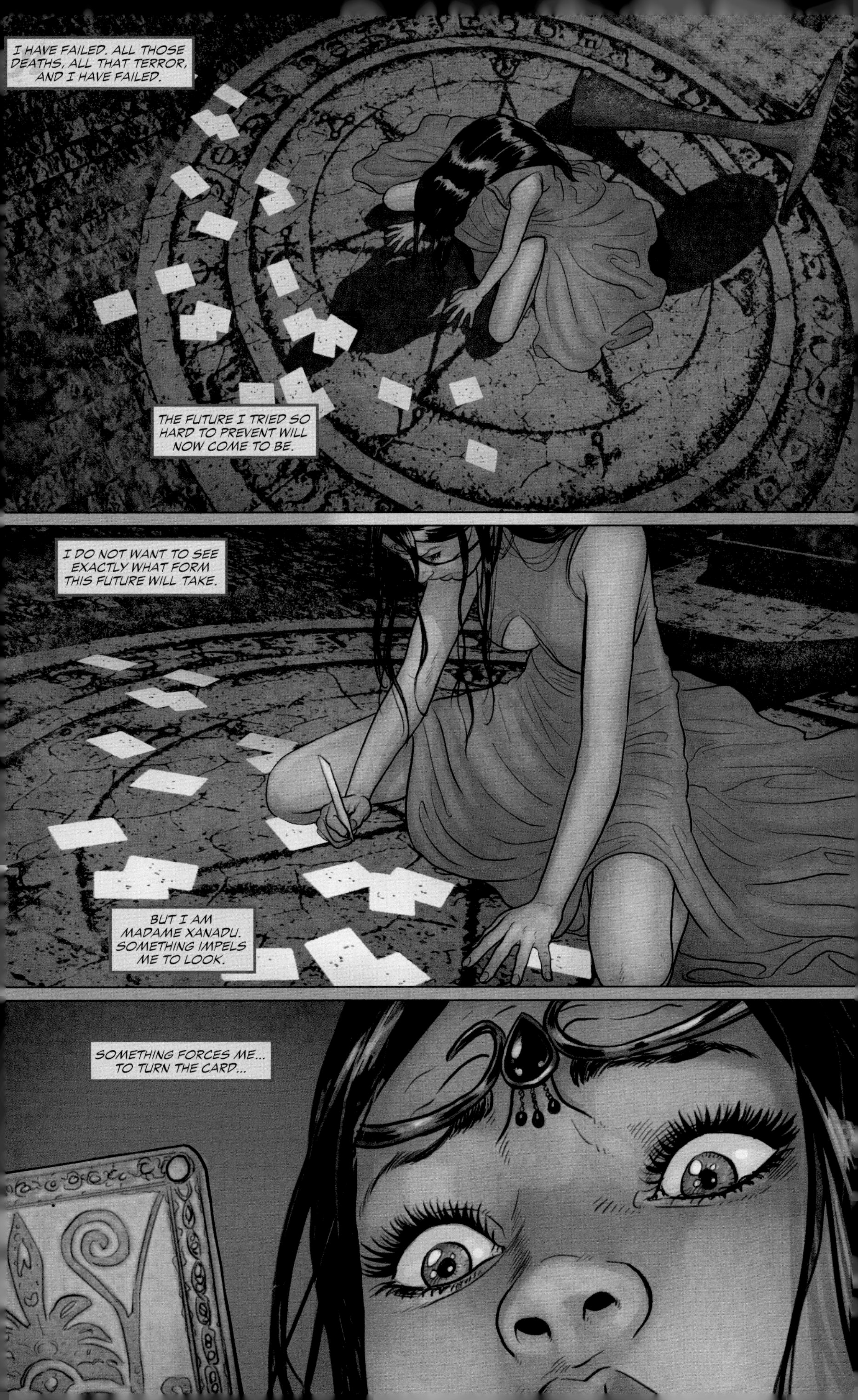
I HAVE FAILED. ALL THOSE DEATHS, ALL THAT TERROR, AND I HAVE FAILED.
THE FUTURE I TRIED SO HARD TO PREVENT WILL NOW COME TO BE.
I DO NOT WANT TO SEE EXACTLY WHAT FORM THIS FUTURE WILL TAKE.
BUT I AM MADAME XANADU. SOMETHING IMPELS ME TO LOOK.
SOMETHING FORCES ME... TO TURN THE CARD...

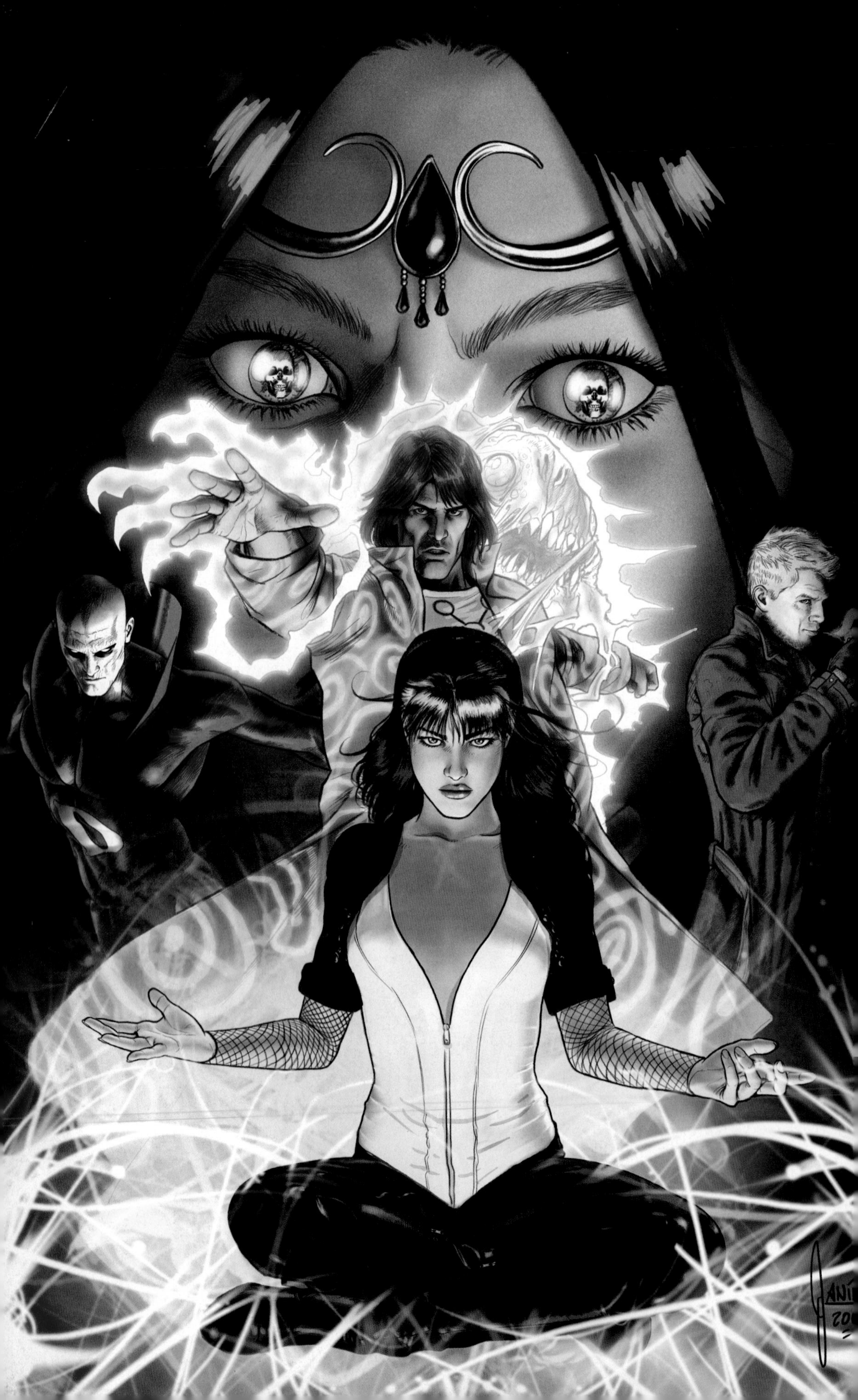

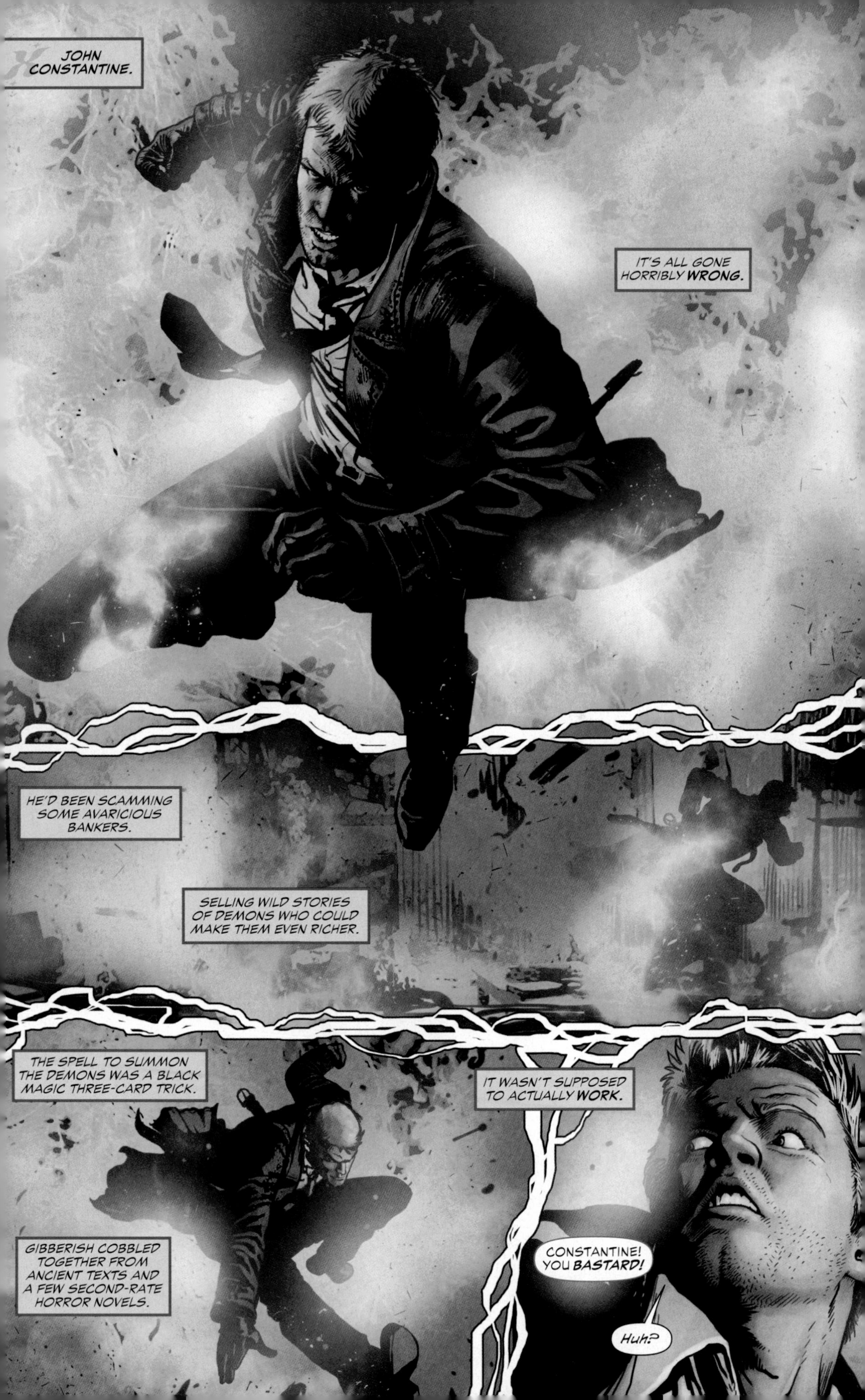
JOHN CONSTANTINE.
IT'S ALL GONE HORRIBLY WRONG.
HE'D BEEN SCAMMING SOME AVARICIOUS BANKERS.
SELLING WILD STORIES OF DEMONS WHO COULD MAKE THEM EVEN RICHER.
THE SPELL TO SUMMON THE DEMONS WAS A BLACK MAGIC THREE-CARD TRICK.
IT WASN'T SUPPOSED TO ACTUALLY WORK.
GIBBERISH COBBLED TOGETHER FROM ANCIENT TEXTS AND A FEW SECOND-RATE HORROR NOVELS.
CONSTANTINE! YOU BASTARD!
Huh?

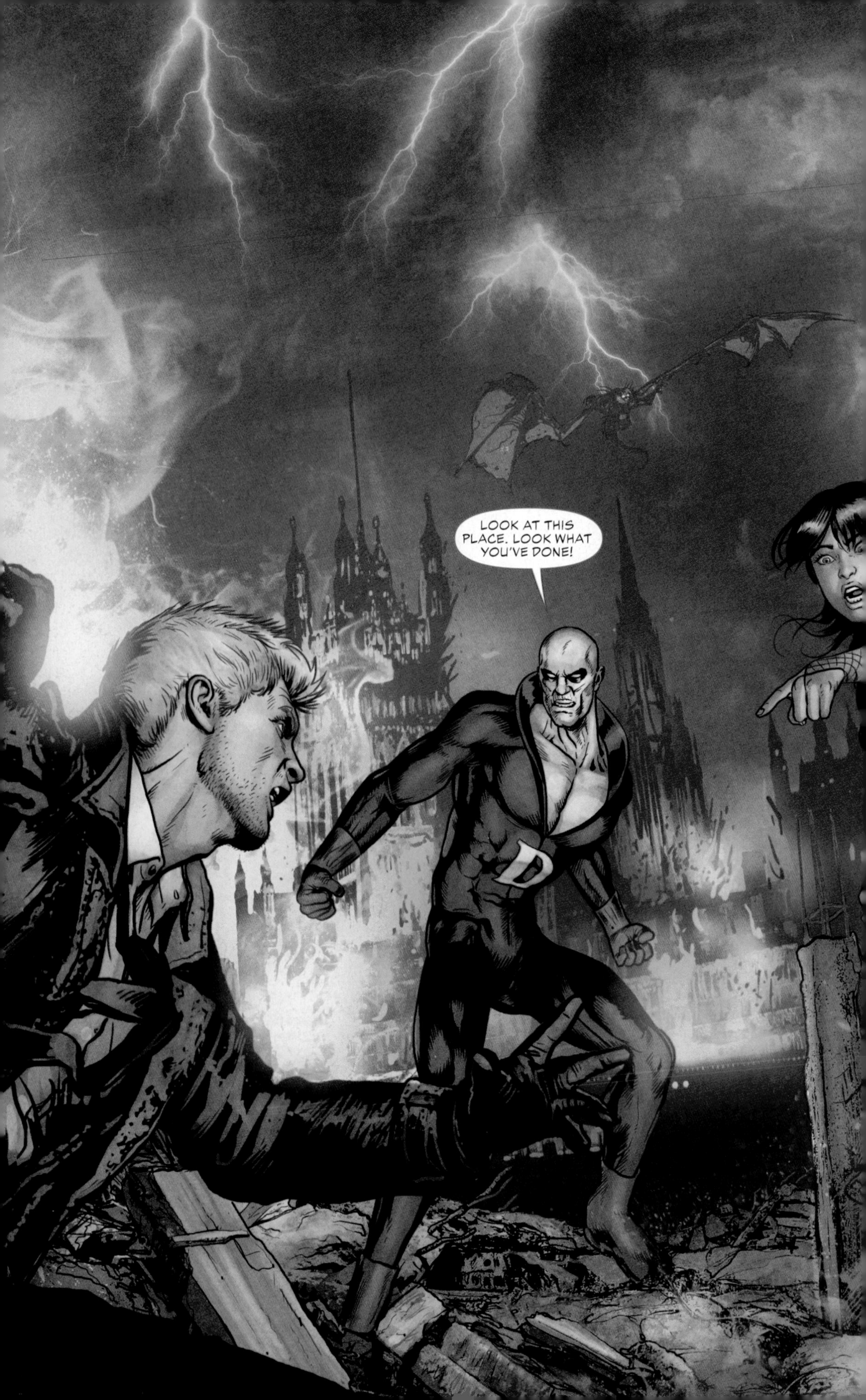
LOOK AT THIS PLACE. LOOK WHAT YOU'VE DONE!

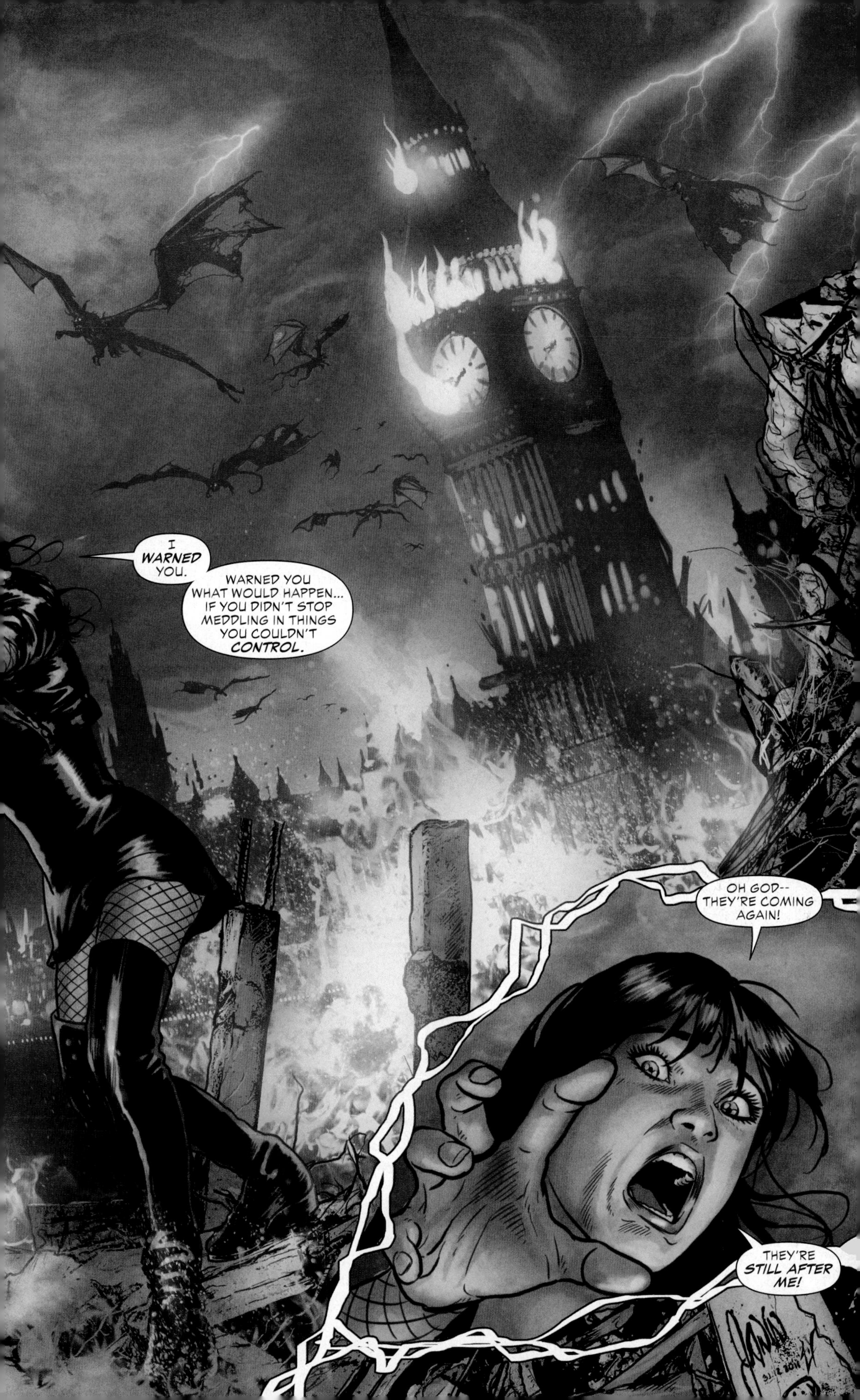
I WARNED YOU.
WARNED YOU WHAT WOULD HAPPEN... IF YOU DIDN'T STOP MEDDLING IN THINGS YOU COULDN'T CONTROL.
OH GOD-- THEY'RE COMING AGAIN!
THEY'RE STILL AFTER ME!

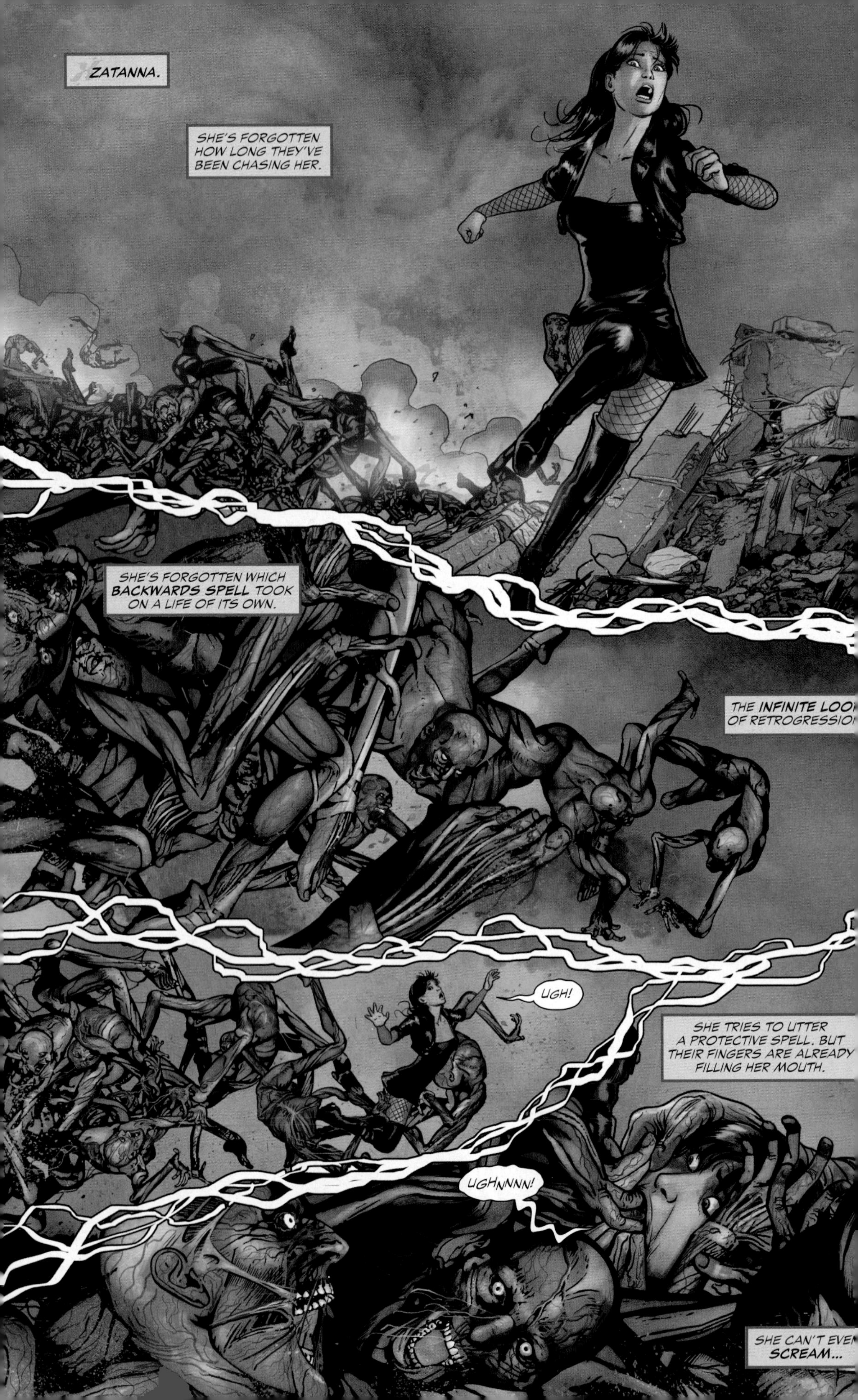
ZATANNA.
SHE'S FORGOTTEN HOW LONG THEY'VE BEEN CHASING HER.
SHE'S FORGOTTEN WHICH BACKWARDS SPELL TOOK ON A LIFE OF ITS OWN.
THE INFINITE LOO
OF RETROGRESSIO
UGH!
SHE TRIES TO UTTER A PROTECTIVE SPELL. BUT THEIR FINGERS ARE ALREADY FILLING HER MOUTH.
UGHNNNN!
SHE CAN'T EVE
SCREAM...

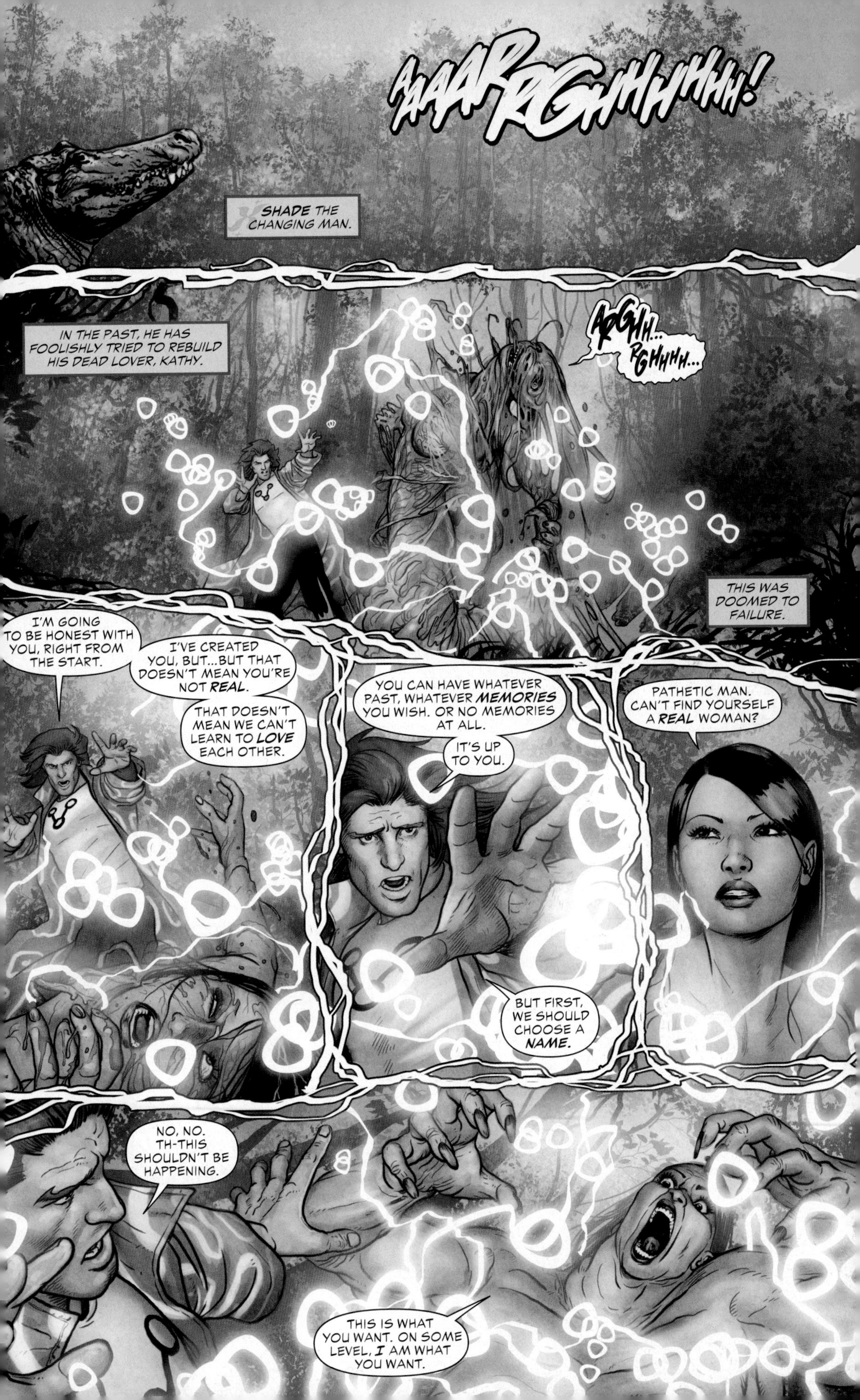

AAAARRGHHHHHH!
SHADE THE CHANGING MAN.
IN THE PAST, HE HAS FOOLISHLY TRIED TO REBUILD HIS DEAD LOVER, KATHY.
ARGHH... RGHHHH...
THIS WAS DOOMED TO FAILURE.
I'M GOING TO BE HONEST WITH YOU, RIGHT FROM THE START.
I'VE CREATED YOU, BUT...BUT THAT DOESN'T MEAN YOU'RE NOT REAL.
THAT DOESN'T MEAN WE CAN'T LEARN TO LOVE EACH OTHER.
YOU CAN HAVE WHATEVER PAST, WHATEVER MEMORIES YOU WISH. OR NO MEMORIES AT ALL.
IT'S UP TO YOU.
BUT FIRST, WE SHOULD CHOOSE A NAME.
PATHETIC MAN. CAN'T FIND YOURSELF A REAL WOMAN?
NO, NO. TH-THIS SHOULDN'T BE HAPPENING.
THIS IS WHAT YOU WANT. ON SOME LEVEL, I AM WHAT YOU WANT.

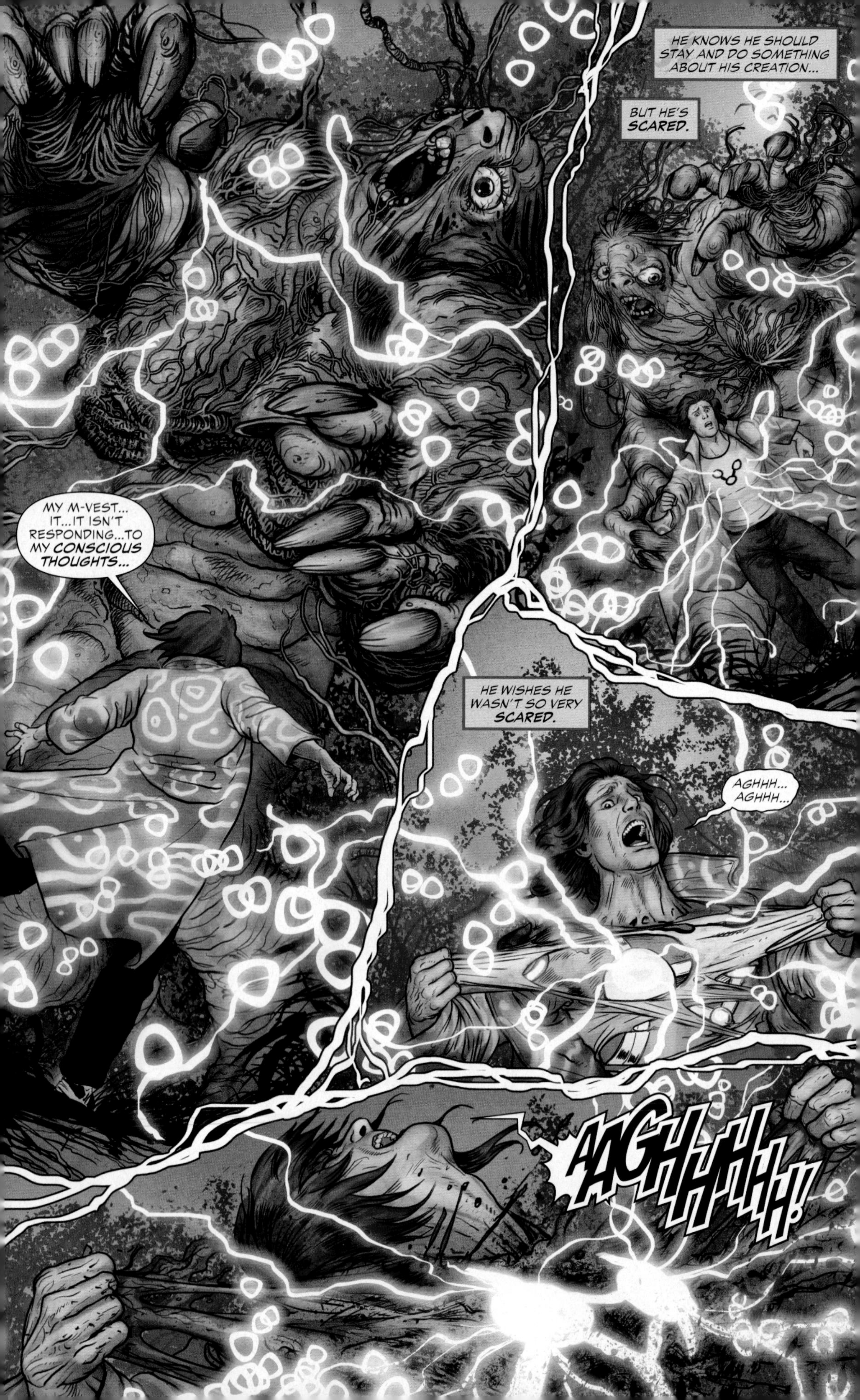
HE KNOWS HE SHOULD STAY AND DO SOMETHING ABOUT HIS CREATION...
BUT HE'S SCARED.
MY M-VEST... IT...IT ISN'T RESPONDING...TO MY CONSCIOUS THOUGHTS...
HE WISHES HE WASN'T SO VERY SCARED.
AGHHH... AGHHH...
AAGHHHHHH!

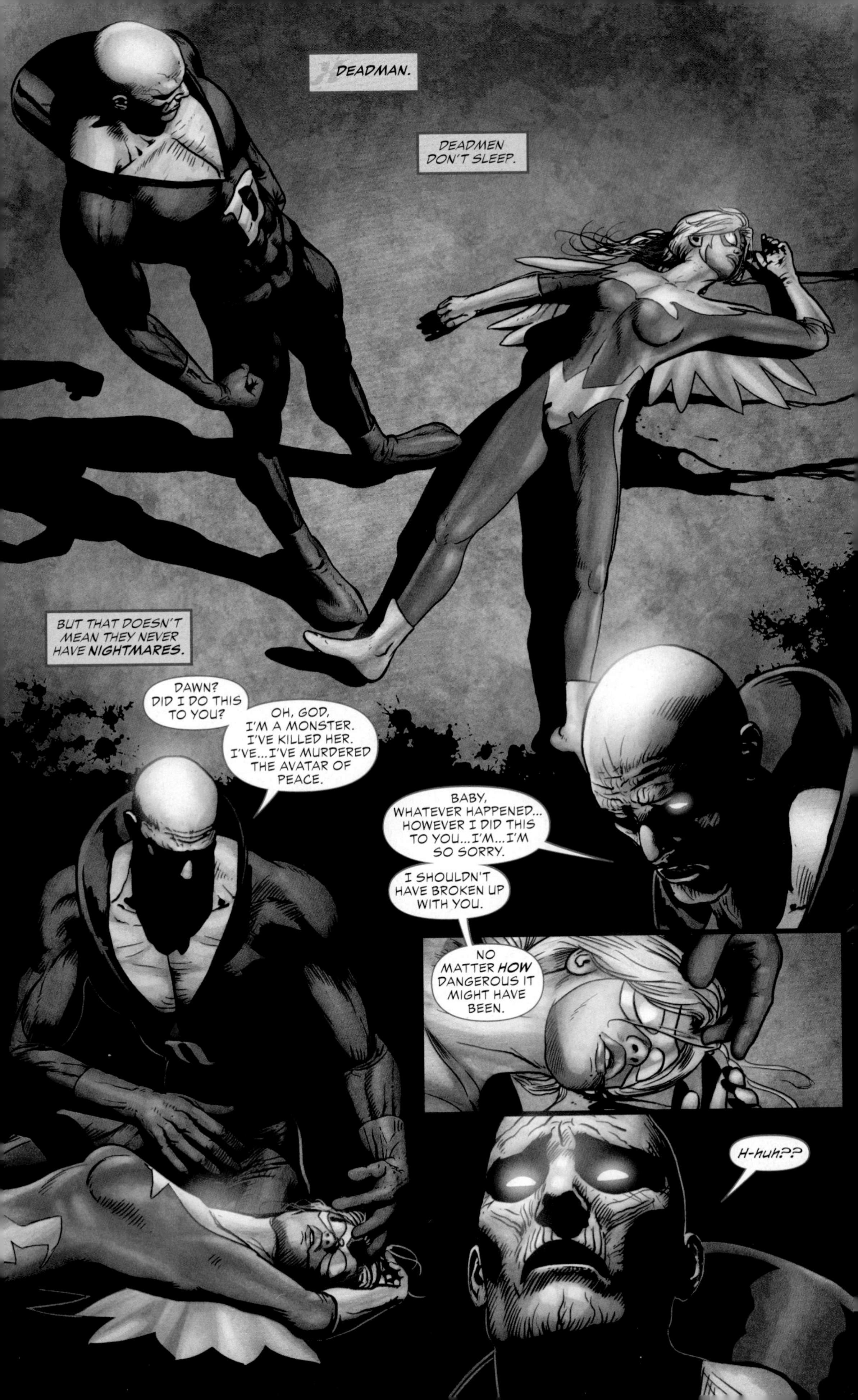
DEADMAN.
DEADMEN DON'T SLEEP.
BUT THAT DOESN'T MEAN THEY NEVER HAVE NIGHTMARES.
DAWN? DID I DO THIS TO YOU?
OH, GOD, I'M A MONSTER. I'VE KILLED HER. I'VE...I'VE MURDERED THE AVATAR OF PEACE.
BABY, WHATEVER HAPPENED... HOWEVER I DID THIS TO YOU...I'M...I'M SO SORRY.
I SHOULDN'T HAVE BROKEN UP WITH YOU.
NO MATTER HOW DANGEROUS IT MIGHT HAVE BEEN.
H-huh??

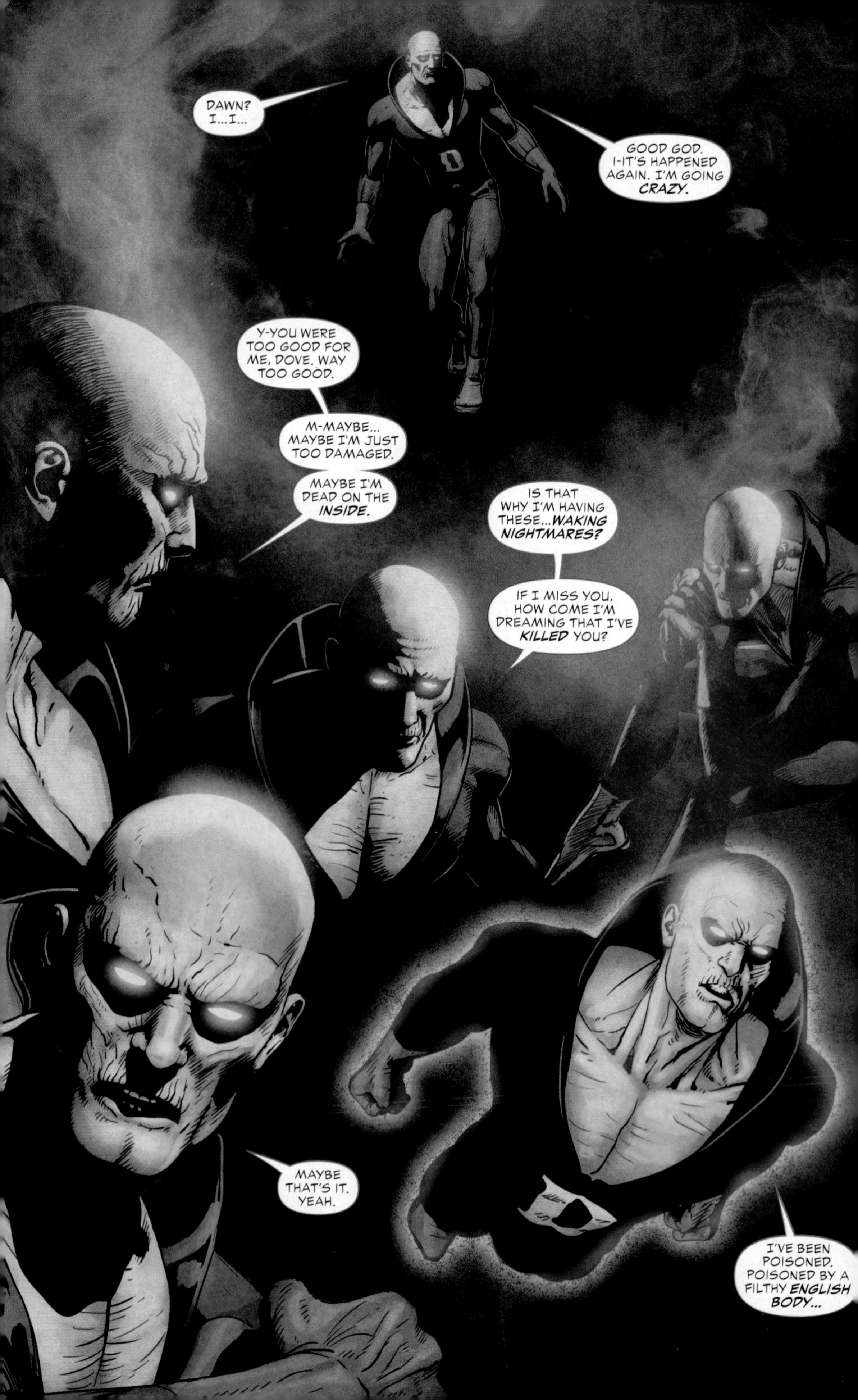
DAWN? I...I...
GOOD GOD. I-IT'S HAPPENED AGAIN. I'M GOING CRAZY.
Y-YOU WERE TOO GOOD FOR ME, DOVE. WAY TOO GOOD.
M-MAYBE... MAYBE I'M JUST TOO DAMAGED.
MAYBE I'M DEAD ON THE INSIDE.
IS THAT WHY I'M HAVING THESE...WAKING NIGHTMARES?
IF I MISS YOU, HOW COME I'M DREAMING THAT I'VE KILLED YOU?
MAYBE THAT'S IT. YEAH.
I'VE BEEN POISONED. POISONED BY A FILTHY ENGLISH BODY...

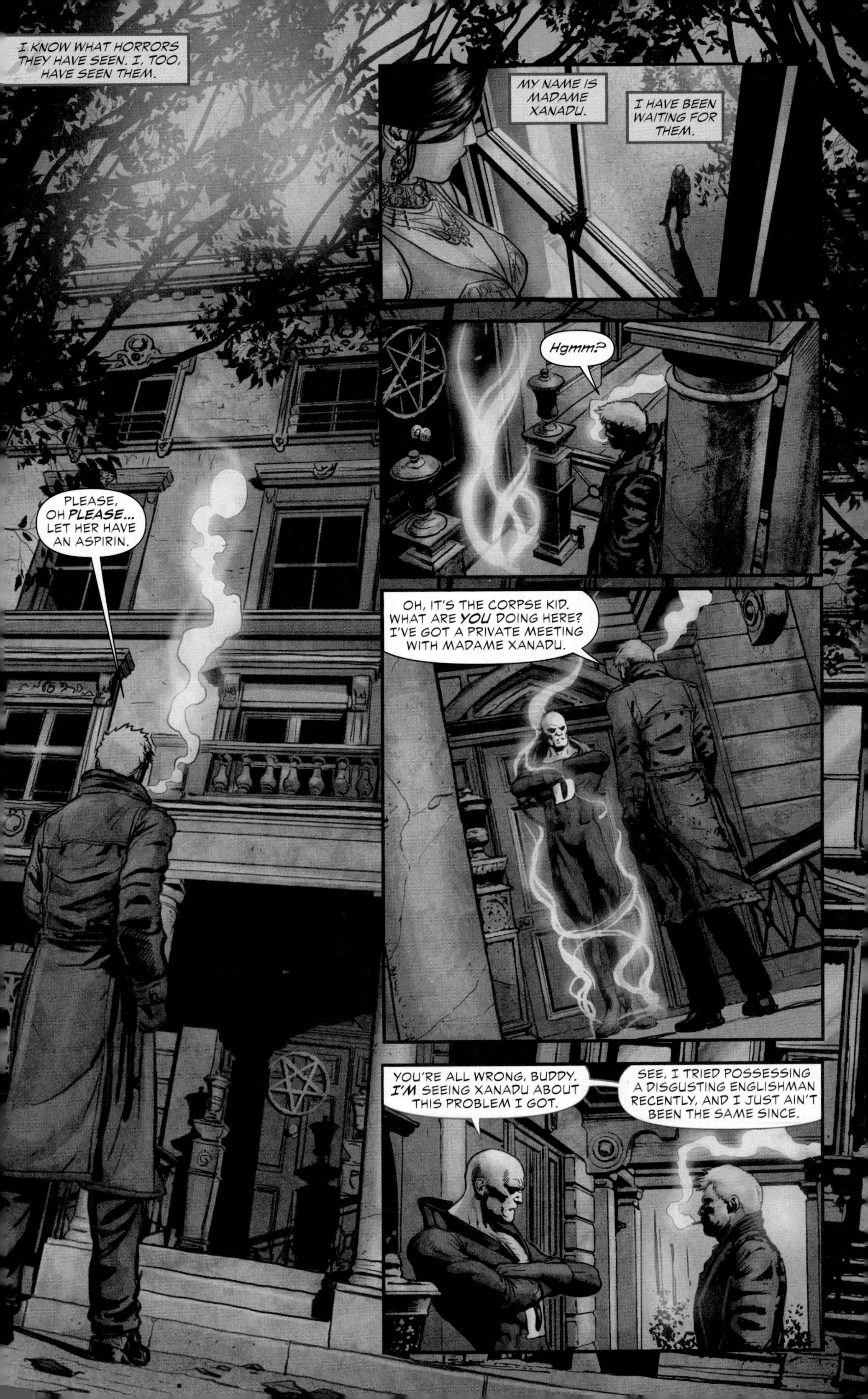
I KNOW WHAT HORRORS THEY HAVE SEEN. I, TOO, HAVE SEEN THEM.
MY NAME IS MADAME XANADU.
I HAVE BEEN WAITING FOR THEM.
PLEASE, OH PLEASE... LET HER HAVE AN ASPIRIN.
Hgmm?
OH, IT'S THE CORPSE KID. WHAT ARE YOU DOING HERE? I'VE GOT A PRIVATE MEETING WITH MADAME XANADU.
YOU'RE ALL WRONG, BUDDY. I'M SEEING XANADU ABOUT THIS PROBLEM I GOT.
SEE, I TRIED POSSESSING A DISGUSTING ENGLISHMAN RECENTLY, AND I JUST AIN'T BEEN THE SAME SINCE.

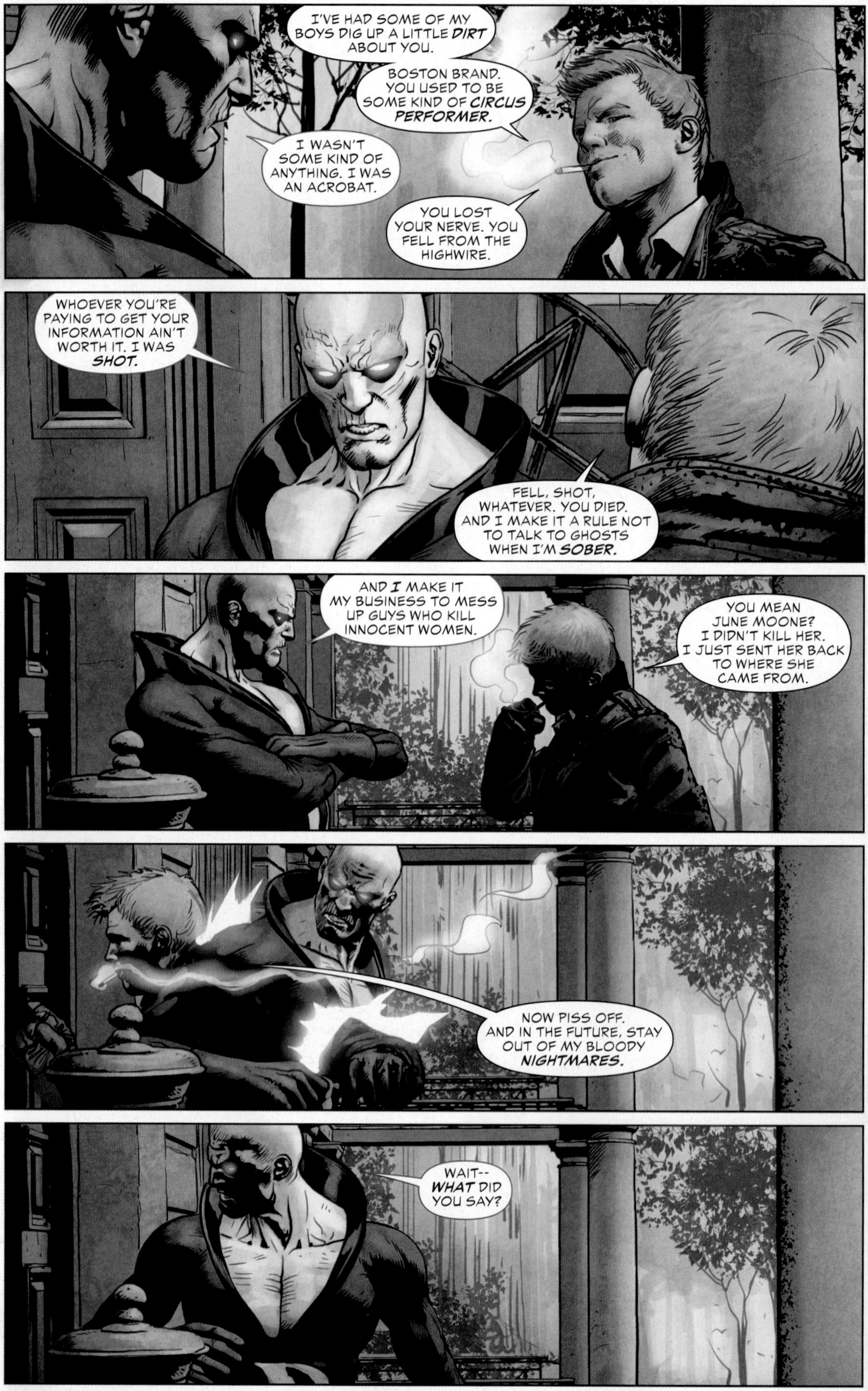
I'VE HAD SOME OF MY BOYS DIG UP A LITTLE DIRT ABOUT YOU.
BOSTON BRAND. YOU USED TO BE SOME KIND OF CIRCUS PERFORMER.
I WASN'T SOME KIND OF ANYTHING. I WAS AN ACROBAT.
YOU LOST YOUR NERVE. YOU FELL FROM THE HIGHWIRE.
WHOEVER YOU'RE PAYING TO GET YOUR INFORMATION AIN'T WORTH IT. I WAS SHOT.
FELL, SHOT, WHATEVER. YOU DIED. AND I MAKE IT A RULE NOT TO TALK TO GHOSTS WHEN I'M SOBER.
AND I MAKE IT MY BUSINESS TO MESS UP GUYS WHO KILL INNOCENT WOMEN.
YOU MEAN JUNE MOONE? I DIDN'T KILL HER. I JUST SENT HER BACK TO WHERE SHE CAME FROM.
NOW PISS OFF. AND IN THE FUTURE, STAY OUT OF MY BLOODY NIGHTMARES.
WAIT-- WHAT DID YOU SAY?

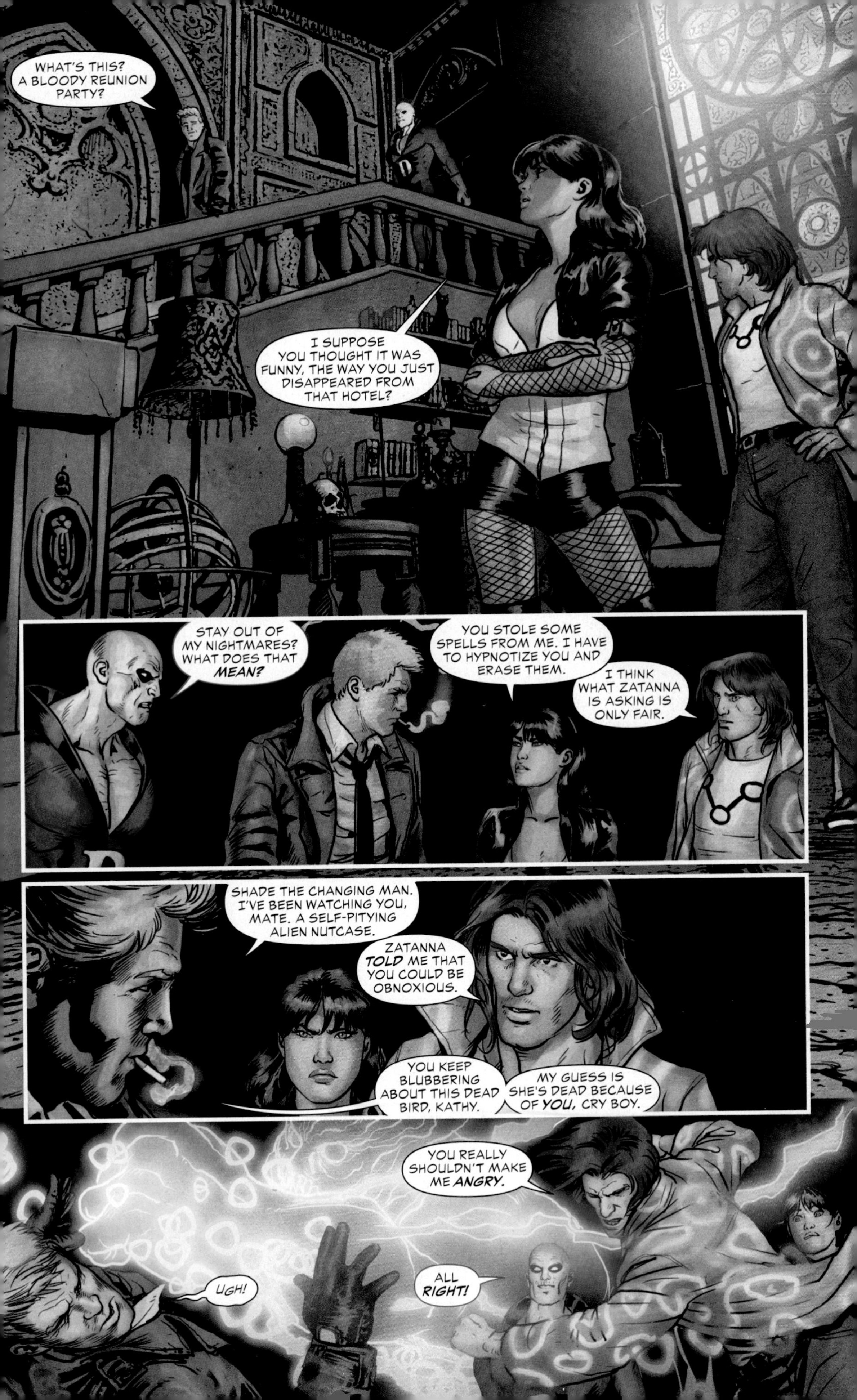
WHAT'S THIS? A BLOODY REUNION PARTY?
I SUPPOSE YOU THOUGHT IT WAS FUNNY, THE WAY YOU JUST DISAPPEARED FROM THAT HOTEL?
STAY OUT OF MY NIGHTMARES? WHAT DOES THAT MEAN?
YOU STOLE SOME SPELLS FROM ME. I HAVE TO HYPNOTIZE YOU AND ERASE THEM.
I THINK WHAT ZATANNA IS ASKING IS ONLY FAIR.
SHADE THE CHANGING MAN. I'VE BEEN WATCHING YOU, MATE. A SELF-PITYING ALIEN NUTCASE.
ZATANNA TOLD ME THAT YOU COULD BE OBNOXIOUS.
YOU KEEP BLUBBERING ABOUT THIS DEAD BIRD, KATHY.
MY GUESS IS SHE'S DEAD BECAUSE OF YOU, CRY BOY.
YOU REALLY SHOULDN'T MAKE ME ANGRY.
UGH!
ALL RIGHT!

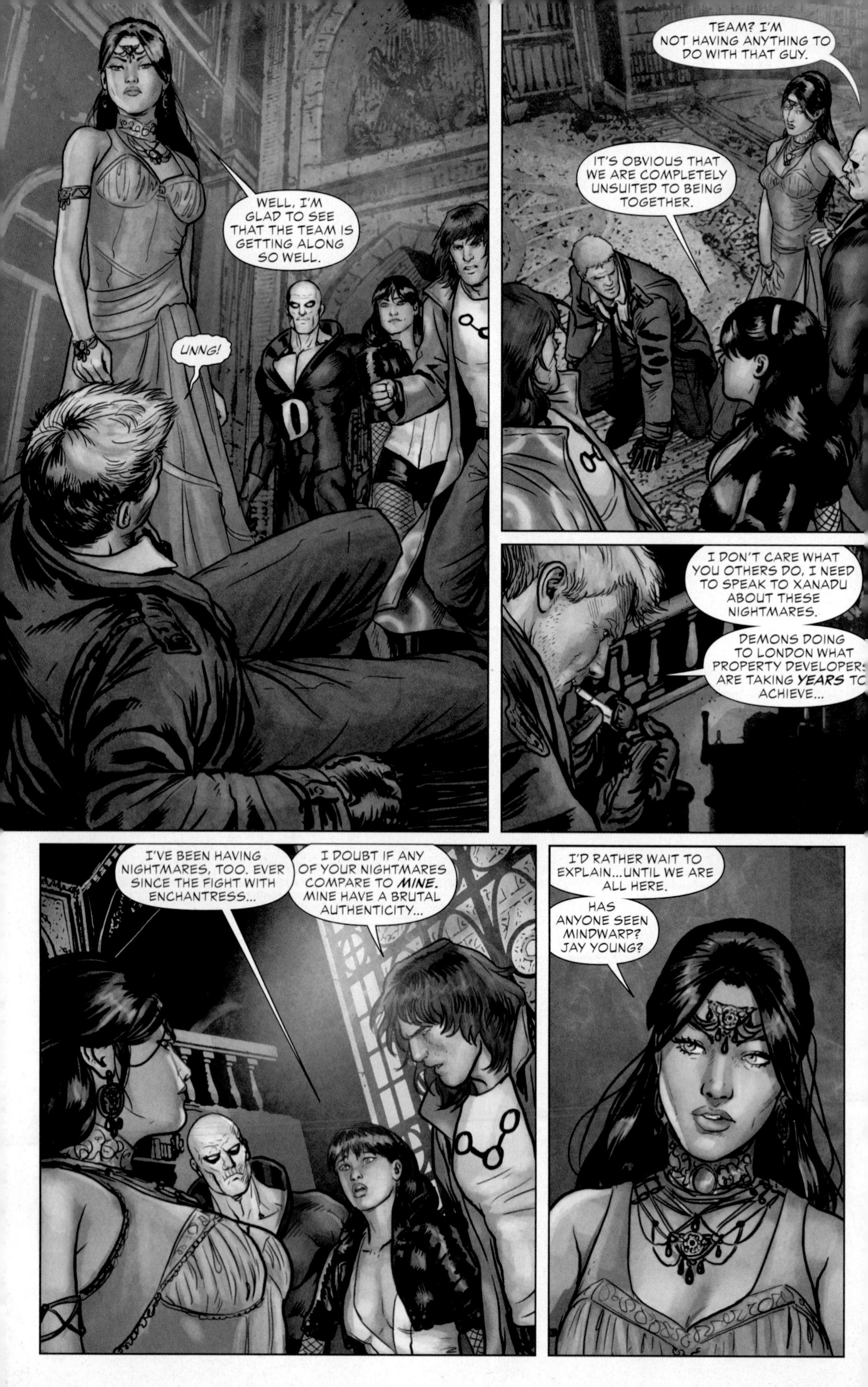
WELL, I'M GLAD TO SEE THAT THE TEAM IS GETTING ALONG SO WELL.
UNNG!
TEAM? I'M NOT HAVING ANYTHING TO DO WITH THAT GUY.
IT'S OBVIOUS THAT WE ARE COMPLETELY UNSUITED TO BEING TOGETHER.
I DON'T CARE WHAT YOU OTHERS DO, I NEED TO SPEAK TO XANADU ABOUT THESE NIGHTMARES.
DEMONS DOING TO LONDON WHAT PROPERTY DEVELOPERS ARE TAKING *YEARS* TO ACHIEVE...
I'VE BEEN HAVING NIGHTMARES, TOO. EVER SINCE THE FIGHT WITH ENCHANTRESS...
I DOUBT IF ANY OF YOUR NIGHTMARES COMPARE TO ***MINE.*** MINE HAVE A BRUTAL AUTHENTICITY...
I'D RATHER WAIT TO EXPLAIN...UNTIL WE ARE ALL HERE.
HAS ANYONE SEEN MINDWARP? JAY YOUNG?

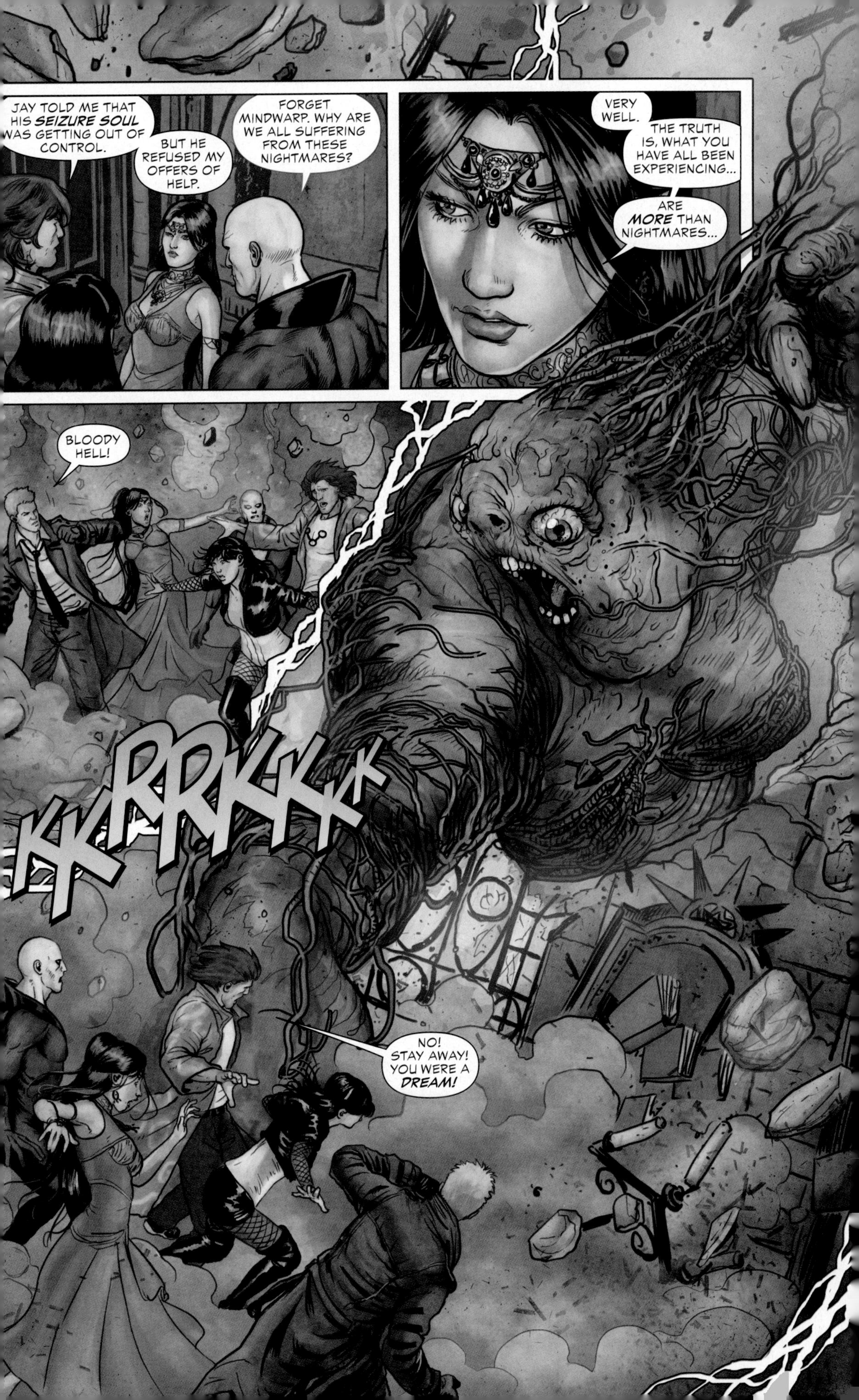
JAY TOLD ME THAT HIS SEIZURE SOUL WAS GETTING OUT OF CONTROL.
BUT HE REFUSED MY OFFERS OF HELP.
FORGET MINDWARP. WHY ARE WE ALL SUFFERING FROM THESE NIGHTMARES?
VERY WELL.
THE TRUTH IS, WHAT YOU HAVE ALL BEEN EXPERIENCING...
ARE MORE THAN NIGHTMARES...
BLOODY HELL!
KKRRKKKK
NO! STAY AWAY! YOU WERE A DREAM!

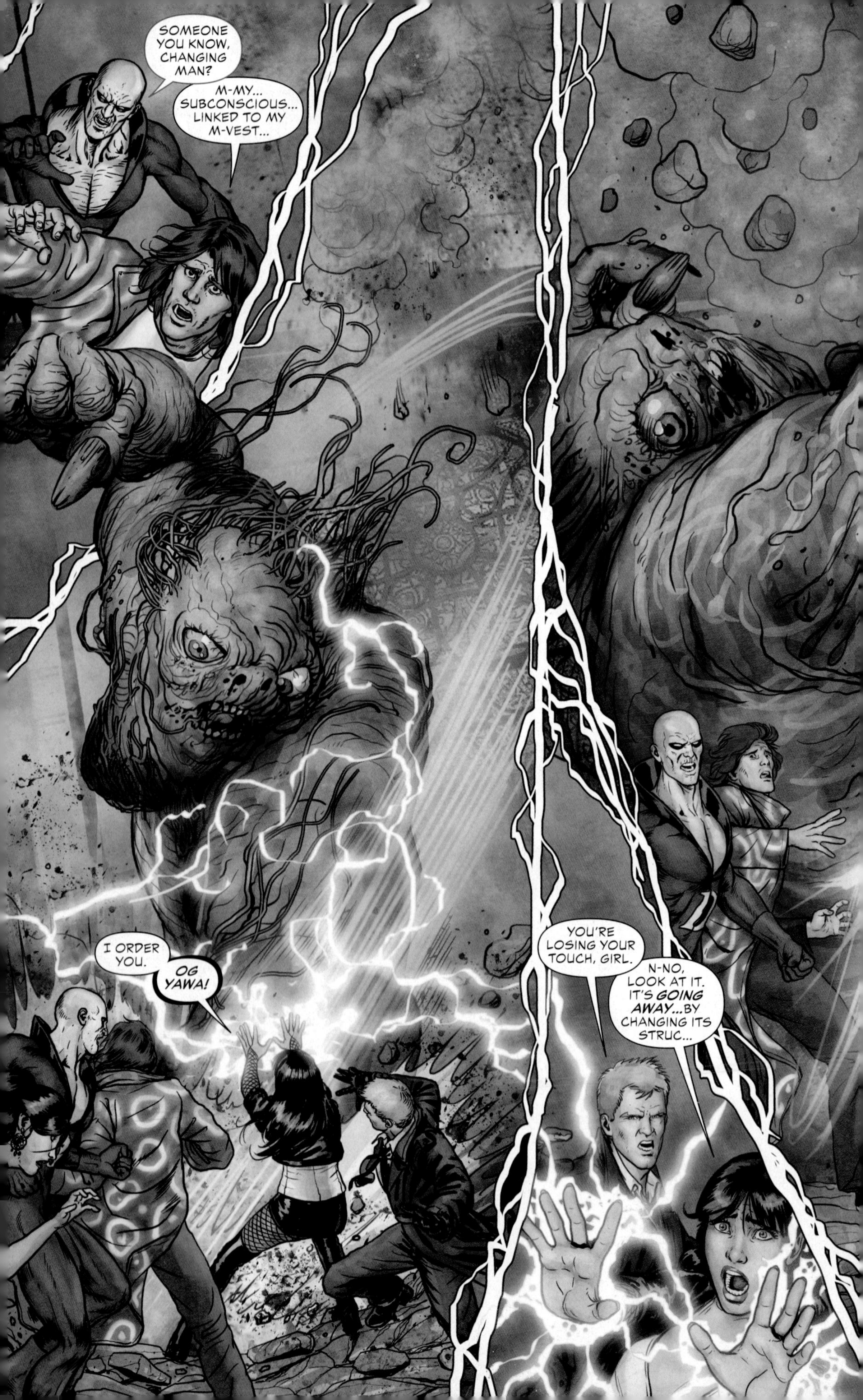
SOMEONE YOU KNOW, CHANGING MAN?
M-MY... SUBCONSCIOUS... LINKED TO MY M-VEST...
I ORDER YOU.
OG YAWA!
YOU'RE LOSING YOUR TOUCH, GIRL.
N-NO, LOOK AT IT. IT'S GOING AWAY...BY CHANGING ITS STRUC...

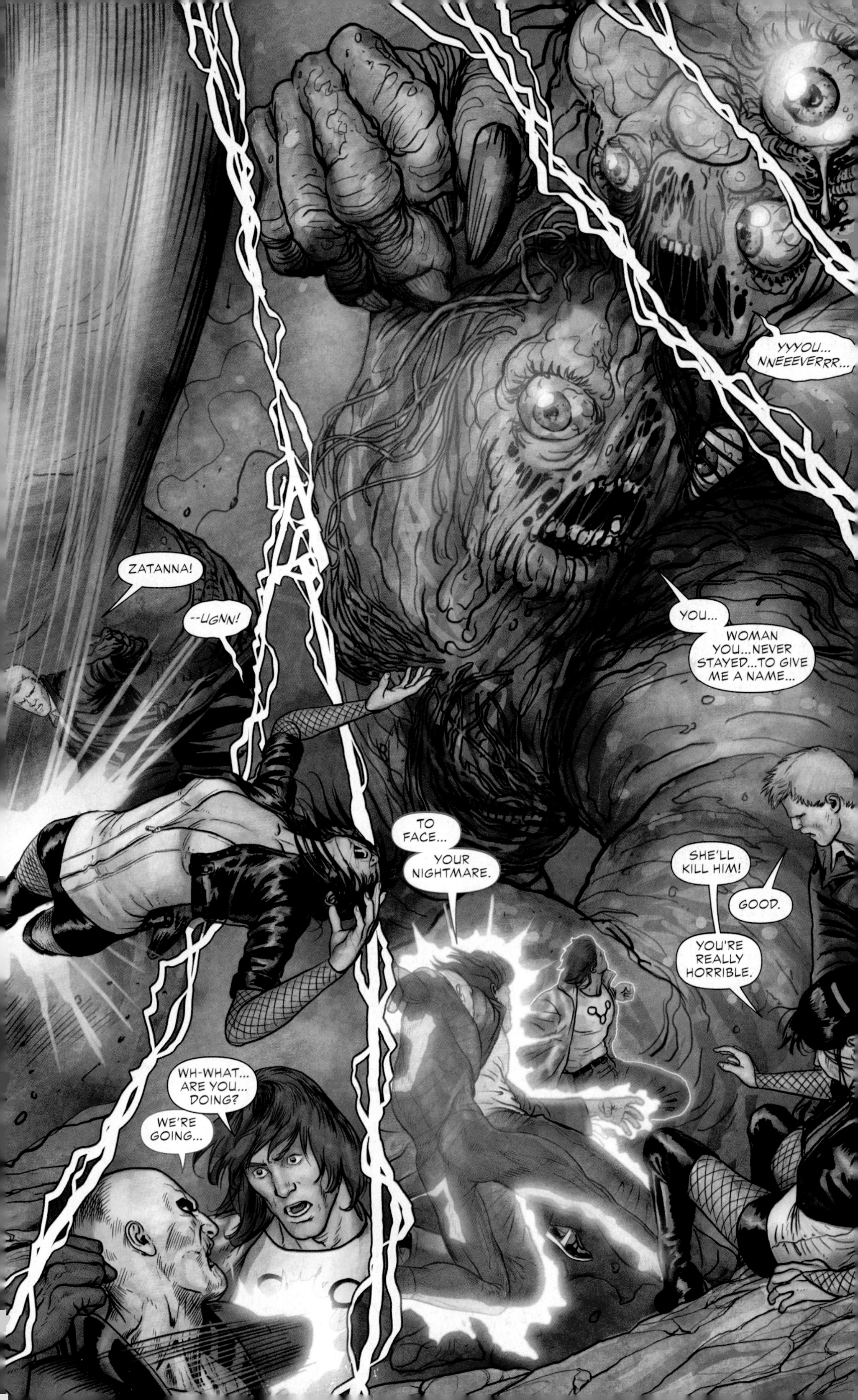
YYYOU... NNEEEVERRR...
ZATANNA!
--UGNN!
YOU...
WOMAN YOU...NEVER STAYED...TO GIVE ME A NAME...
TO FACE...
YOUR NIGHTMARE.
SHE'LL KILL HIM!
GOOD.
YOU'RE REALLY HORRIBLE.
WH-WHAT... ARE YOU... DOING?
WE'RE GOING...

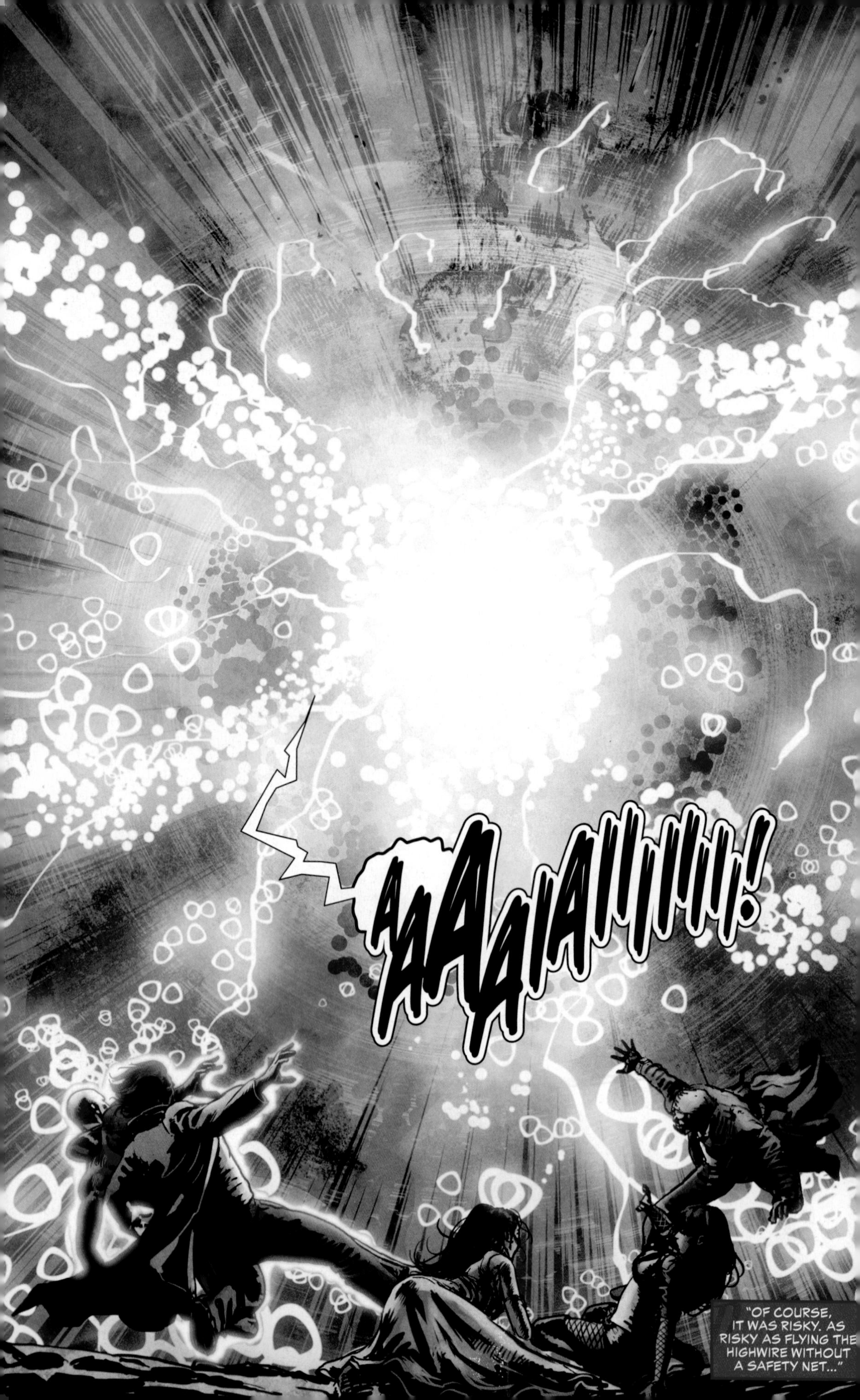
ZZAAAIIIIIIIII!
"OF COURSE, IT WAS RISKY. AS RISKY AS FLYING THE HIGHWIRE WITHOUT A SAFETY NET..."

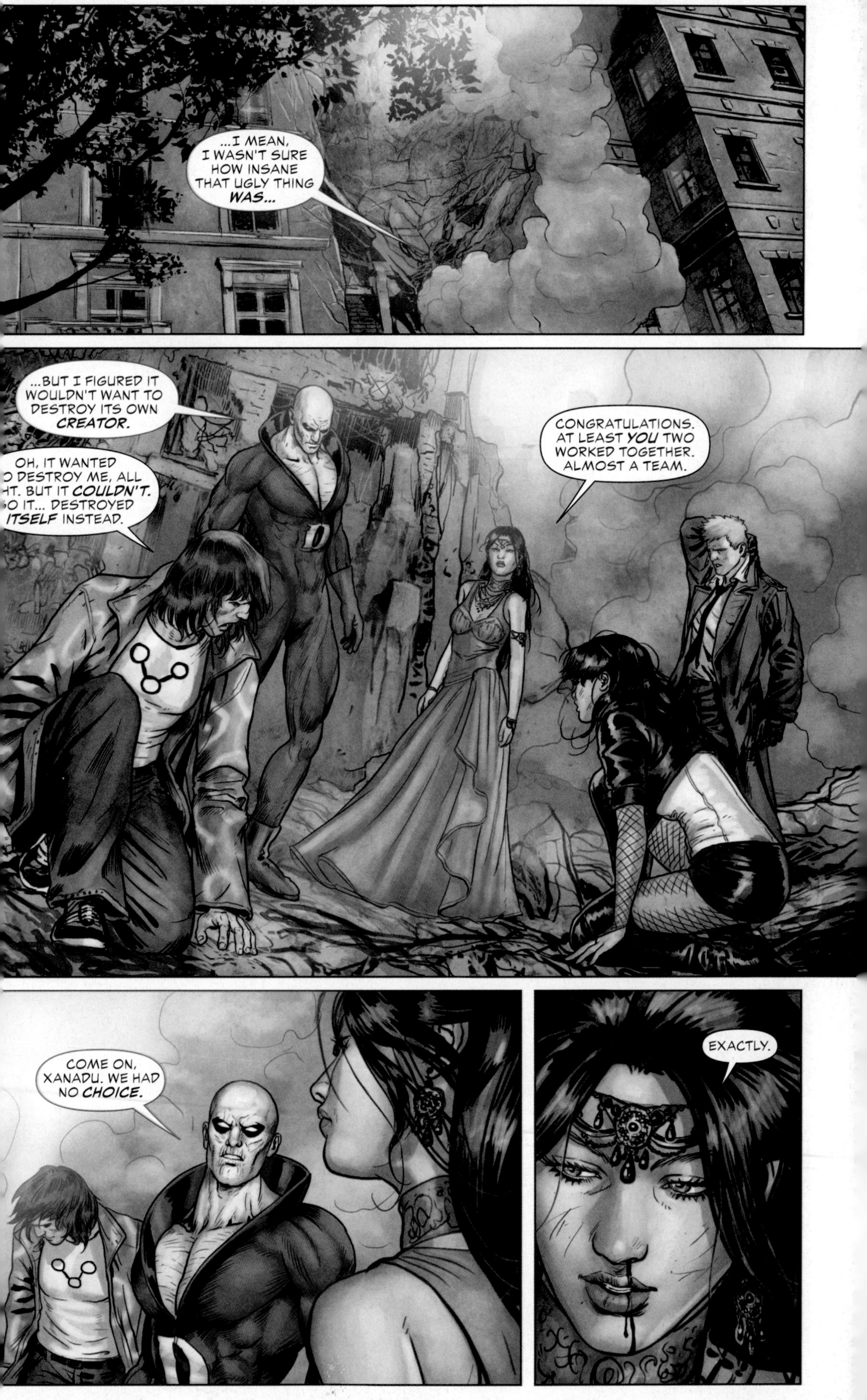
...I MEAN, I WASN'T SURE HOW INSANE THAT UGLY THING WAS...
...BUT I FIGURED IT WOULDN'T WANT TO DESTROY ITS OWN CREATOR.
OH, IT WANTED O DESTROY ME, ALL HT. BUT IT COULDN'T. O IT... DESTROYED ITSELF INSTEAD.
CONGRATULATIONS. AT LEAST YOU TWO WORKED TOGETHER. ALMOST A TEAM.
COME ON, XANADU. WE HAD NO CHOICE.
EXACTLY.

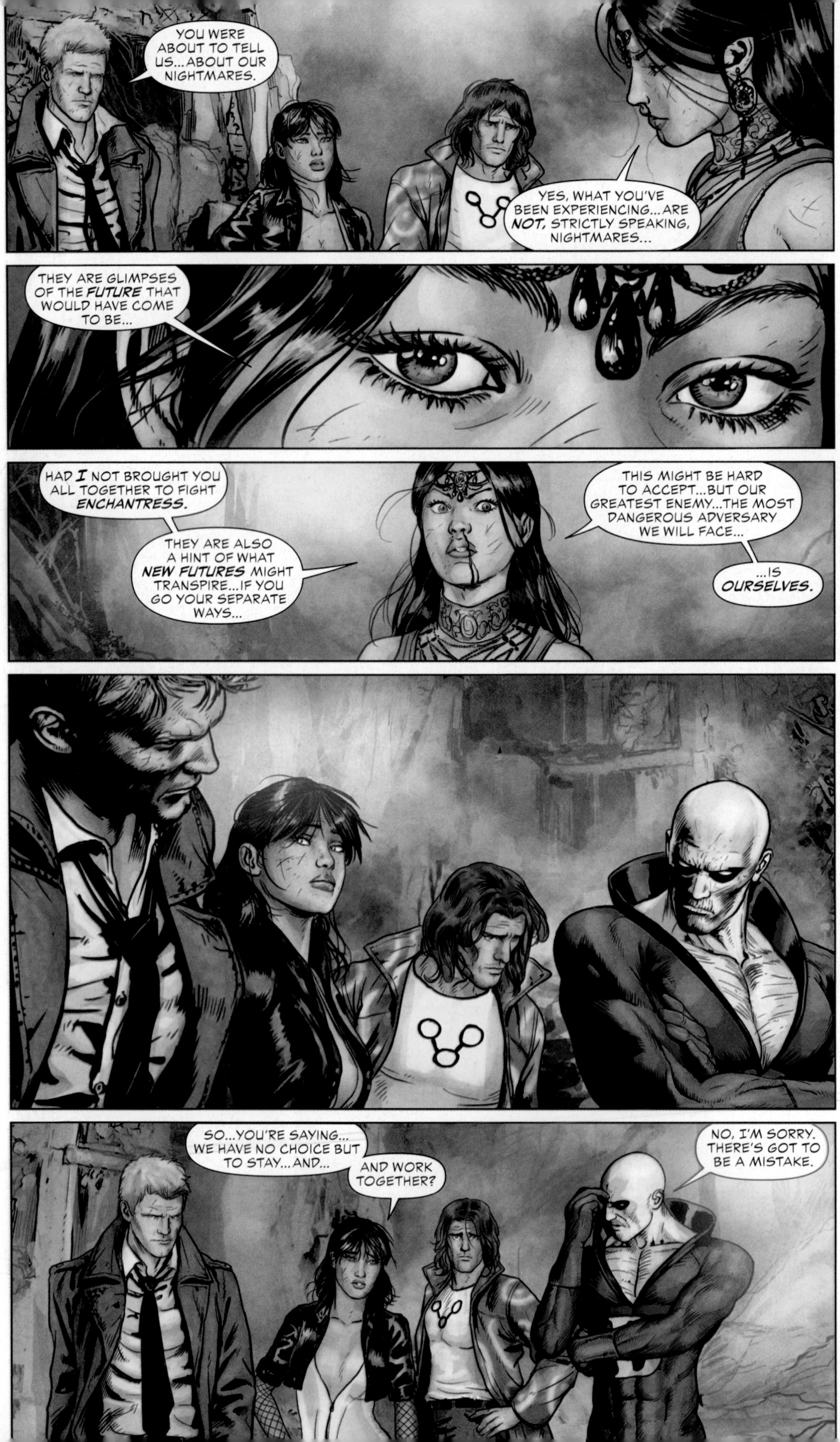
YOU WERE ABOUT TO TELL US...ABOUT OUR NIGHTMARES.
YES, WHAT YOU'VE BEEN EXPERIENCING...ARE NOT, STRICTLY SPEAKING, NIGHTMARES...
THEY ARE GLIMPSES OF THE FUTURE THAT WOULD HAVE COME TO BE...
HAD I NOT BROUGHT YOU ALL TOGETHER TO FIGHT ENCHANTRESS.
THEY ARE ALSO A HINT OF WHAT NEW FUTURES MIGHT TRANSPIRE...IF YOU GO YOUR SEPARATE WAYS...
THIS MIGHT BE HARD TO ACCEPT...BUT OUR GREATEST ENEMY...THE MOST DANGEROUS ADVERSARY WE WILL FACE...
...IS OURSELVES.
SO...YOU'RE SAYING... WE HAVE NO CHOICE BUT TO STAY...AND...
AND WORK TOGETHER?
NO, I'M SORRY. THERE'S GOT TO BE A MISTAKE.

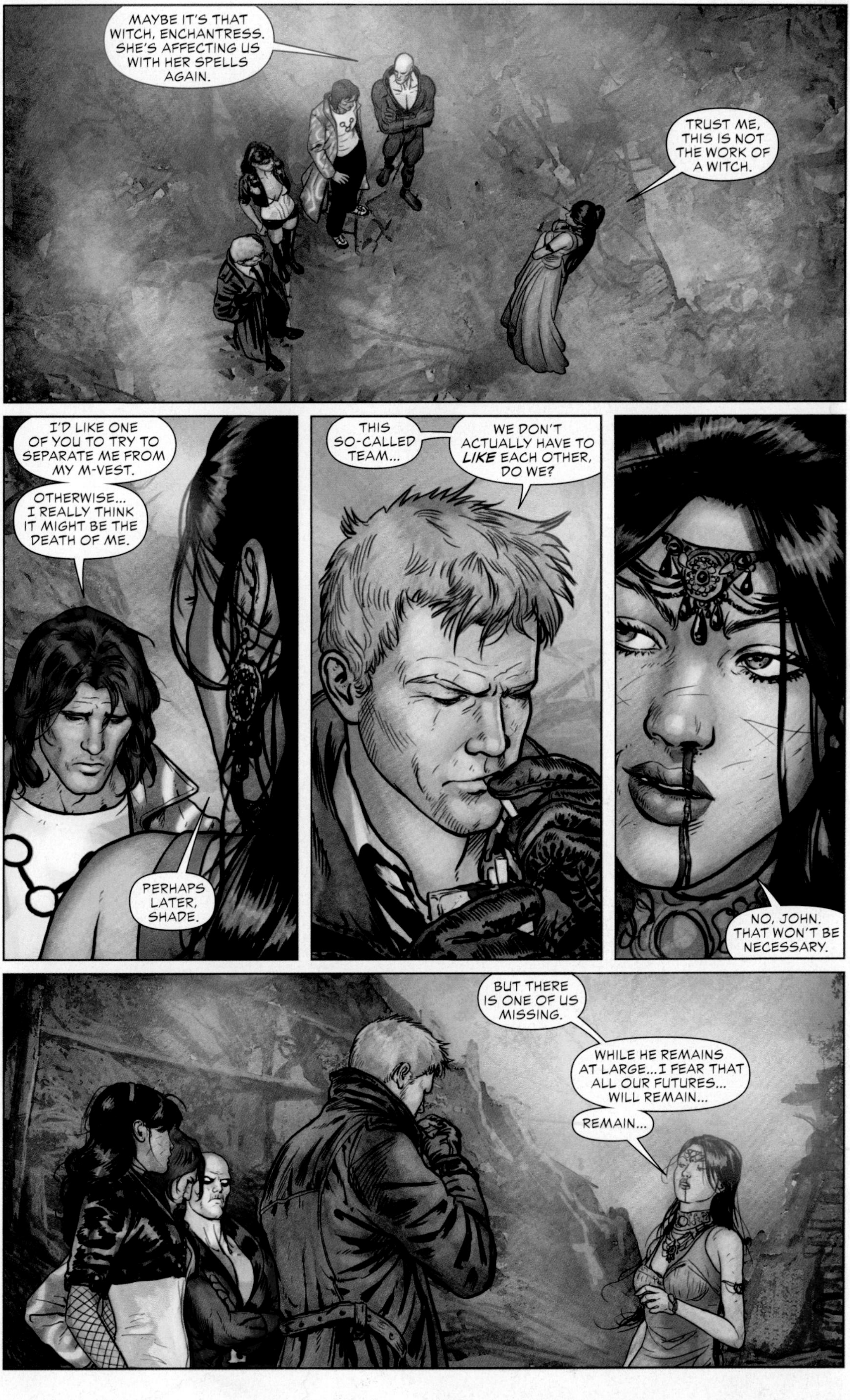
MAYBE IT'S THAT WITCH, ENCHANTRESS. SHE'S AFFECTING US WITH HER SPELLS AGAIN.
TRUST ME, THIS IS NOT THE WORK OF A WITCH.
I'D LIKE ONE OF YOU TO TRY TO SEPARATE ME FROM MY M-VEST.
OTHERWISE... I REALLY THINK IT MIGHT BE THE DEATH OF ME.
PERHAPS LATER, SHADE.
THIS SO-CALLED TEAM...
WE DON'T ACTUALLY HAVE TO *LIKE* EACH OTHER, DO WE?
NO, JOHN. THAT WON'T BE NECESSARY.
BUT THERE IS ONE OF US MISSING.
WHILE HE REMAINS AT LARGE...I FEAR THAT ALL OUR FUTURES... WILL REMAIN...
REMAIN...

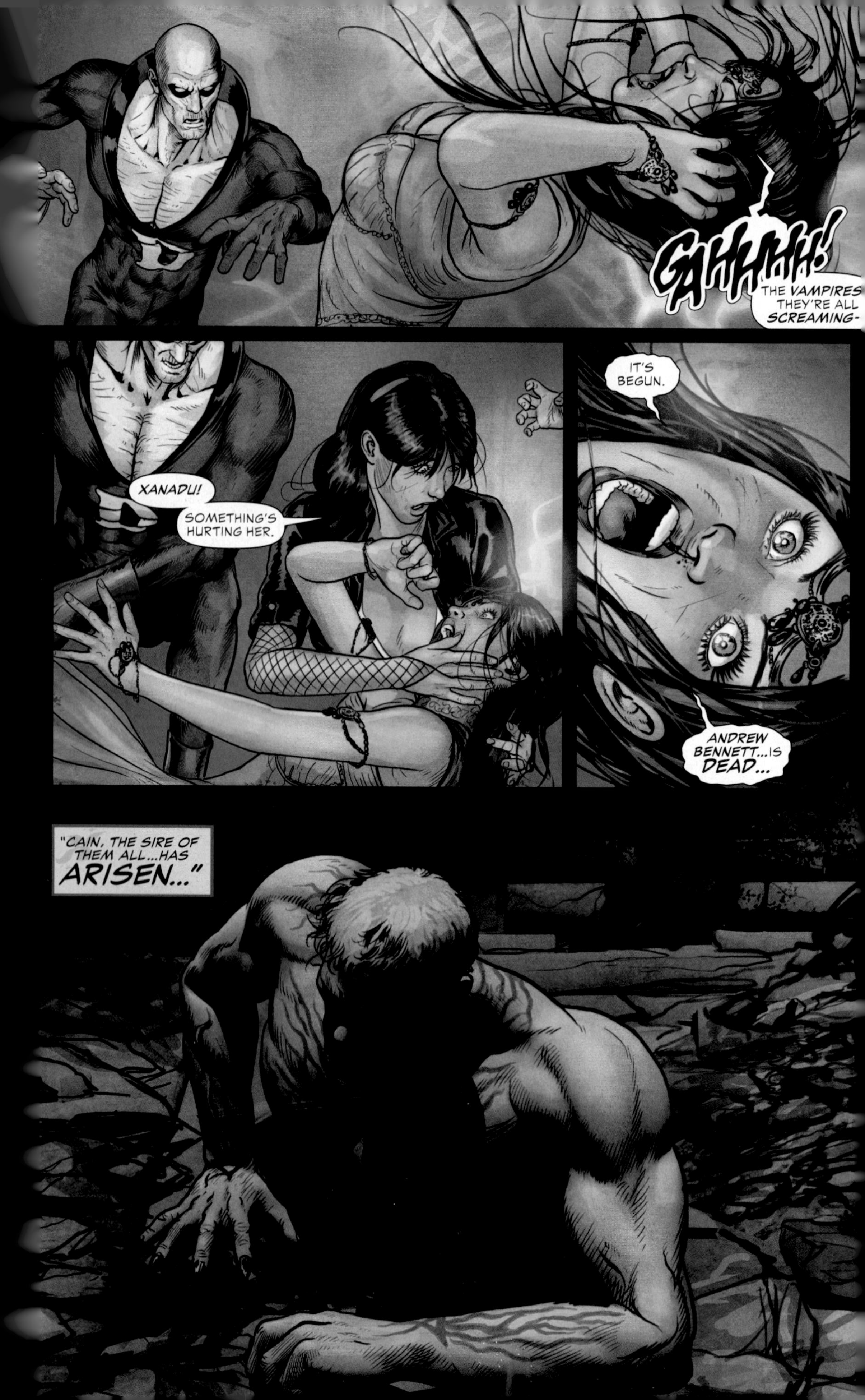
GAHHHHH!
THE VAMPIRES THEY'RE ALL SCREAMING-
XANADU!
SOMETHING'S HURTING HER.
IT'S BEGUN.
ANDREW BENNETT...IS DEAD...
"CAIN, THE SIRE OF THEM ALL...HAS ARISEN..."

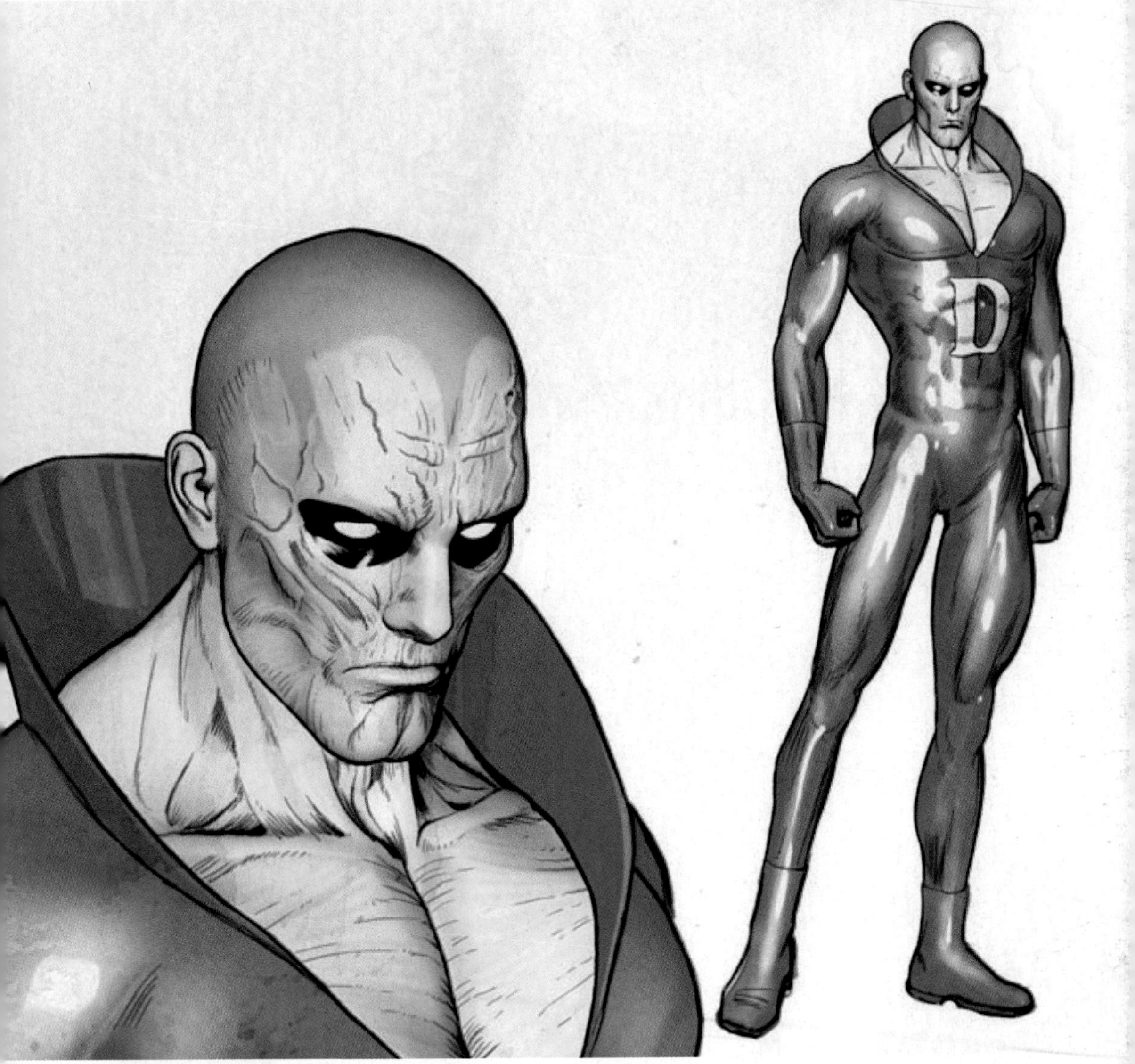
D

Deadman

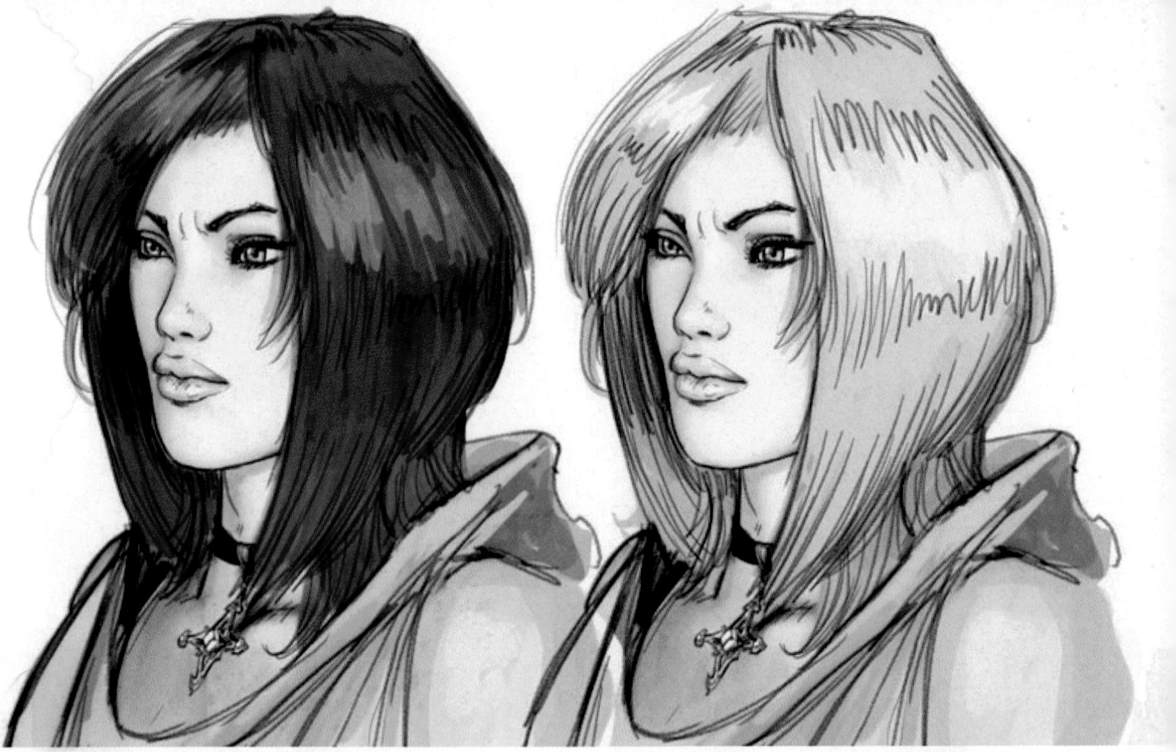

June Moone / Enchantress

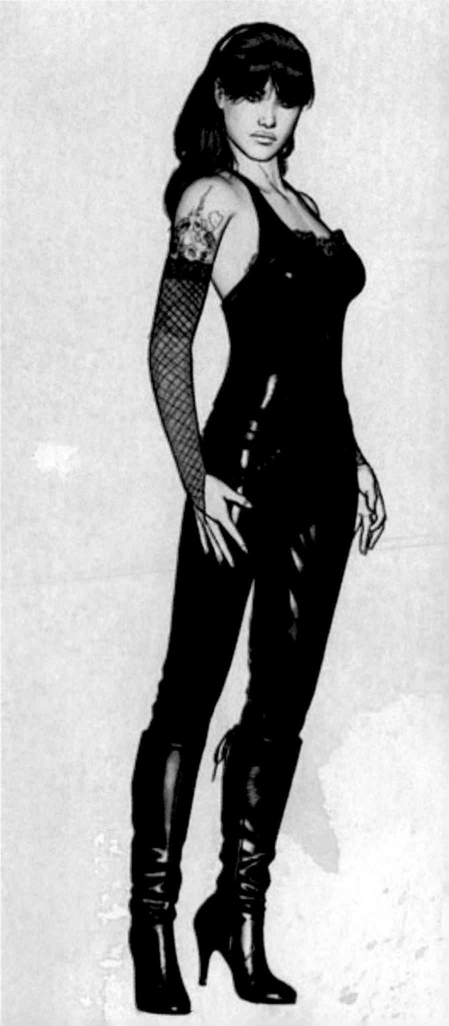

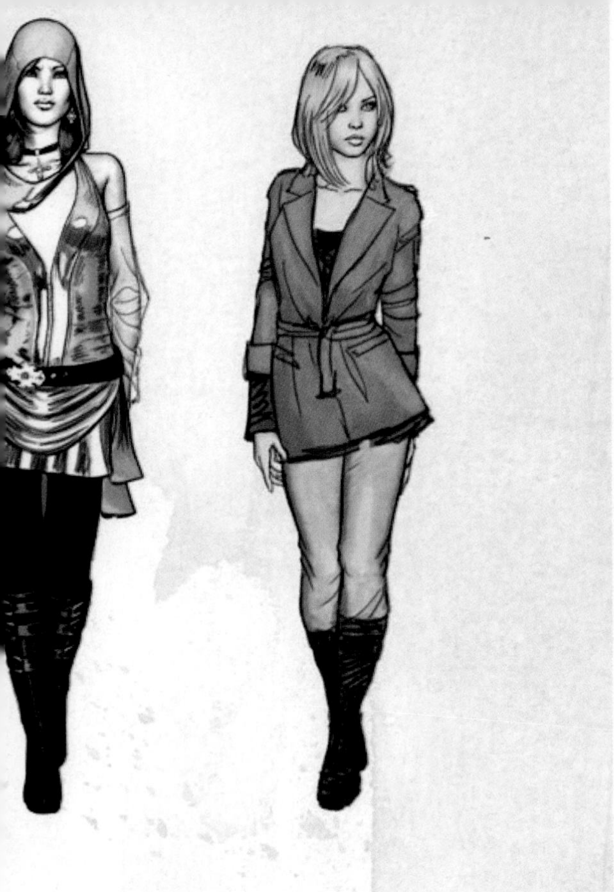

Zatanna

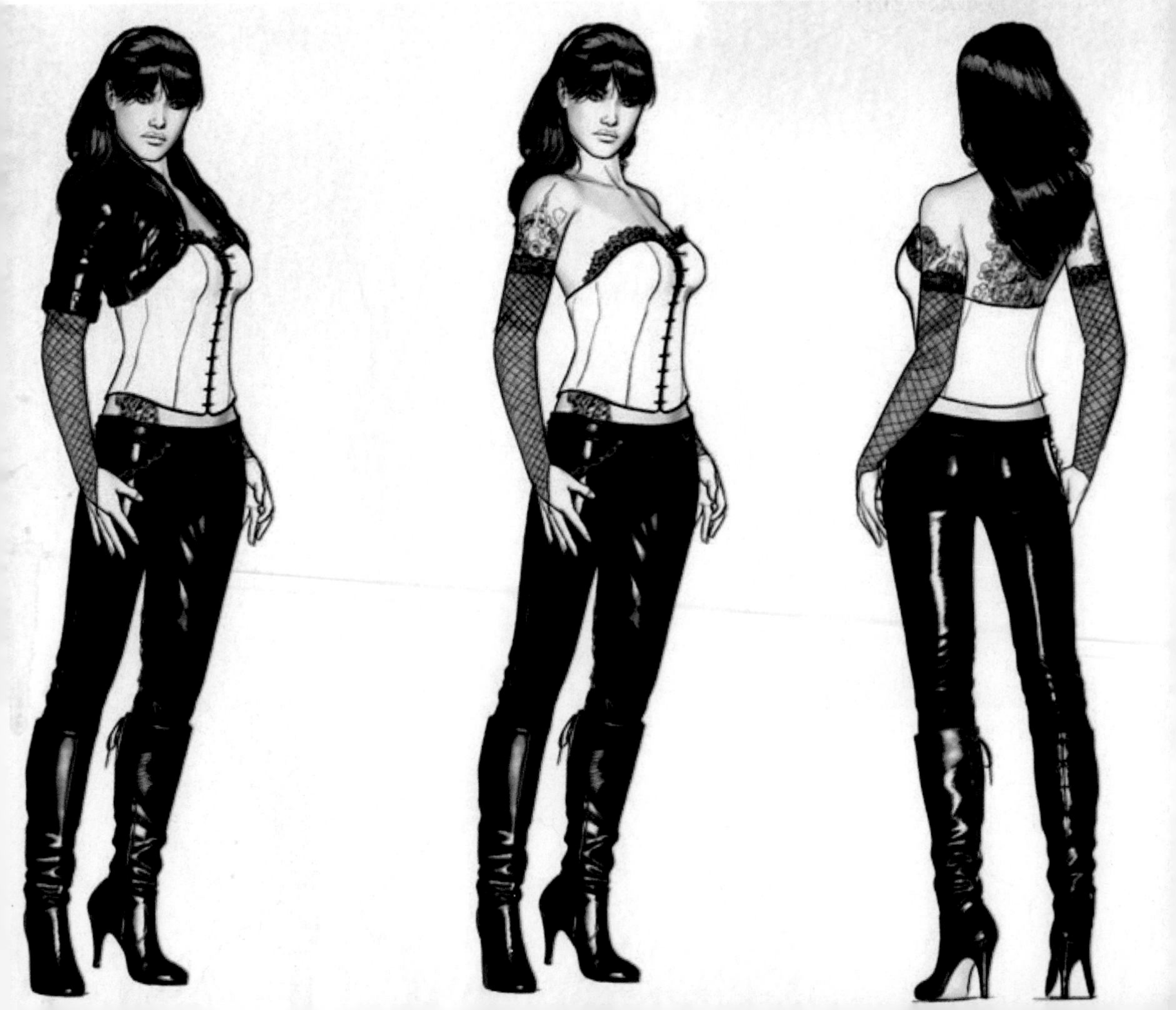

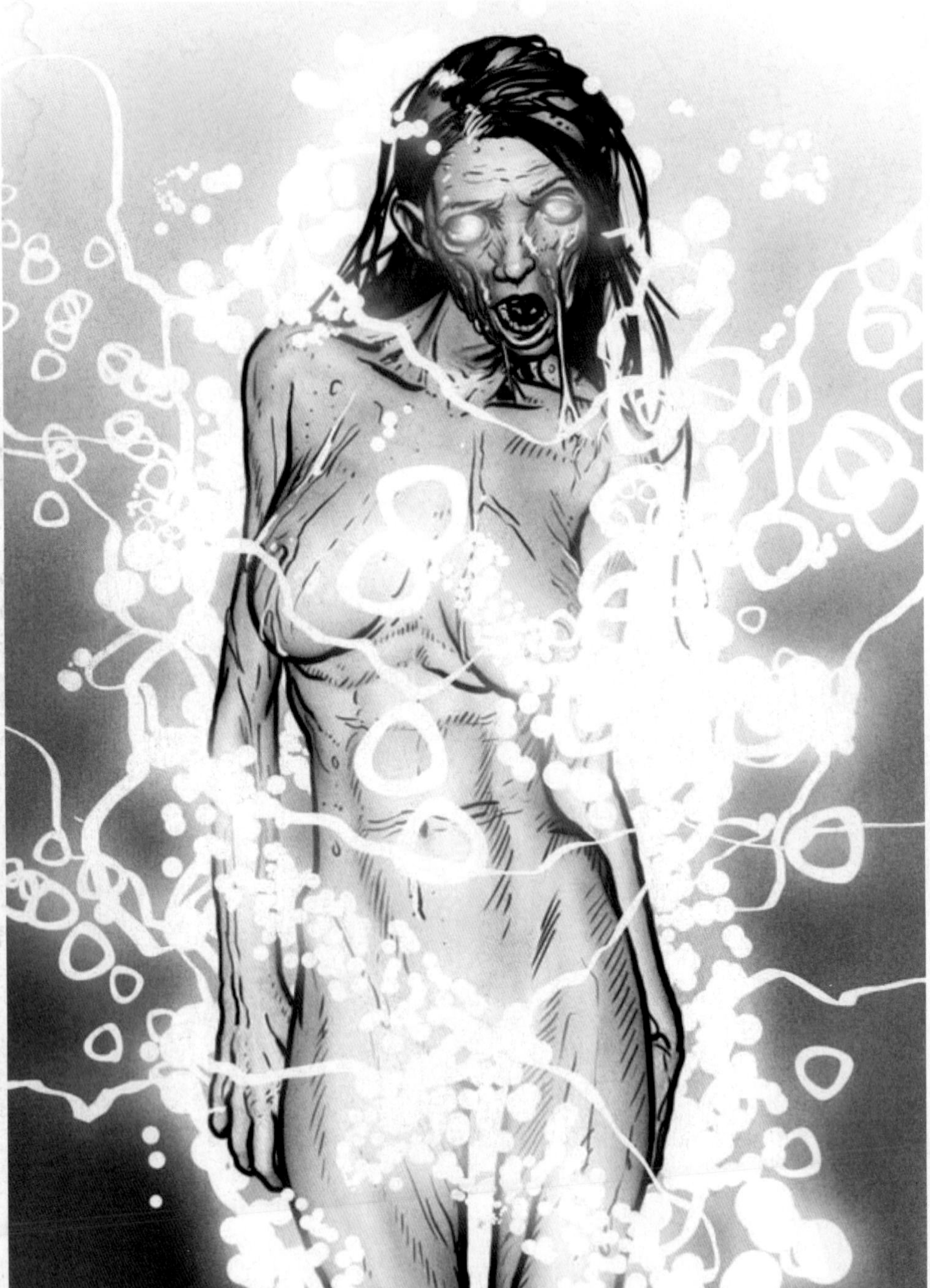

Kathy sketch

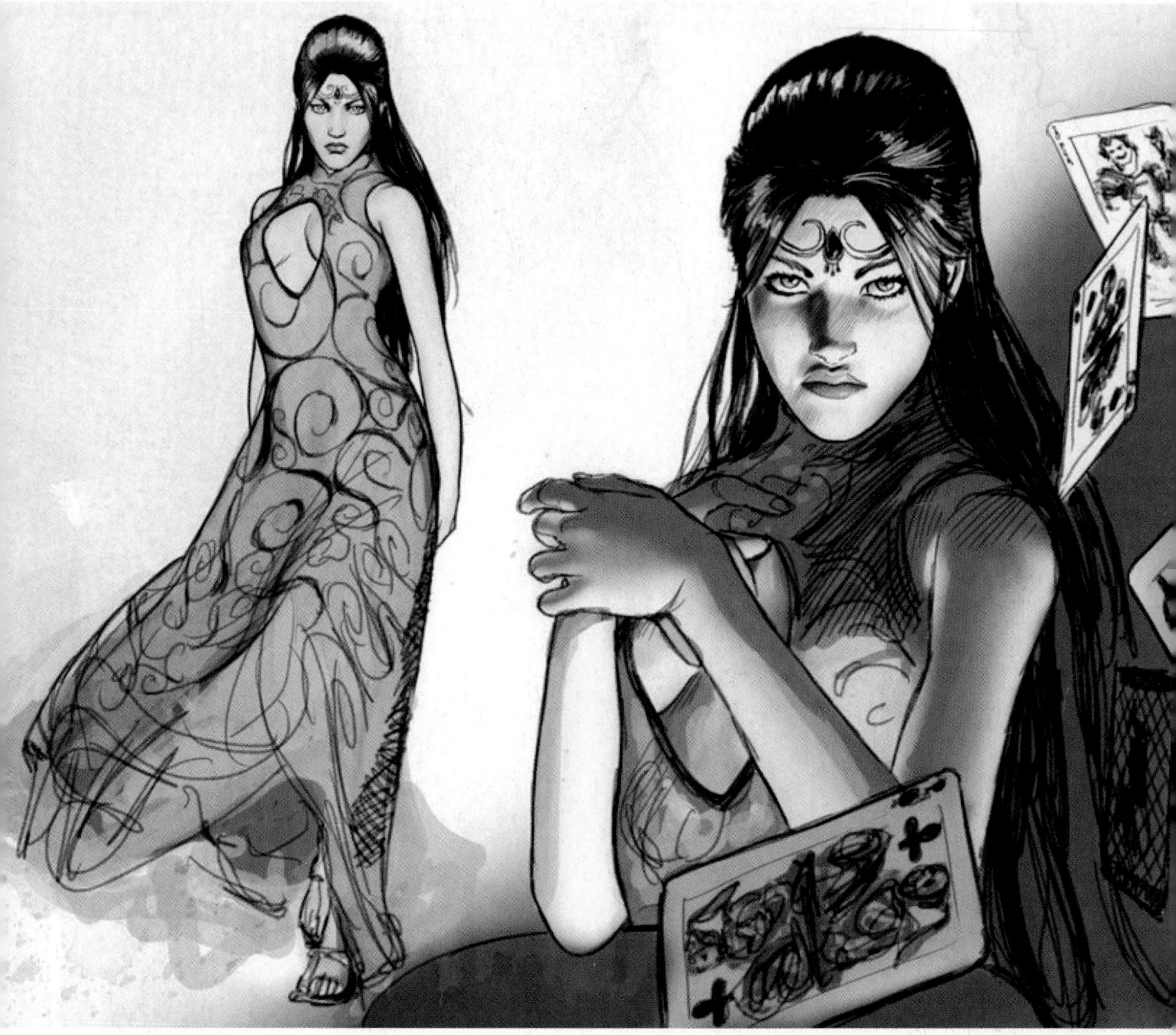

Madame Xanadu

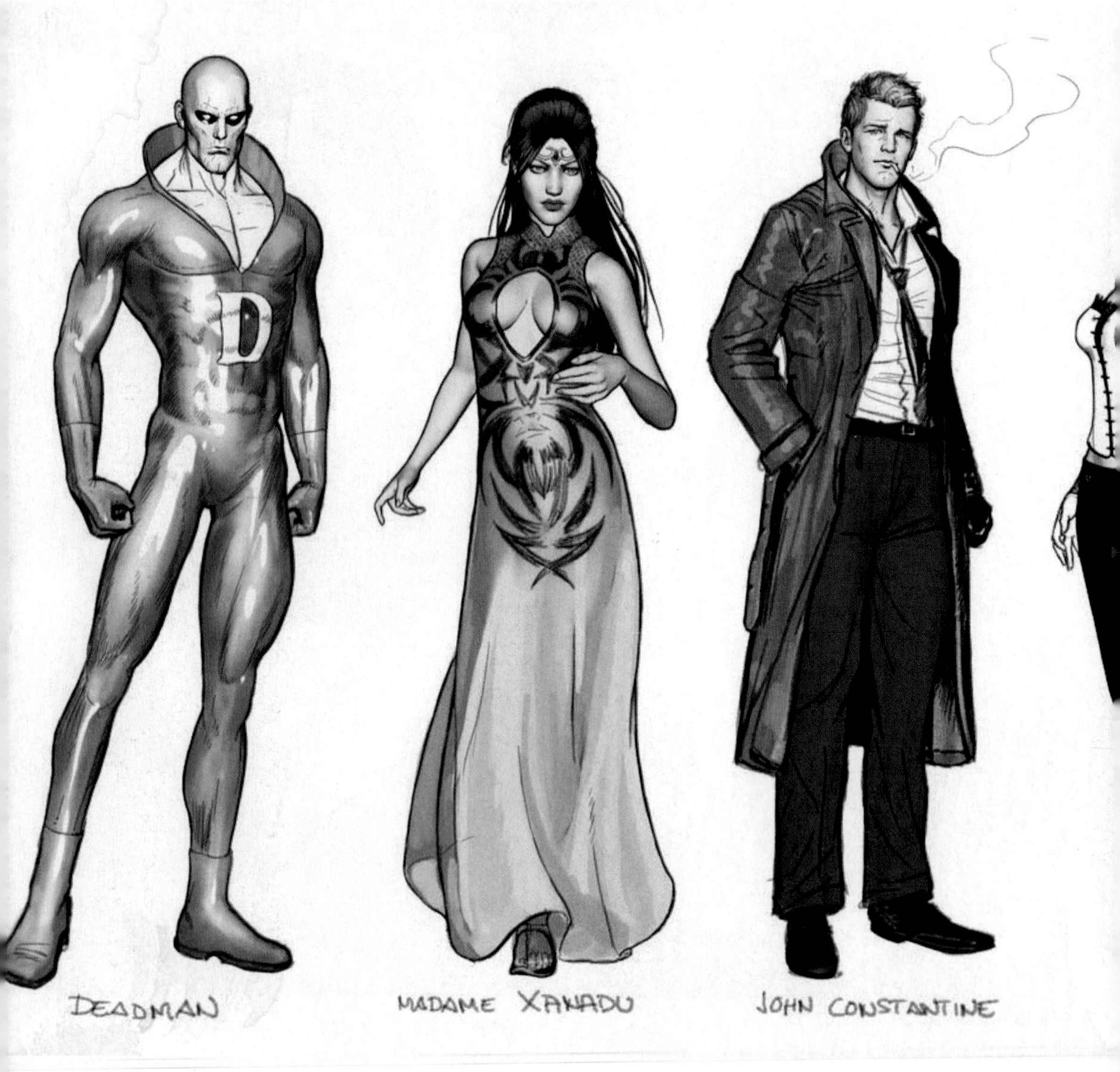
D
DEADMAN
MADAME XANADU
JOHN CONSTANTINE

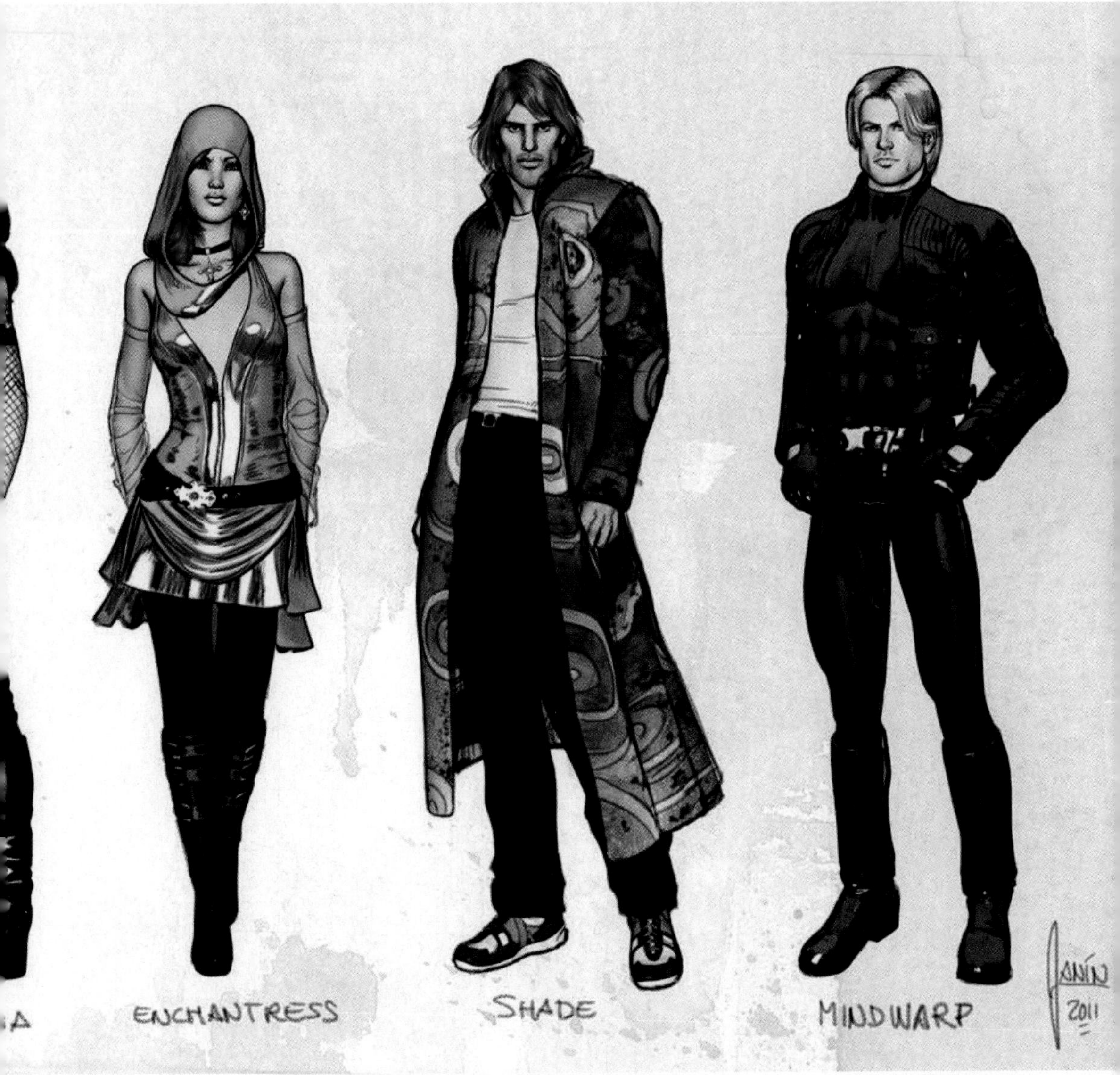
ENCHANTRESS
SHADE
MINDWARP
JANÍN
2011

JUSTICE LEAGUE DARK
ART BY MIKEL JANIN

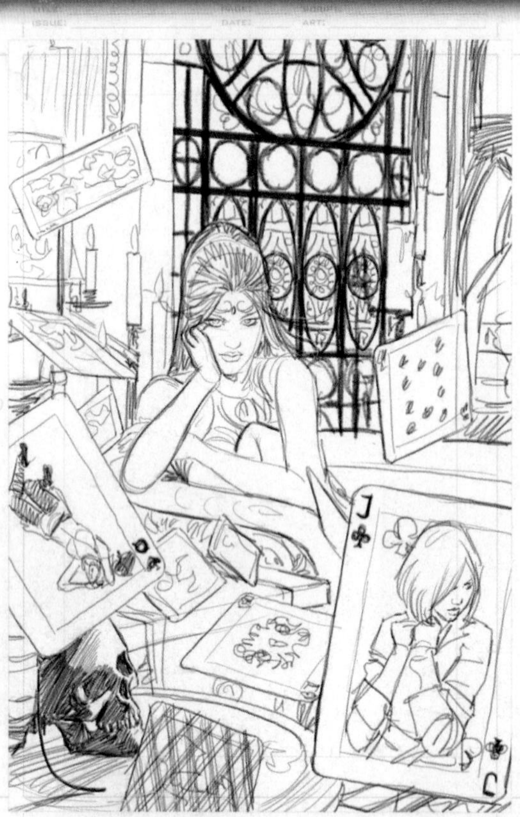

Rough sketch JUSTICE LEAGUE DARK #1 PAGE 1

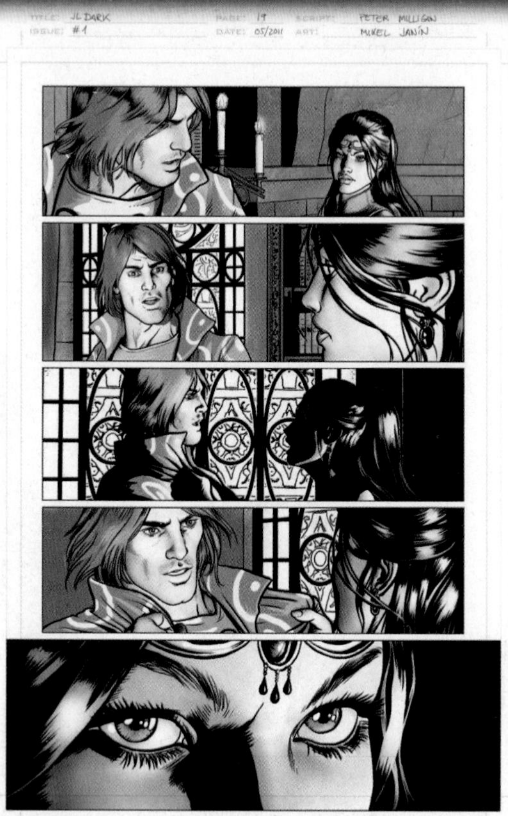
TITLE: JL DARK
PAGE: 19
SCRIPT: PETER MILLIGAN
ISSUE: #1
DATE: 05/2011
ART: MIKEL JANIN

JUSTICE LEAGUE DARK #1 PAGE 19

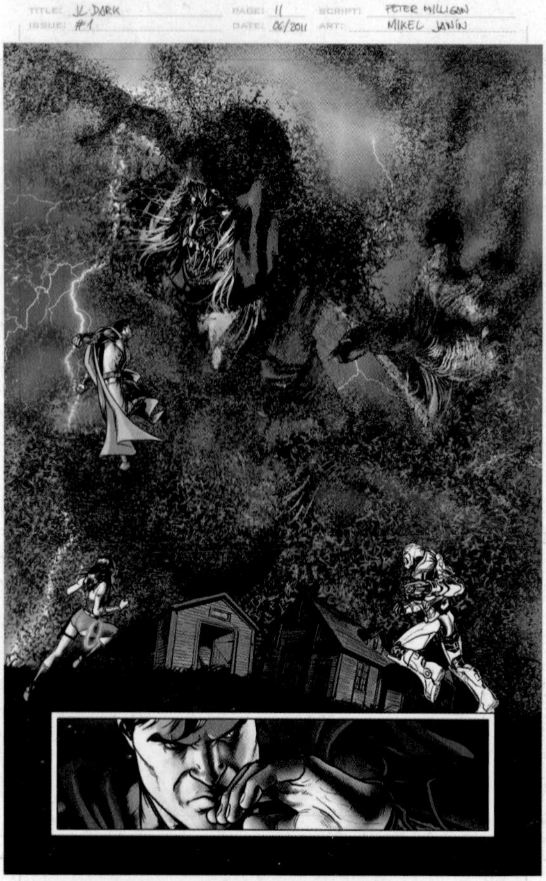
TITLE: JL DARK
PAGE: 11
SCRIPT: PETER MILLIGAN
ISSUE: #1
DATE: 06/2011
ART: MIKEL JANIN

JUSTICE LEAGUE DARK #1 PAGE 11

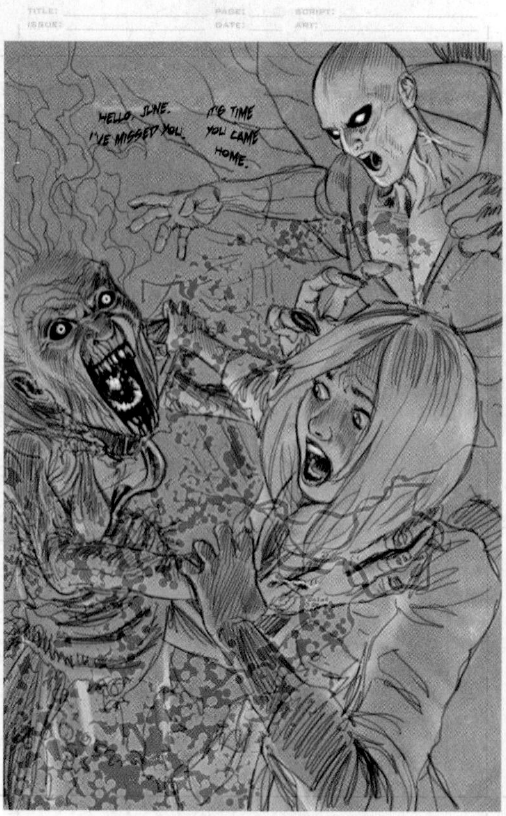
HELLO, JUNE. I'VE MISSED YOU.
IT'S TIME YOU CAME HOME.

JUSTICE LEAGUE DARK #3 PAGE 20